Pandemics in the Age of Social Media

This book offers insights into social media practices and challenges in developing nations during the COVID-19 pandemic. Covering different aspects of social media during the pandemic, the book offers new frameworks, concepts, tools and techniques for integrating social media to support national development.

Thematically organized chapters from a global team of scholars address the different aspects of social media during the pandemic. The book begins by looking at ICT for development and how development agencies have used social media platforms, before looking at engagement with these social media campaigns and the spread of misinformation. Further chapters cover the practical uses of social media in healthcare and virtual medicine, mental health issues and challenges, remote education and government policies.

This timely volume will be of interest to scholars and students of social media, health communication, global development studies and NGO communication.

Vikas Kumar received an MSc and PhD from Kurukshetra University, India. Along with 15 books, he has more than 100 research papers to his credit in various national and international conferences and journals. Dr. Kumar is presently serving at Central University of Haryana, India and is a visiting professor at the Indian Institute of Management, Indore and University of Northern Iowa, USA. His areas of interest include information systems, business analytics and ICT for development.

Mohit Rewari received a bachelor of engineering degree from MD University, India and further MBA from Guru Jambheshwar University of Science and Technology, India. He has authored two books in the area of business management and published a number of papers in international journals of repute. He has widely presented in a number of national and international conferences. He is presently serving at Indira Gandhi University, Rewari, India. His areas of interest include entrepreneurship development, social media and ICT in business.

Routledge Studies in New Media and Cyberculture

51 Smartphone Communication
Interactions in the App Ecosystem
Francisco Yus

52 Upgrade Culture and Technological Change
The Business of the Future
Adam Richard Rottinghaus

53 Digital Media and Participatory Cultures of Health and Illness
Stefania Vicari

54 Podcasting as an Intimate Medium
Alyn Euritt

55 On the Evolution of Media
Understanding Media Change
Carlos A. Scolari

56 Digital Ageism
How it operates and approaches to tackling it
Andrea Rosales, Mireia Fernández-Ardèvol & Jakob Svensson

57 Queer Reflections on AI
Uncertain Intelligences
Michael Klipphahn-Karge, Ann-Kathrin Koster & Sara Morais dos Santos Bruss

58 Pandemics in the Age of Social Media
Information and Misinformation in Developing Nations
Edited by Vikas Kumar and Mohit Rewari

For more information about this series, please visit: https://www.routledge.com/Routledge-Studies-in-New-Media-and-Cyberculture/book-series/RSINC

Pandemics in the Age of Social Media

Information and Misinformation in Developing Nations

Edited by Vikas Kumar and Mohit Rewari

LONDON AND NEW YORK

First published 2024
by Routledge
4 Park Square, Milton Park, Abingdon, Oxon OX14 4RN

and by Routledge
605 Third Avenue, New York, NY 10158

Routledge is an imprint of the Taylor & Francis Group, an informa business

© 2024 selection and editorial matter, Vikas Kumar and Mohit Rewari; individual chapters, the contributors

The right of Vikas Kumar and Mohit Rewari to be identified as the authors of the editorial material, and of the authors for their individual chapters, has been asserted in accordance with sections 77 and 78 of the Copyright, Designs and Patents Act 1988.

All rights reserved. No part of this book may be reprinted or reproduced or utilised in any form or by any electronic, mechanical, or other means, now known or hereafter invented, including photocopying and recording, or in any information storage or retrieval system, without permission in writing from the publishers.

Trademark notice: Product or corporate names may be trademarks or registered trademarks, and are used only for identification and explanation without intent to infringe.

British Library Cataloguing-in-Publication Data
A catalogue record for this book is available from the British Library

Library of Congress Cataloging-in-Publication Data
Names: Kumar, Vikas (Social media analyst), editor. |
    Rewari, Mohit, editor.
Title: Pandemics in the age of social media : information and
    misinformation in developing nations / edited by Vikas Kumar
    and Mohit Rewari.
Description: Abingdon, Oxon ; New York, NY : Routledge, 2024. |
    Series: Routledge studies in new media and cyberculture |
    Includes bibliographical references and index.
Identifiers: LCCN 2023016304 (print) | LCCN 2023016305 (ebook) |
Subjects: LCSH: Internet—Social aspects—Developing countries. |
    Social media—Developing countries. | COVID-19 Pandemic,
    2020—Developing countries. | Misinformation—Developing
    countries.
Classification: LCC HN981.I56 P36 2024 (print) | LCC HN981.I56
    (ebook) |
DDC 302.23/1—dc23/eng/20230626
LC record available at https://lccn.loc.gov/2023016304
LC ebook record available at https://lccn.loc.gov/2023016305

ISBN: 978-1-032-32393-0 (hbk)
ISBN: 978-1-032-32484-5 (pbk)
ISBN: 978-1-003-31527-8 (ebk)

DOI: 10.4324/9781003315278

Typeset in Sabon
by Apex CoVantage, LLC

Contents

List of Figures	*vii*
List of Tables	*viii*
List of Contributors	*ix*
Acknowledgements	*xi*
Preface	*xii*
VIKAS KUMAR AND MOHIT REWARI	
Foreword	*xv*
JAKOB SVENSSON	
Foreword	*xvii*
AGUS EKO SUJIANTO	

1 **Social Media as an Enabler to Combat Misinformation** 1
AASHISH BHARDWAJ AND VIKAS KUMAR

2 **Science Versus Populism: Social Media's Strengthening of
Public's Stance on Scientific Controversy** 16
IKBAL MAULANA

3 **COVID-19 Pandemic and Economic Inequalities: Analysis of
the Discourses of Turkish Political Parties on Twitter** 35
AYŞE FULYA ŞEN

4 **Social Media for Knowledge Sharing and Pandemics: A
Systematic Literature Review** 54
PALLAVI VYAS AND UJJAL MUKHERJEE

5 **Infodemic Management in India: A Social Media Perspective** 85
RITU BAJAJ, MAITRI, AND SANGEETA GUPTA

vi *Contents*

6 **The Role of Trust in Disaster Management Using Social Media: COVID-19 Perspective** 99
GABRIEL AYODEJI OGUNMOLA AND UJJWAL DAS

7 **Social Media and Trust Management During the Pandemic** 120
MANJU LATA AND SAURABH MITTAL

8 **Telegram as a Pedagogical Tool During the COVID-19 Pandemic** 136
KERSHNEE SEVNARAYAN

9 **Social Media–Based Learning Platforms and the Pandemic: A Comparative Analysis** 153
POOJA NANDA AND ANU GUPTA

10 **The Scope and Challenges of Learning Through Social Media Sites During the Pandemic: What Really Matters** 172
IRTIFA MUKHTER, RICHA CHOUDHARY, AASIM UR REHMAN GANIE, AND SYED SEERATH MUKHTER

Index 189

Figures

1.1	Approach to prevent spread of misinformation on social media	10
2.1	Terawan, Vaksin Nusantara, BPOM, and IDI as search terms of Google search engine	23
2.2	The topic distribution of the comments of a YouTube video	26
4.1	PRISMA methodology followed for the selection of research papers	59
4.2	Themes developed on the usage of SM on KS	74
6.1	Intelligence gathering model	109
8.1	The four interrelated presences of a community of inquiry	139
8.2	Lecturers' pinned messages on the Telegram group	145
8.3	Lecturer's use of polls to understand students' content needs	146
8.4	The use of casual language by the lecturer on Telegram	147
8.5	The use of memes by the lecturer	148
8.6	Lecturer being accessible on Telegram	149
8.7	Lecturer directing students to their Moodle LMS	150

Tables

1.1	Number of social media users in June 2022	1
1.2	Number of active users on popular social media sites (worldwide)	2
1.3	Production process for traditional media and social media	5
1.4	Misinformation incidents on social media	7
2.1	YouTube videos from which the comments were collected	20
3.1	Frequency distribution of the keywords on the tweets of the political parties	45
3.2	Thematic coding of CHP's tweets (@herkesicinCHP)	46
3.3	Thematic coding of AK Party's tweets (@Akparti)	47
4.1	Inclusion and exclusion criteria	58
4.2	List of scientific papers on social media and knowledge sharing used in the current literature review (2018–2022)	61
4.3	Geographical focus of the literature	63
4.4	Methodology-based clustering of the literature	63
4.5	Summary of gap analysis and scope for future research	66
4.6	Proposed scope for future research	75
5.1	Indian government initiatives for the people and by the people	89
5.2	Demographic profile of the respondents	91
6.1	Quasi-journalistic verification model	110
6.2	Crowdsourcing model	113

Contributors

Ritu Bajaj Department of Management, IGU, Meerpur, Rewari, Haryana, India

Aashish Bhardwaj Guru Tegh Bahadur Institute of Technology, New Delhi, India

Richa Choudhary Department of Social Work, B.R. Ambedkar College, University of Delhi, New Delhi, India

Ujjwal Das Department of Business Administration, Faculty of management, Sharda University Uzbekistan

Ayşe Fulya Şen Department of Journalism, Firat University, Elazig, Turkey

Aasim Ur Rehman Ganie Department of Psychiatric Social Work, NIMHANS Bengaluru, India

Anu Gupta Guru Jambheshwar University of Science & Technology, Hisar, Haryana, India

Sangeeta Gupta Department of Management, MERI, New Delhi, India

Vikas Kumar Central University of Haryana, Jant-Pali, Mahendergarh, Haryana, India

Manju Lata Chaudhary Bansi Lal University, Bhiwani, Haryana, India

Maitri Department of Management, Graphic Era (Deemed-to-be) University, Dehradun, Uttrakhand, India

Ikbal Maulana The National Research and Innovation Agency (BRIN), Indonesia

Saurabh Mittal Fore School of Management, Qutab Institutional Area, New Delhi, India

Ujjal Mukherjee Faculty of Management Studies, CMS Business School, Jain (Deemed-to-be) University, Bangalore

Irtifa Mukhter Department of Social Work, University of Delhi, India

x *Contributors*

Syed Seerath Mukhter Independent Researcher Pampore Pulwama, India

Pooja Nanda Sushant University, Gurugram, Haryana, India

Gabriel Ayodeji Ogunmola Department of Business Administration, Faculty of management, Sharda University Uzbekistan

Mohit Rewari Indira Gandhi University, Meerpur, Rewari, Haryana, India

Kershnee Sevnarayan University of South Africa

Agus Eko Sujianto Islamic State University of Sayyid Ali Rahmatullah, Tulungagung, Indonesia

Jakob Svensson Department of Computer Science and Media Technology, Malmö University, Sweden

Pallavi Vyas Faculty of Management Studies, CMS Business School, Jain (Deemed-to-be) University, Bangalore

Acknowledgements

We would like to express our heartfelt gratitude to all individuals and groups who have contributed to this book and supported us in different ways. Our sincere thanks to Prof. Tankeshwar Kumar (Vice Chancellor, Central University of Haryana) and Prof. J.P. Yadav (Vice Chancellor, Indira Gandhi University) for their constant support and motivation to take up this project.

We really got wonderful support from the Routledge team. The administrative and editorial staff helped us at every stage to serve as editors for this academic project. We owe an enormous debt of gratitude to all the reviewers, who gave us detailed and constructive reviews for improving the chapters, without which a quality project wouldn't have been possible. We are indebted to all the authors and contributors for sending their original contributions and working as per the tight deadlines.

We wish to acknowledge the support from our colleagues: Prof. Raj Kovid and Dr. Rachna Bansal (Sharda University), Dr. Christine Schrage (University of Northern Iowa), Dr. Subagyo and Dr. Gesty (Nusantara PGRI University), Dr. Gaurav Gupta (Amity University), Dr. Pawan Gupta and Dr. Sunita Bharatwal (Chaudhary Bansi Lal University), Dr. G.K. Sethi (MLN College), Dr. Surender Kumar (Jaipuria Institute of Management) and other peers from academia who have motivated and helped us a lot in this project.

Finally, we would love to mention our parents, family members and friends for their support and motivation to complete this project.

Vikas Kumar and Mohit Rewari

Preface

Data and information are the key enablers to success in the present-day technology-driven world. However, a lot of data-related complications were seen at the time of the pandemic. The sudden outbreak of the COVID pandemic, accompanied with explosion of information and misinformation on the social media platforms, forced the government and public health system to deal with both the pandemic and infodemic. The detonation of unchecked information and the spread of misinformation amplified the global crisis. A lot of stories prevailed on social media, which included 5G technologies has caused the pandemic; covid can be cured by drinking cow urine or hot water or neat alcohol or with whiskey and honey, etc. All such stories were, however, baseless, and they only leveraged the large user base of social media.

Millions of people have been affected directly or indirectly as Covid-19 emerged as the greatest threat to mankind, and a series of lockdowns were imposed by countries without worrying much about the economy. The spread of fake and misleading information during the pandemic raised the concern that we were not only fighting the pandemic but also an infodemic. Hence, major steps were required to be taken for effective solutions to tackle such issues. The social media platforms were utilized for spread of false claims, half-baked conspiracy theories and pseudoscience health therapies, diagnosis, treatment, prevention from the virus. At the same time, many politicians, world leaders, celebrities, prominent public figures used social media to reach the general public and shared information and appeals to fight with the pandemic. The present book offers a collection of chapters covering the different aspects of social media usage during the pandemic.

The first chapter, "Social Media as an Enabler to Combat Misinformation", by Bhardwaj and Kumar, focuses on the power of social media to combat the spread of the false and misleading information. It emphasizes that misinformation can be stopped by educating the users which is the best defense to counter the proliferation of fake information. The chapter also presents different examples of rumours and deliberate misinformation on social media during the COVID-19 pandemic. The three-stage model has been proposed by the authors to prevent the spread of misinformation.

Preface xiii

The second chapter, "Science versus Populism: Social Media's Strengthening of Public's Stance on Scientific Controversy", by Maulana, differentiates the science legitimacy and public knowledge on the complex and uncertain situations. The vaccines were developed following all necessary measures, and taking care of all possible repercussions was internationally accepted. But the people of all arenas who may or may not have had adequate knowledge on the topic could still express their views and designs to disrepute the scientific approach. This chapter presents how populist sentiment, which is not necessarily orchestrated by a particular group, interferes with the controversy of vaccine development, and how populist rhetoric discursively overrides the scientific arguments.

The third chapter by Ayşe Fulya Şen, "COVID-19 Pandemic and Economic Inequalities: Analysis of the Discourses", presents the political discourses on economic issues intensified during the COVID-19 period, and discussed the limitations and capacities of the political discourses and Twitter as a public sphere. Example of ruling and opposition party in Turkey has been chosen with specific examples of the tweets. The study is very interesting and presents the real economic discourse through social media.

The fourth chapter by Vyas and Mukherjee identified the developments in knowledge sharing using social media platforms. It discussed how organizations are leveraging social media for knowledge sharing and how employers are continually looking for methods to incorporate SM into their operations. The chapter identified the important research gaps and provided very valuable inputs on theoretical, contextual, and methodological understanding of social media usage for knowledge sharing.

The next chapter, "Infodemic Management in India: A Social Media Perspective", enumerates the initiatives taken by Indian government to combat COVID-19 and the role of social media in this reference. The chapter focuses on use of social media for engaging and empowering communities to take positive action during the pandemic in India and illustrates the effectiveness of measures taken by the government of India during the pandemic. The chapter suggests how the government used social media platforms to communicate its initiatives effectively and efficiently.

The sixth chapter, "The Role of Trust in Disaster Management Using Social Media: Covid-19 Perspective", by Ayodeji Ogunmola, is about misleading information spread about COVID-19 which raised the trust issues on global public health management during the tough times and led to the unintended fatalities and self-harm. The chapter evaluates the models for using social media platforms during emergency for collection and management of information for building of trust in public. Trust becomes an important aspect considering the large number of social media users and fast spread of both the information and misinformation. It also affects the privacy and security to a larger extent.

Lata and Mittal, in their findings in the seventh chapter, "Social Media and Trust Management during the Pandemic", described the key aspects

xiv *Preface*

of entrusting and managing users' trust using social media strategies. They found that, in turbulent times, the role of social media becomes much more important as the platforms can contribute in providing authentic information. The chapter highlighted the use of social media as a communication tool during the pandemic. A responsible social media approach has been illustrated by the authors to enhance the user trust on social media.

The chapter "Telegram as a Pedagogical Tool During the COVID-19 Pandemic", by Kershnee Sevnarayan, investigates the potential benefits of social media platforms during teacher-student interactions and, most importantly, its integration in the pedagogy. The observations of a live Telegram group has been used to understand the perception about the specific social media platform and its importance to the students and teachers. The study describes the use of telegram application in assisting the students and how new pedagogical methodologies can be implemented using such platforms in the future.

The ninth chapter is based on the comparative analysis of various learning platforms by Nanda and Gupta and presents an exploratory approach to investigate the role of social media–based tools to support learning during the pandemic. The study describes how social media learning platforms can support learning with suitability of time, place and speed and better accommodate the needs of learners. In this chapter, a comparative analysis has also been done to identify the features of various social media–based educational tools and their implications in learning. A number of commercially available tools have been taken up by the authors, and their suitability has been assessed.

The last chapter, "The Scope and Challenges of Learning through Social Media Sites during the Pandemic: What Really Matters", elaborates the scope of social media adoption by students to enhance the academic learning. This chapter presents a review the use of various social media platforms and tools, applicability and functioning of social media in learning over the past few years and during Covid-19 pandemic. Authors highlighted that social media should be adopted as part of higher education teaching and learning curriculum only after in-depth analysis, when the clear guidelines for using such tools are provided for both the instructors and learners.

We sincerely hope that the book covers the different aspects of social media usage during the pandemic. It presents both the theoretical and practical perspectives from different parts of the world and offers opportunities to develop new models. The interdisciplinary approach of the chapters will be useful for the researchers, students, practitioners, policymakers and anybody interested in social media applications. The chapters will serve as material for policymaking and development of communication strategies during times of emergency. The book will serve as a wonderful academic reference for the researchers and academicians, and at the same time, it will serve as a comprehensive resource for the practitioners.

Vikas Kumar and Mohit Rewari

Foreword

The corona pandemic hit the globe with full force in 2019 and affected our lives in ways we were unfamiliar with. Many of us had to invent strategies to navigate our everyday life, work life, and social life in a time full of uncertain and unprecedented regulations and restrictions. We were presented with new forms of expertise and predictions novel to most (if not all) of us. While the effects and consequences of COVID-19 have varied, (social) media has been central in news and knowledge dissemination, but also as tools in how we adapted to this new normal with distance work and non-physical sociality. That social media was adopted, adapted and appropriated across the globe prior to the pandemic no doubt put these services and platforms in a privileged position when the pandemic hit. While governments and agencies worked hard to manage the challenges posed by COVID-19 with their worked-up routines, available tools, channels and platforms, other types of organizations and lay persons put their emphasis on social media to spread information, communicate and maintain a basic level of sociality and interconnectivity. Social media use also comes with its challenges, such as the quick spread of misinformation and so-called "fake news". Hence, the pandemic gives us an opportunity to study social media communication, good practices, less successful ones and what we can learn in terms of effective and sustainable communication during what was arguably the first global pandemic in the age of social media. Hence the volume you hold in your hands, or read on your tablet, is titled *Pandemics in the Age of Social Media*.

The subtitle is *Information and Misinformation in Developing Nations*. This is of particular importance as I, a scholar residing in the globalized North, often tend to forget voices from the global South, unwillingly generalising my experiences as global. It is therefore refreshing and important for a volume to give ample space for other voices to be heard than usual suspects. Edited by Vikas Kumar and Mohit Rewari, *Pandemics in the Age of Social Media: Information and Misinformation in Developing Nations* offers insights from academics in India, Indonesia, South Africa, Turkey and Uzbekistan. The chapters highlight innovative social media uses during the pandemic and approach them in a contextually appropriate manner. And regardless where we live and from where we act, we can learn from meaningful xvi *Foreword*

insights and practical solutions to the problems and challenges discussed in these chapters. As such, I believe this volume to be a resource for practitioners, communications officers, policymakers as well as academics and their students.

Jakob Svensson,
Department of Computer Science and Media Technology,
Malmö University,
Malmö, Sweden

Foreword

The impact of the Covid-19 pandemic on this world cannot be measured in terms of numbers. The crisis prevailed for a longer duration, and not only the human beings but the animals and nature also became a stakeholder to the same. A lot of physical restrictions came into place, hence communication played a vital role. Both organizations and individuals used social media as a prime mode of communication for spreading pandemic-related information. This, however, led to a number of instances of fake news and fake information being spread, which put forward a big challenge towards the trust on social media. Although this is true for both developed and developing nations, there may be instances, which seek different treatment for different countries.

The book volume *Pandemics in the Age of Social Media: Information and Misinformation in Developing Nations*, edited by Vikas Kumar and Mohit Rewari, presents a number of chapters which capture real-life insights on the use of social media at time of unprecedented crisis in the form of the corona pandemic, and suggest communication strategies to deal with the pandemic. Both the positive and negative aspects of social media communication have been taken up in the book, and a number of case studies have been presented from different parts of the world.

I opine that the book enriches the existing understanding of social media–based communication and, most importantly, the relevance of social media at the time of the pandemic. The research-based chapters of the book provide very interesting and meaningful insights into the social media response of different communities. This volume contributes to offering communication-based solutions to a number of problems society has faced during the pandemic. A group of practitioners and academicians came together to contribute chapters on a variety of contexts such as healthcare, education and politics, among others. The coverage and depth of book chapters is very comprehensive to be considered as a reference book related to different dimensions of the pandemic. This special volume has a great potential to be a meaningful resource for policymakers, practitioners, students and academicians who need communication strategies to deal with challenging situations in the pandemic and post pandemic time.

xviii *Foreword*

I feel proud to congratulate the chapter authors and editors of the book for coming-up with this piece of excellent resource. I am very sure that the readers will get deep insights and knowledge from the collection of chapters in this book.

Agus Eko Sujianto
Islamic State University of Sayyid Ali Rahmatullah
Tulungagung, Indonesia

1 Social Media as an Enabler to Combat Misinformation

Aashish Bhardwaj and Vikas Kumar

1. Introduction

The proliferation of social networks is very deep in the current scenario relating to government interactions with citizens, police organizations for preventing crimes, people sharing incidents of phishing, etc. There are two faces of a social network; one is a primary source of information, and the other is a vehicle to disinformation or fake news. It can be used to collect, analyze and visualize user data to differentiate between legitimate and forged. As per Statista (www.statista.com/statistics/278341/number-of-social-network-users-in-selected-countries/), the number of social media users in June 2022 in some of the selected countries is shown in Table 1.1.

Some of the popular social media used worldwide include Facebook, YouTube, WhatsApp, Instagram, Twitter and Snapchat. The number of active users for popular social media sites worldwide as of January 2022 (www.statista.com/statistics/272014/global-social-networks-ranked-by-number-of-users/) are presented in Table 1.2.

The use of social media and new digital technologies (since 1990s) allow large numbers of amateur individuals to post online with little or no filters and gatekeepers (Kumar & Malhotra, 2020). The social media has reduced the gatekeeping power of media production and has increased the capacity of various kinds of actors (Gilardi et al., 2022). The four type of actors are, first, personality actors, which use their own personality to post information on social media. Second type is creative actors, who enhance information by

Table 1.1 Number of social media users in June 2022

S. No.	Country	Social Media Users (Millions)
1	China	1,021.96
2	India	755.47
3	United States	302.25
4	Indonesia	217.53
5	Brazil	165.45
6	Russia	115.05

DOI: 10.4324/9781003315278-1

2   *Aashish Bhardwaj and Vikas Kumar*

Table 1.2 Number of active users on popular social media sites (worldwide)

S. No.	News Process	Active Users (Millions)
1	Facebook	2,910
2	YouTube	2,562
3	WhatsApp	2,000
4	Instagram	1,478
5	WeChat	1,263
6	Snapchat	557

upgrading themselves and even go against their own personality as well. Third type is chameleon actors, who play a wide range of roles, even ones which are unrelated to their personalities. Last type is nonprofessional actors, who add realism to the existing information to make media interesting (Shawky et al., 2022). Prior to this, in the1970s and 1980s, the media production contained all the contents and information needed to be approved before it was aired or published. This approval was done by traditional gatekeepers like newspaper editors, publishers and news shows (Bhardwaj & Kumar, 2022c; Lynch, 2022). This trend caused only a small handful of media corporations to reach a mass audience but prevents anything controversial, distasteful or too oppositional to be sent across people. Also the independent voices were kept out of conversation, and there were incidents of false consensus as well (Rhodes, 2022). There was a video on YouTube channel 11th February 2019 calling some journalists to "be hanged". The prominent journalists include Mohammed Zubair of Alt News; Rana Ayyub of the *Washington Post*, Barkha Dutt of The Wire, Faye D'Souza of Mojo Story and several other news agencies. This was done because of claiming a "money trail" between journalists and "anti-India conspiracy". Later the claims in the video were found to by fake, but still that it was read by many people (Henry & Plantan, 2022). Also, false consensus is amplified using social media platforms, which causes people to overestimate with others who are like them. Jency Jacob had admitted that their platform on Facebook is utilized by some parties for political reasons, although they had not created the platform for that (Kwon et al., 2022). Thousands of groups are created by political parties for messaging on WhatsApp to build fake consensus, which is most popular in India (Jain et al., 2022). Also, Instagram is used, which is a popular social media platform to attract first-time voters—about 90 million in India (Bhattacharya, 2022).

During the COVID-19 pandemic, social media was used to create awareness through its role in quick dissemination of information (Kumar & Malhotra, 2021). It has also helped in connecting with people when the whole world was shut down and was maintaining social distance to avoid infections related to coronavirus (Kumar & Gupta, 2021). The usage of social media was done to pass the time by the general population of the world, celebrities, professional and world leaders in the same way alike (Mheidly & Fares,

2020). Social media has also played a vital role in raising health awareness and prevention of infectious disease during the COVID-19 pandemic (Kovid & Kumar, 2022). For example, medical descriptions and preventive measures were sent to a large population using videos on YouTube which were more beneficial as compared to written prescriptions of medical professionals (Basch et al., 2020). Also Twitter, MySpace, blogs and Wikipedia were used extensively to as references to clinics, health specialists, patients and pharmaceutical companies (Sattar & Arifuzzaman, 2021). At the same time, misinformation was also spread using social media during the pandemic, which was a major societal issue. As per the World Health Organization (WHO), in the first three months of the year 2020, approximately 6,000 people were hospitalized, and it was found that around 800 people have died due to misinformation (www.who.int/news-room/feature-stories/detail/fighting-misinformation-in-the-time-of-covid-19-one-click-at-a-time). This is because the wrong information, which spreads like wildfire, can even kill. There were many preventive measures as well to stop the spread of misinformation, like when BBC World Television started a website and app named "Stop the Spread" in May and June 2020 to raise public awareness and cross-check the misinformation related to the novel coronavirus (Kim et al., 2021). WHO had also identified many myths related to COVID-19 transmission (Dutta et al., 2020) as mentioned below:

- COVID-19 is transmitted through goods produced in countries where the disease is spreading.
- The infectious disease is transmitted through mosquitoes.
- Coronavirus is also spreading through clothes.
- Drinking alcohol prevents infection from coronavirus.
- COVID-19 is spread in cold climate, whereas hot and humid climate kills the virus.
- Digital thermometers are not effective in detecting corona-infected patients.
- Ultraviolet lamps which are used for disinfecting can also kill coronavirus.
- Spraying alcohol and chlorine on human body kills coronavirus.
- Eating garlic, which has anti-microbial bodies, can kill coronavirus.
- Vaccines used to prevent pneumonia can also be used to prevent coronavirus.
- Rinsing your nose with saline solution, which prevents the common cold, can also prevent coronavirus.

When COVID-19 infection was on its peak, wreaking havoc on the whole world, with many countries greatly affected, there were many alternative cures and home remedies circulating on social media which did not have any scientific evidence, and some are mentioned below:

- Eating frozen foods like ice cream, spring roll and soya chaap spreads coronavirus.

4 Aashish Bhardwaj and Vikas Kumar

- Adding pepper to meals, soups and juice before consuming can prevent coronavirus.
- Drinking a lot of water every 15 minutes can help to flush out coronavirus from the body.
- Turmeric and lemon can prevent diseases originating from coronavirus.
- COVID-19 infection can be cured by gargling with hot water mixed with salt and vinegar.
- Eating garlic, which is a healthy food, can prevent coronavirus.
- COVID-19 can be cured by drinking fresh gourd juice.
- Eating chicken, even when hygienically prepared, spreads coronavirus.
- Cooking with the use of mustard oil helps to prevent coronavirus.
- Fruits and vegetables should be washed with soap and water to prevent coronavirus infection.

All these misinformation and myths are usually spread through forwarded messages or by word-of-mouth, which should not be believed. Rather people should focus on information from official sources only and any battle can be won with corporation and commitment (Wan et al., 2020).

2. Media Production

The five stages of media production involves creation, editing, publishing, amplifying and consumption for any article (Hatano et al., 2022). In traditional media production, different professionals create information in the first stage, which had self-censorship (Kumar & Svensson, 2015). This includes their vast experiences in the field with data collected and their foreseeing impact on society as well (Bhardwaj & Kumar, 2022a). In the second phase of editing, the editorial policy was used to find the gaps or additions in the created material of the first stage. The editorial policy has a set of guidelines by which the organization operates (Öztürk & Mihçiokur, 2022). It includes the organization's attitudes towards society and helps editors to make correct decisions. Next, the third stage, is the publishing stage, which has a control of state censorship filter for every media production like speech, public communication or other information. The printing and publishing of news in periodicals or newspapers in India are governed by the Press and Registration of Books Act, 1867 and the Registration of Newspaper Rules, 1956. In order to ensure the compliance of conditions prescribed in the act, the government of India has also appointed the Registrar of Newspapers for registration of newspapers and periodicals published in India. The media is checked at this stage for harmful, objectionable, sensitive or inconvenient information. The state censorship is conducted by governments, private institutions or other apex controlling bodies (Shomova, 2022). All these three stages make it sure to publish only reasonable, responsible and liable publishing material for society. The fourth stage is the amplifying stage, which refers to promoting and distributing contents through various media channels like paid, owned

Table 1.3 Production process for traditional media and social media

S. No.	Production Process	Traditional Media	Social Media
1	Creation	Professionals	Amateurs and professionals
2	Edit	Editorial policy	No liable policy
3	Publish	State censorship	Self-censorship
4	Amplify	Extra efforts, breaking news	Consumers amplify themselves
5	Consumption	Slow speed	Very fast speed

and earned media campaigns. The difference in media production process for traditional and social media is shown in Table 1.3.

Such amplifications include paid social advertisements and naturally searched advertisements (Kumar & Bhardwaj, 2018). The next stage is the final stage of media production, which is consumption by readers, viewers or listeners. This is the sum of information and entertainment media consumed by individual or groups. The activities in this stage include reading books, magazines, newspaper; watching television or films; listening to radio or interacting with new media (Kumar & Bhardwaj, 2020a). With the advent of the internet, or as the internet enters the media production process, there is drastic change in traditional media (Sun & Wu, 2022). The internet has changed all the ways people create and experience all the media. It has affected all the media types like application, audio, image, text and video (Bhardwaj & Kumar, 2022b). A social media layer is created which tells the section of society what they like, what they watch, who and what they pay attention to and the location of people when they are doing something (Nguyen et al., 2022). With internet as a tool, anyone can publish, anyone can amplify and even anyone can edit the information which are shared in public. All these have created a stage in which editors have gone, or writers don't require their expertise and there is no trash can as well (Bhardwaj & Kumar, 2021). The information posted on the internet cannot be taken back by the creator. With the development of the internet age media or social media, the process of media production in all five stages have changed a lot. The creation stage has got amateurs added along with professionals to create media information (Bhardwaj & Kumar, 2014). They have self-censorship, controlled by their own best knowledge as a control over the information to be sent in public. The next three stages of editing, publishing and amplification is done by the means of the internet (Näsi et al., 2021). These include much less or almost negligible censorship from the state or any private organization. These three stages are also not controlled by any liable policies as done by traditional media production (Kumar & Bhardwaj, 2020b). The same is true of the consumption stage, which is augmented by the internet and is amplified by the consumers themselves at a very fast speed (First et al., 2021).

6   Aashish Bhardwaj and Vikas Kumar

3.   Social Media and Misinformation

Social media is the main driver for spreading misinformation (all false or inaccurate information on social media) as compared to established websites of news, e-commerce, educational, portfolio, corporate, entertainment or blogs (Luo et al., 2022; Kumar & Nanda, 2019). As per Statista (www.statista.com/statistics/381455/most-trusted-sources-of-news-and-info-worldwide/) the least trusted source of general news and information worldwide from 2011 to 2021 is social media, then owned media, then traditional media, and the most trusted are search engines. The misinformation has drastic impacts on society as it leads people to question science, true or legitimate news and society norms. Such misinformation is sometimes affecting election results in forming governments worldwide, changing opinions on serious subjects, redefining truths, principles and evidences (Olan et al., 2022). In the last few years, misinformation has increased via social media platforms like Facebook, Twitter, WhatsApp, YouTube, etc. Some of the examples include drawing a similarity between COVID-19 and World War III, with characterization of heaps of coffins, mass burials, overloaded crematoria, empty streets, closed market places and worship places (Gurevitz, 2021). Misinformation related to origin of coronavirus, rumours related to public health institutions and health recommendations to prevent or cure diseases related to the novel coronavirus. Some of those includes alkaline diet, drinking wine and drinking alkaline as it kills virus. Also, sanitizers have big percentage of wine in them (Mian & Khan, 2020). Another misinformation on social media was related to COVID-19 vaccine side effects like infertility, chronic diseases, DNA changes, acute illness, physical deformity and that the vaccine itself causes COVID-19 illness and have poisonous effects (Loomba et al., 2021). Misinformation related to conspiracy, with claims that coronavirus is a man-made disease with intentions to enforce vaccination, a side effect of 5G technology, an attempt by Big Pharma companies for depopulation, etc. (Ferrara et al., 2020). Other misinformation was related to the development of vaccines related to coronavirus, like crucial trials skipped in its fast development, vaccines were developed before the disease spread out and the contents related to vaccines (Lockyer et al., 2021). All such misinformation spread fast on social media because of its online presence and fast sharing mechanism. This mechanism of social media augments misinformation which are false information, but when a person conveys it, others feel that it is true and shares with others (Wang et al., 2022). The misinformation can be of different forms like fabricated contents, memes, satire, false connection, imposter contents and misrepresentation of facts (Salaverría & León, 2022). The sharing of misinformation is not always done by the persons knowing that it is fake but sometimes due to its novel contents, concern for friends and family, sometimes for political, sociological reasons, business interests or just for fun (Baptista & Gradim, 2022; Mehta et al., 2022). Some of the examples where misinformation has been spread using social media are shown in Table 1.4.

Social Media as an Enabler to Combat Misinformation   7

Table 1.4 Misinformation incidents on social media

S. No.	Incident of Misinformation on Social Media	Reference
1	"Pizzagate" conspiracy on Twitter where a false story was fabricated mentioning that sexually abused children were hidden in a pizza parlor at Washington, D.C. It was also mentioned that Mrs. Hillary Clinton also has the information about this sex ring. The story seemed so real that Edgar Welch, a man from north Carolina, went to the place with his assault weapon to protect the abused kids.	Batzdorfer et al. (2022); Kang et al. (2016)
2	"Boston Marathon bombing" was a local terrorist attack during annual marathon in 2013 at Boston, United States. Two brothers implanted a home-made pressure cooker bomb near the finish line, killing three people and injuring many others. But as the information spread, it was full of rumours which were full of misinformation. Many of the reports which were circulated during that time were proved to be false, including the misidentification of one of the bombers.	Regan (2022)
3	"Hurricane Sandy", a massive storm which came and went in Washington D.C. with a four-day weekend and power outages in some thousands. But the social media sites were full of fake photos and misinformation. There were photos of sharks swimming in New York streets and flooding scenes of New York Stock Exchange. News of shutting down of power in Manhattan and shutting down of NYC subway for rest of the week. All bridges to and from Manhattan to be shut down and zombies reigning the street.	Singh and Sharma (2022)
4	"COVID-19 myths" are common myths circulated on social media related to the pandemic, which include eating onions with rock salt can cure COVID-19 infection, plant-based diet prevents corona infection, putting lemon drops in nostrils kills Covid, drinking alcohol kills virus, steam with peppermint oil kills Covid virus, inhaling camphor, ajwain increases oxygen levels, cow dunk and urine are effective in Covid and micronutrients like Vitamin D, C and zinc cures COVID-19 disease.	Challenger et al. (2022)

It's not that social media only spread misinformation; there are incidents when social media has helped in saving lives of people like in the case of a plane doing a crash landing in Hudson River. On 15th January 2009, U.S. Airways Flight 1549 got partially submerged in the Hudson River due to an accident. Janis Krums uploaded its photograph for the first time on Twitter

8 Aashish Bhardwaj and Vikas Kumar

and then started rescuing passengers of the plane. Many emergency services rushed to the site because of that tweet to save the plane's passengers. The information was spread quickly because of a social media site, even faster than FlightStats information website which showed downing of the flight 26 minutes later and Google's similar trending service (Boarini, 2022). This was even true with other previous disasters like China earthquakes to Mumbai terrorist's attacks, where social media has been on the forefront of disseminating and breaking news. Social media provides real-time accuracy, analysis and commentary of incidents faster than traditional media (Ruan et al., 2022; Abramova et al., 2022). The amplification and dissemination of information with a very fast speed is sometimes done by automated "bots". Such bots are trending on social media sites like Twitter where they are providing online crowds for legitimacy (Heidari et al., 2021). They help to generate more traffic as with digital contents; the more the posts are shared or liked, the more traffic is generated. Such things help to feast even fake information over the "digital means of communication" quickly. This is same as graphic contents with provocative comments that travel faster and become viral as compared to original posts (Xu & Sasahara, 2022). Such bots are banned by major social sites like Facebook as they spread rumours, misinformation, malware and noise (Urman & Katz, 2022). It is also observed that such bots have exploited opinions of people, misled and have even manipulated election results throughout world. These mysterious bots infiltrate unaware population of humans and manipulate their perception of reality for unpredictable results. With more advanced versions, bots can even engage people in complex interactions, amplify their influence, echo them with like-minded people and affect conversations nationally or internationally (Mbona & Eloff, 2022).

3.1 Dissemination of Misinformation

The dissemination of misinformation on social media like rumours (may be verified or unverified), fake news (same format as of legitimate news), spams (a large number of recipients) and trolls have become an immense problem throughout the world in recent years (Kumar & Nanda, 2019). The dissemination of misinformation may be due to unintentional spread to deceive some of its recipients. People receive such information from their friends, relatives or family members and pass it on to others due to novelty or their concerns. The same is done in case of widespread information about COVID-19 (Vraga & Bode, 2021) and Ebola (Sell et al., 2020). Sometimes misinformation is also spread intentionally by any individual or a group of people to gain popularity or making conspiracies. Such things were trending during the 2016 United States presidential elections, like the fake news of Paul Horner claiming credit of some news (Verstraete et al., 2021). Sometimes a troll is also used for dissemination of misinformation, which is to cause an argument or disruption for an individual or a group of people (Wu et al., 2022). The misinformation on the social media works as people interpret new information

Social Media as an Enabler to Combat Misinformation 9

in ways that encourage existing beliefs and worldviews. Also, people are engaged in motivated reasoning and confirmation bias unintentionally. One of the reasons for dissemination of misinformation is the backfire effect, which is a cognitive bias that affects the ability to change people's opinion and ability to rationally process information (Wood & Porter, 2019).

3.2 Social Media Combating Misinformation

Social media can be used to stop the spread of misinformation in different ways like putting restrictions on their platforms and implementing strategies to deal with misinformation particularly related to fake news and hate speech (Luo et al., 2022). Previously, these companies have provided their platforms as free hand to the users just like white paper where anything can be written. At those times they were not held responsible for the contents published on their platforms. Now this is not the case; social media is becoming news media for the latest updates, so it is becoming more responsible as well towards their users (Montag et al., 2021). These platforms have themselves implemented editorial policies which are human intervened and automated as well to filter the contents. The editorial challenges for these platforms are very many due to the volume of contents presented on them. Some of the contents posted on social media which invite violence or incite others to commit crime are posted without censorship or any hesitation from the user. One such incident is from New Zealand where a shooter broadcasted live their violent crime on Facebook (Geeng et al., 2020). For preventing such contents on its platform, Facebook is monitoring all the contents through humans 24 hours to check if there is any violation of its terms of use (Chiu, 2022). Also, any of the content that reaches a particular level of popularity is also monitored by human beings. For monitoring text, images and videos quickly, an artificial intelligence–based system is also deployed. On the same track, Yahoo has deployed algorithm to detect offensive and inappropriate images in public domain (Dib et al., 2022). In combating misinformation, social media companies are employing either restrictions or bans to the misinformation as done by Pinterest and Facebook. Alternatively, they are providing real or correct information to expose the misinformation as done by YouTube (Laforet et al., 2022). A three-stage approach to combat misinformation on social media is presented in Figure 1.1.

In Stage 1, humans can work as fact checkers from industry and business models to identify misinformation. Human-machine teamwork is an important aspect as machines can identify potential misinformation which can be double-checked by humans (Bhardwaj & Cyphert, 2020). Only machines can use artificial intelligence to check misinformation on social networks. This can be done in two stages—one at content level, based on knowledge and style (Ng, 2021). At social level, it is based on stance and propagation. Intervention in content can be done by the group of experts on different topics of science, history, geography, etc., to prevent spread of fake news. Also,

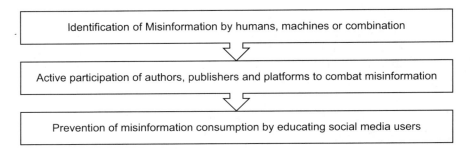

Figure 1.1 Approach to prevent spread of misinformation on social media

development of algorithms, which can inadvertently identify and halt the spread of hate speeches. In Stage 2, active participation of authors, publishers and platform is done to combat misinformation. Stopping authors to publish misinformation by threatening to imprison them by framing laws as done by Polish anti-holocaust law, locking them up like what was done in Turkey and demonetizing them by not allowing them to advertise at fake sites. Publishers can help in disseminating misinformation by denying it for hosting, as done by GoDaddy and Google to notorious neo-Nazi site, by denying listing in DNS (Domain Name System) directory as done by Catalan independence websites by Spanish government and blocking internet traffic to fake sites as done by the great firewall of China (i.e. Bloomberg to block access to selected foreign sites) (Chen, 2022). Finally, public platforms like Facebook, Google, Twitter can provide label, augment, hide or remove misinformation as labeling of fake news is done by Facebook, Google or down-ranking (pushing down) misinformation on search results with help from outside fact checkers, augmenting misinformation with legitimate information and warning users before sharing misinformation. Removal of misinformation can be done, as done by YouTube and *The Guardian*, and private messaging platforms Viber, Snapchat or WeChat can listen to private conservation as per the limits of privacy laws as done by Chinese social media to control shared contents online and prevents spread of misinformation. At Stage 3, prevention of consuming misinformation by educating the social media users as people forget misinformation very quickly just like the non-existent news. Users need critical thinking and material skills to combat misinformation on the social media platforms. Most of the time these days, young people are more active on social media as they spend significant time for blogging, chatting, listening to online music, watching online movie, posting photographs and connecting to friends (Bailey et al., 2022). This makes them more vulnerable to misinformation as they rely on more online information of the world which has perceived a reality to them. Therefore a concrete education on social media literacy and information should be made a part of the school and higher education institutions (Kumar & Lata, 2022). For imparting such education, teachers should be well-trained to educate students with necessary competencies in dealing with misinformation on social media. There should be projects within group of students at national and international levels to build critical thinking of young people in identifying truth and determining biases (Hayes, 2022).

4. Conclusion

Social networks have no official editors who can control the contents shared on media, but individuals are themselves the creators and editors. The most efficient technology to disturb the circulation of misinformation is through the platform. The misinformation is very hazardous as it can affect public opinions and election results nationally and internationally. This is because of the information flow with social pressure seen on trusted platforms that misinformation is taken seriously by the viewers. As most users are young people on social media, continuous education programme should be done to make them aware of online misinformation. The solution in such a scenario is to have a guerrilla war on misinformation. The chapter has presented a three-stage approach to combat misinformation on social media. Also, every member of society has a responsibility to battle with misinformation both offline and online. The members of society includes investigating journalism, general public for digital literacy and reducing financial incentives for misinformation on any platform.

References

Abramova, O., Batzel, K., & Modesti, D. (2022, January). Coping and regulatory responses on social media during health crisis: A large-scale analysis. In *HICSS* (pp. 1–10). Retrieved May 25, 2023, from https://scholarspace.manoa.hawaii.edu/items/8c080a34-8a9b-4913-9daf-1bdcb1891a23

Bailey, E., Boland, A., Bell, I., Nicholas, J., La Sala, L., & Robinson, J. (2022). The mental health and social media use of young Australians during the COVID-19 pandemic. *International Journal of Environmental Research and Public Health*, *19*(3), 1077.

Baptista, J. P., & Gradim, A. (2022). Online disinformation on Facebook: The spread of fake news during the Portuguese 2019 election. *Journal of Contemporary European Studies*, *30*(2), 297–312.

Basch, C. H., Hillyer, G. C., Zagnit, E. A., & Basch, C. E. (2020). YouTube coverage of COVID-19 vaccine development: Implications for awareness and uptake. *Human Vaccines & Immunotherapeutics*, *16*(11), 2582–2585.

Batzdorfer, V., Steinmetz, H., Biella, M., & Alizadeh, M. (2022). Conspiracy theories on Twitter: Emerging motifs and temporal dynamics during the COVID-19 pandemic. *International Journal of Data Science and Analytics*, *13*(4), 315–333.

Bhardwaj, A., & Cyphert, D. (2020). Direct benefit transfer using Aadhaar: Improving transparency and reducing corruption. In *Examining the roles of IT and social media in democratic development and social change* (pp. 185–210). IGI Global Publications.

Bhardwaj, A., & Kumar, V. (2014). Identity management practices in cloud computing environments. *International Journal of Cloud Computing*, *3*(2), 143–157.

Bhardwaj, A., & Kumar, V. (2021). Electronic healthcare records: Indian vs. International Perspective on standards and privacy. *International Journal of Service Science, Management, Engineering, and Technology (IJSSMET)*, 12(2), 44–58.

Bhardwaj, A., & Kumar, V. (2022a). A framework for enhancing privacy in online collaboration. *International Journal of Electronic Security and Digital Forensics (IJESDF)*, 14(4), 413–432.

Bhardwaj, A., & Kumar, V. (2022b). Privacy and healthcare during COVID-19. In *Cybersecurity crisis management and lessons learned from the COVID-19 pandemic* (pp. 82–96). IGI Global Publications.

Bhardwaj, A., & Kumar, V. (2022c). Web and social media approach to marketing of engineering courses in India. *International Journal of Business Innovation and Research (IJBIR)*, 27(4), 541–555.

Bhattacharya, J. (2022). Political deification of Lord Parshuram: Tracing Brahminic masculinity in contemporary North India. *Religion*, 1–26.

Boarini, M. (2022). Disruptive communication: Challenges and opportunities of the 21st century. In *Navigating digital communication and challenges for organizations* (pp. 39–57). IGI Global Publications.

Challenger, A., Sumner, P., & Bott, L. (2022). COVID-19 myth-busting: An experimental study. *BMC Public Health*, 22(1), 1–13.

Chen, F. (2022). Image-oriented design control in China: A case study from Nanjing. *Urban Design International*, 1–13.

Chiu, Y. P. (2022). An elaboration likelihood model of Facebook advertising effectiveness: Self-monitoring as a moderator. *Journal of Electronic Commerce Research*, 23(1), 33–44.

Dib, F., Mayaud, P., Chauvin, P., & Launay, O. (2022). Online mis/disinformation and vaccine hesitancy in the era of COVID-19: Why we need an eHealth literacy revolution. *Human Vaccines & Immunotherapeutics*, 18(1), 1–3.

Dutta, S., Acharya, S., Shukla, S., & Acharya, N. (2020). COVID-19 Pandemic-revisiting the myths. *SSRG-IJMS*, 7, 7–10.

Ferrara, E., Cresci, S., & Luceri, L. (2020). Misinformation, manipulation, and abuse on social media in the era of COVID-19. *Journal of Computational Social Science*, 3(2), 271–277.

First, J. M., Shin, H., Ranjit, Y. S., & Houston, J. B. (2021). COVID-19 stress and depression: Examining social media, traditional media, and interpersonal communication. *Journal of Loss and Trauma*, 26(2), 101–115.

Geeng, C., Yee, S., & Roesner, F. (2020, April). Fake news on Facebook and Twitter: Investigating how people (don't) investigate. In *Proceedings of the 2020 CHI conference on human factors in computing systems* (pp. 1–14). Association for Computing Machinery.

Gilardi, F., Gessler, T., Kubli, M., & Müller, S. (2022). Social media and political agenda setting. *Political Communication*, 39(1), 39–60.

Gurevitz, M. (2021). Has World War III begun. *Journal of Clinical Research and Reports*, 7(2), 2690–1919.

Hatano, J., Kusama, S., Tanaka, K., Kohara, A., Miyake, C., Nakanishi, S., & Shimakawa, G. (2022). NADPH production in dark stages is critical for cyanobacterial photocurrent generation: A study using mutants deficient in oxidative pentose phosphate pathway. *Photosynthesis Research*, 1–8.

Heidari, M., James Jr, H., & Uzuner, O. (2021, April). An empirical study of machine learning algorithms for social media bot detection. In *2021 IEEE international IOT, electronics and mechatronics conference (IEMTRONICS)* (pp. 1–5). IEEE.

Henry, L., & Plantan, E. (2022). Activism in exile: How Russian environmentalists maintain voice after exit. *Post-Soviet Affairs*, 38(4), 274–292.

Jain, G., Sreenivas, A. B., Gupta, S., & Tiwari, A. A. (2022). The dynamics of online opinion formation: Polarization around the vaccine development for COVID-19. In *Causes and symptoms of socio-cultural polarization* (pp. 51–72). Springer.

Kang, C., & Goldman, A. (2016). In Washington pizzeria attack, fake news brought real guns. *New York Times*, 5(2016), A1.

Kim, J. E., Lee, J. H., Lee, H., Moon, S. J., & Nam, E. W. (2021). COVID-19 screening center models in South Korea. *Journal of Public Health Policy*, 42(1), 15–26.

Kovid, R. K., & Kumar, V. (Eds.). (2022). *Cases on emerging markets responses to the COVID-19 pandemic*. IGI Global Publications.

Kumar, V., & Bhardwaj, A. (2018). Identity management systems: A comparative analysis. *International Journal of Strategic Decision Sciences (IJSDS)*, 9(1), 63–78.

Kumar, V., & Bhardwaj, A. (2020a). Deploying cloud-based healthcare services: A holistic approach. *International Journal of Service Science, Management, Engineering, and Technology (IJSSMET)*, 11(4), 87–100.

Kumar, V., & Bhardwaj, A. (2020b). Role of cloud computing in school education. In *Handbook of research on diverse teaching strategies for the technology-rich classroom* (pp. 98–108). IGI Global Publications.

Kumar, V., & Gupta, G. (Eds.). (2021). *Strategic management during a pandemic*. Routledge; Taylor & Francis Group.

Kumar, V., & Lata, M. (Eds.). (2022). *The future of e-commerce*. Nova Science Publishers.

Kumar, V., & Malhotra, G. (Eds.). (2020). *Examining the role of IT and social media in democratic development and social change*. IGI Global Publications.

Kumar, V., & Malhotra, G. (Eds.). (2021). *Stakeholder strategies for reducing the impact of global health crises*. IGI Global Publications.

Kumar, V., & Nanda, P. (2019). Social media to social media analytics: Ethical challenges. *International Journal of Technoethics (IJT)*, 10(2), 57–70.

Kumar, V., & Svensson, J. (Eds.). (2015). *Promoting social change and democracy through information technology*. IGI Global Publications.

Kwon, K. H., Shao, C., Walker, S., & Vinay, T. (2022, January). Mobilizing consensus on Facebook: Networked framing of the US gun-control movement on Facebook. In *HICSS* (pp. 1–10). Retrieved May 26, 2023, from https://scholarspace.manoa.hawaii.edu/communities/32d42543-f8b4-45fb-8c50-11a42cb8fe9a

Laforet, P. E., Basch, C. H., & Tang, H. (2022). Understanding the content of COVID-19 vaccination and pregnancy videos on YouTube: An analysis of videos published at the start of the vaccine rollout. *Human Vaccines & Immunotherapeutics*, 1–8.

Lockyer, B., Islam, S., Rahman, A., Dickerson, J., Pickett, K., Sheldon, T., & Bradford Institute for Health Research Covid-19 Scientific Advisory Group. (2021). Understanding COVID-19 misinformation and vaccine hesitancy in context: Findings from a qualitative study involving citizens in Bradford, UK. *Health Expectations*, 24(4), 1158–1167.

Loomba, S., de Figueiredo, A., Piatek, S. J., de Graaf, K., & Larson, H. J. (2021). Measuring the impact of COVID-19 vaccine misinformation on vaccination intent in the UK and USA. *Nature Human Behaviour*, 5(3), 337–348.

Luo, M., Hancock, J. T., & Markowitz, D. M. (2022). Credibility perceptions and detection accuracy of fake news headlines on social media: Effects of truth-bias and endorsement cues. *Communication Research*, 49(2), 171–195.

Lynch, K. S. (2022). Fans as transcultural gatekeepers: The hierarchy of BTS' Anglophone Reddit fandom and the digital East-West media flow. *New Media & Society*, 24(1), 105–121.

Mbona, I., & Eloff, J. H. (2022). Feature selection using Benford's law to support detection of malicious social media bots. *Information Sciences*, 582, 369–381.

Mehta, N., Pacheco, M. L., & Goldwasser, D. (2022, May). Tackling fake news detection by continually improving social context representations using Graph Neural networks. In *Proceedings of the 60th annual meeting of the association for computational linguistics* (Volume 1: Long Papers, pp. 1363–1380). Retrieved May 26, 2023, from https://aclanthology.org/events/acl-2022/#2022acl-long

Mheidly, N., & Fares, J. (2020). Leveraging media and health communication strategies to overcome the COVID-19 infodemic. *Journal of Public Health Policy*, 41(4), 410–420.

Mian, A., & Khan, S. (2020). Coronavirus: The spread of misinformation. *BMC Medicine*, 18(1), 1–2.

Montag, C., Hegelich, S., Sindermann, C., Rozgonjuk, D., Marengo, D., & Elhai, J. D. (2021). On corporate responsibility when studying social media use and well-being. *Trends in Cognitive Sciences*, 25(4), 268–270.

Näsi, M., Tanskanen, M., Kivivuori, J., Haara, P., & Reunanen, E. (2021). Crime news consumption and fear of violence: The role of traditional media, social media, and alternative information sources. *Crime & Delinquency*, 67(4), 574–600.

Ng, T. K. (2021). New interpretation of extracurricular activities via social networking sites: A case study of artificial intelligence learning at a secondary school in Hong Kong. *Journal of Education and Training Studies*, 9(1), 49–60.

Nguyen, M. H., Hunsaker, A., & Hargittai, E. (2022). Older adults' online social engagement and social capital: The moderating role of Internet skills. *Information, Communication & Society*, 25(7), 942–958.

Olan, F., Jayawickrama, U., Arakpogun, E. O., Suklan, J., & Liu, S. (2022). Fake news on social media: The impact on society. *Information Systems Frontiers*, 1–16.

Öztürk, D., & Mihçiokur, H. (2022). Production of innovative magnetic adsorbent Fe3O4@ PEI® Tween 85 and removal of oxytetracycline from aqueous media. *Separation Science and Technology*, 57(7), 1030–1042.

Regan, J. (2022). Pathways of radicalization: Contrasting the Boston Marathon Bombers and Mohamad Merah. *Behavioral Sciences of Terrorism and Political Aggression*, 1–21.

Rhodes, S. C. (2022). Filter bubbles, echo chambers, and fake news: How social media conditions individuals to be less critical of political misinformation. *Political Communication*, 39(1), 1–22.

Ruan, T., Kong, Q., McBride, S. K., Sethjiwala, A., & Lv, Q. (2022). Cross-platform analysis of public responses to the 2019 Ridgecrest earthquake sequence on Twitter and Reddit. *Scientific Reports*, 12(1), 1–14.

Salaverría, R., & León, B. (2022). Misinformation beyond the media: "Fake news" in the big data ecosystem. In *Total journalism* (pp. 109–121). Springer.

Sattar, N. S., & Arifuzzaman, S. (2021). COVID-19 vaccination awareness and aftermath: Public sentiment analysis on Twitter data and vaccinated population prediction in the USA. *Applied Sciences*, *11*(13), 6128.

Sell, T. K., Hosangadi, D., & Trotochaud, M. (2020). Misinformation and the US Ebola communication crisis: Analyzing the veracity and content of social media messages related to a fear-inducing infectious disease outbreak. *BMC Public Health*, *20*(1), 1–10.

Shawky, S., Kubacki, K., Dietrich, T., & Weaven, S. (2022). The multi-actor perspective of engagement on social media. *International Journal of Market Research*, *64*(1), 19–37.

Shomova, S. (2022). "Hieroglyphs of protest": Internet memes and the protest movement in Russia. *Problems of Post-Communism*, *69*(3), 232–241.

Singh, B., & Sharma, D. K. (2022). Detecting image forgery over social media using residual neural network. In *International conference on artificial intelligence and sustainable engineering* (pp. 393–400). Springer.

Sun, M., & Wu, Y. (2022). Changing family styles in China: The influence of traditional media and internet use on the acceptance of premarital cohabitation. *The American Journal of Family Therapy*, 1–18.

Urman, A., & Katz, S. (2022). What they do in the shadows: Examining the far-right networks on Telegram. *Information, Communication & Society*, *25*(7), 904–923.

Verstraete, M., Bambauer, D. E., & Bambauer, J. R. (2021). Identifying and countering fake news. *Hastings Law Journal*, 73.

Vraga, E. K., & Bode, L. (2021). Addressing COVID-19 misinformation on social media preemptively and responsively. *Emerging Infectious Diseases*, *27*(2), 396.

Wan, S., Xiang, Y. I., Fang, W., Zheng, Y., Li, B., Hu, Y., & Yang, R. (2020). Clinical features and treatment of COVID-19 patients in northeast Chongqing. *Journal of Medical Virology*, *92*(7), 797–806.

Wang, X., Zhang, M., Fan, W., & Zhao, K. (2022). Understanding the spread of COVID-19 misinformation on social media: The effects of topics and a political leader's nudge. *Journal of the Association for Information Science and Technology*, *73*(5), 726–737.

Wood, T., & Porter, E. (2019). The elusive backfire effect: Mass attitudes' steadfast factual adherence. *Political Behavior*, *41*(1), 135–163.

Wu, B., Li, F., Zhou, L., Liu, M., & Geng, F. (2022). Are mindful people less involved in online trolling? A moderated mediation model of perceived social media fatigue and moral disengagement. *Aggressive Behavior*, *48*(3), 309–318.

Xu, W., & Sasahara, K. (2022). Characterizing the roles of bots on Twitter during the COVID-19 infodemic. *Journal of Computational Social Science*, *5*(1), 591–609.

2 Science Versus Populism

Social Media's Strengthening of Public's Stance on Scientific Controversy

Ikbal Maulana

1. Introduction

The COVID-19 outbreak has become a global pandemic that has lasted more than two years, indicating the insufficiency of the international community's capacity, including the knowledge capacity, to deal with the virus (Kovid & Kumar, 2022). It has overburdened the healthcare system of almost every country and crippled their economy. The complex, multidimensional, and massive impacts of the pandemic make it a concern for everyone (Kumar & Malhotra, 2021). Everyone is affected, not just by being sick or having to take care of sick loved ones but also by experiencing economic and social hardship like never before.

Although governments and societies around the world were unprepared for the scope and magnitude of the COVID-19 pandemic, it was not unanticipated by scholars of various disciplines (Lasco, 2020; Kumar & Gupta, 2021). Previous experiences with the 2002–2004 SARS outbreak and the 2010 MERS-CoV outbreak informed them of the possible nature of the pandemic, its social and economic consequences, and the required multi-level governance structure to deal with it. These experiences can guide society to survive the pandemic when all important knowledge is yet to be collected and vaccines to be developed. But, for the general public, the uncertain situation of a pandemic is not tolerable and can cause anxiety (Taha et al., 2014). And the anxiety can only be reduced or eliminated either by increasing control over events or by increasing knowledge that can make sense of the situation they face (Miceli & Castelfranchi, 2005). Either they can influence reality or they understand how reality works and survive navigating through it. The COVID-19 pandemic impacts everyone requiring simultaneous local, national, and international measures. All these measures have limited knowledge of the virus and how it spreads. It confused the general public, which has to balance the protection from virus infection and the sustaining of life by assuring access to basic needs, such as food.

Science is expected to reduce confusion. However, during the pandemic, many things were unknown. Even so-called experts or scientists could not give the public a complete or sound explanation (Maulana, 2021). Facing

DOI: 10.4324/9781003315278-2

highly stressful events, such as the pandemic, people may feel a loss of control over and the predictability of the life they have to live. Consequently, they attempt meaning-making, which is a form of cognitive readjustment to "restore a sense of the world as meaningful and their own lives as worthwhile" (Park, 2010: 258).71). If they do not have access to and enough time to search for knowledge, they will be vulnerable to any disinformation or conspiracy theory that can give them a sense of order in the chaotic world (Bergmann, 2018). In current political contestation, populism has been attractive to many people because it gives an interpretive framework that makes the world more comprehensible to them, even though their position in the interpretation is the one in misfortune, which is however caused by other people. Often the elites have ignored their interest (McKee et al., 2021). During the COVID-19 pandemic, in some countries, populism has fuelled the spread of the virus, particularly through their denialism. COVID-19 has led to the strengthening of populism due to their simplistic grasp of theory that blames others as the cause of the problem (McKee et al., 2021). With respect to dealing with the pandemics, the harm of populism is the contempt for institutions, including scientific institutions. For example, the accusation that the current institutions have been dictated to by foreign interests.

This chapter discusses how populist sentiment, which is not necessarily orchestrated by a particular group, interferes with the controversy of vaccine development, and how populist rhetoric discursively overrides scientific arguments. It does not see the problem as black and white. Given the epistemic limits of non-experts, public reasons are sound in some cases. This chapter also seeks to reveal the role of politics and media in shaping how the issue is developing.

2. Scientific Legitimation

The borderless nature of the COVID-19 pandemic necessitates local, national, and international communities to coordinate with each other (Bhardwaj & Kumar, 2022). This coordination by different stakeholders requires different levels of knowledge. The quality of coordination is determined by the quality of institutional logic that is triggered during the coordination process. Institutional logic offers a framework for actor orientation they specify: issues they address, what is significant to them, and how they assess situations before acting (Hustedt & Danken, 2017).

While it is easy to agree that scientific knowledge is important to deal with the pandemic, determining what knowledge and whose knowledge are valued can be problematic, because there are many aspects of the pandemic which are scientifically unknown (Maulana, 2021). In developing countries, where empirical testing and tracing cannot be maximally conducted due to the limited resources, scientists have to make reasoned guesses based on available data. Besides, no single scientific knowledge or expert is sufficient to solve the problem; scientists need to combine their knowledge, which requires

18 *Ikbal Maulana*

complex scientific governance. Governments also cannot provide medicine and vaccine supplies on their own. Facing a pandemic that has multidimensional impacts, governments may also suffer governance failure, incapacity to offer systematic direction to the public, and incapacity to orchestrate interventions in multiple domains (Peters, 2015). These problems can weaken the established scientific and state institutions in front of the public that demands fast and accurate responses from them.

Compared to other disciplines, scientific governance in medical science is relatively stronger. It can be said that there is a global consensus about how knowledge should be developed and put into practice. Through the approach of evidence-based medicine (EBM), medical scientific communities can determine the globally agreed-upon assessment of the evidence of a claim (Kaefer et al., 2019; Kamradt-Scott, 2012). Scientific publication in respected journals is an important instrument for knowledge development, enabling scientists to assess, evaluate, validate as well as learn from each other. By implementing EBM, medical scientific communities can gain epistemic authority because their claim can be transparently assessed by their fellow scientists (Kerridge, 2010).

In general, the public does not know about EBM. Medical practitioners generally enjoy public trust through services that give the latter recognizable benefits, such as saving a patient's life, recovering from sickness, and minimizing pain. However, during the COVID-19 pandemic, when scientists still struggled to understand how the virus spread and the cure for it, the public was not easy to convince. People wanted clarity that the scientists or health institutions could not give. It gave the opportunity for populism and conspiracy theories to thrive and flourish because they readily gave a clear and comprehensible explanation (Bergmann, 2018).

3. Public Knowledge

During the pandemic, many people were feeling anxious due to the complex and uncertain situation they had to face, while government institutions often did not provide comforting information. Facing a serious threat of the virus but not being fully knowledgeable of it is often unbearable (Maulana, 2021). Anxiety evokes the need for control; if one does not possess pragmatic control over the situation, at least one has epistemic control, allowing one to foresee what will happen (Miceli & Castelfranchi, 2005). If they cannot control the world they face, at least they expect to fully know what is threatening them (Kumar & Svensson, 2015). They need a complete narrative or explanation that allows them to safely navigate the pandemic. Hence, they need to fill the gap in their own narrative (Ylä-Anttila, 2018).

To many people, having a full narrative without any gaps is more important than having an accurate but incomplete explanation of the situation. They need information that allows them to make sense of the situation, regardless of its truthfulness or accuracy. Since scientists or academics are not readily accessible to the public, people rely more on media as an alternative source of knowledge (Arnoldi, 2007). Even worse, people rely on social media, with no editorial filter, as their main source of information (Kumar & Geethakumari, 2014).

When people desperately need a full explanation regardless of its truthfulness, they become the vulnerable targets of disinformation or conspiracy theories. Conspiracy theories fulfil a human need for the comprehension of social complexity by "a state of affairs as products of covert plots of evil elites who, in secret, are systematically working to advancing their own narrow and often personal interests while harming the innocent and generally unknowing ordinary public" (Bergmann, 2018: 49). During the pandemic, people compared experts' explanation with their own experiential knowledge. With respect to the risk they had to face at work or the side effect they suffer after taking a vaccine, they believed they had legitimate experiential knowledge (Iles & Montenegro de Wit, 2020). They may not have been able to draw the limit of its legitimacy, but as long as they felt they could make sense of any challenges they faced, they could rely on it.

In times of crisis, populism offers simple explanations that are emotionally charged, making it immensely appealing to everyday people. Populism seeks to sympathize with people who feel anxious or resentful with either their own condition or country. The problem is populism frames the economic problems with the issue of identity, and views that their problem is caused by others, either elite, immigrant, or minority group (Head & Banerjee, 2020). Populism creates a dichotomy between the people and the elite, that can be extended into a broader dichotomy between in-group versus out-group (Hopster, 2021). It also convinces people not to trust public institutions, which are accused of being the cause of their problem. This distrust can even undermine public authority of scientific knowledge and institutions (Goldenberg, 2019).

4. Methodology

This chapter discusses how populism takes over science in the discourse of COVID-19 vaccines circulated among the Indonesian elite and public. The focus of the discussion is the controversy around Vaksin Nusantara (VN), a vaccine which is developed using a different scientific approach, that is, based on the dendritic cell (DC) vaccine therapy (Saadeldin et al., 2021). To understand the discourse among the elite, this chapter analyzed the news provided by major online news sites, such as Kompas.com, Tempo.co, and TheJakartaPost.com, which are parts of reputable and established media corporations. The news being collected was from 2021, when VN first got public attention because the result of its trial was not approved by the Agency for Food and Drug Control, or the Indonesian FDA (BPOM), and immediately attracted support from some members of parliament. This chapter also uses the material taken from the content of YouTube videos produced by major TV stations, as well as from a blog owned by Dahlan Iskan, a former CEO of

20 Ikbal Maulana

a big media corporation, who actively writes and produces YouTube videos commenting on any matter.

Public sentiment and responses were gathered from the comments on YouTube videos on debates about VN uploaded by major reputable news sites. These videos are selected because they present the two opposing parties.

Table 2.1 YouTube videos from which the comments were collected

Channel and Video Titles	Date	Views	Like	Comments	URL
Najwa Shihab (8.48M subscribers)					
Vaksin Cap Dalam Negeri— KASAD: Kami Siap Bantu Penelitian Vaksin (Part 1)	4/22/2021	386,073	4.6K	1,344	www.youtube.com/ watch?v=jGVTTK o9o_Q&t=3s
Vaksin Cap Dalam Negeri: Bela Vaksin Nusantara, Dahlan Iskan: Apa Salahnya? (Part 2)	4/22/2021	535,692	6.1K	2,507	www.youtube.com/ watch?v=1NdtWGJcLn0
Dahlan Iskan: Vaksin Nusantara itu Bapaknya Amerika, Ibunya Indonesia (Part 3)	4/22/2021	226,910	1.5K	1,096	www.youtube.com/ watch?v=wXM8Fy_XgIY
Vaksin Cap Dalam Negeri: Vaksin Mana yang Jadi Prioritas Negara? (Part 4)	4/22/2021	66,333	490	428	www.youtube.com/ watch?v=VdNnhc6OfSA
KompasTV (12.3M subscribers)					
Peneliti Utama Jawab Kontroversi Vaksin Nusantara— ROSI (1)	4/16/2021	708,212	7.2K	4,423	www.youtube.com/ watch?v=r8ZgB1jB 7FY&t=15s
Ramai-ramai Jadi Relawan Vaksin Nusantara, Apa yang Ingin Ditunjukan Anggota DPR?— ROSI (2)	4/16/2021	28,863	281	311	www.youtube.com/ watch?v=VBSJ1hFrCDw

(Continued)

Science Versus Populism   21

Table 2.1 (Continued)

Channel and Video Titles	Date	Views	Like	Comments	URL
Uji Klinis Vaksin Nusantara Tak Diizinkan, BPOM Dianggap Berlebihan?— ROSI (3)	4/16/2021	325,611	2.6K	2,242	www.youtube.com/ watch?v=wNGNzBIq 73g&t=2s
Jangan Bikin Bingung! BPOM & Peneliti Vaksin Nusantara Harus Bertemu—ROSI (4)	4/16/2021	9,976	101	51	www.youtube.com/ watch?v=ZVgmdm No40Q
TVOneNews (8.72M subscribers)					
dr. Tirta: dari Vaksin Merah Putih sampai Vaksin Nusantara, Kita Sangat Apresiasi I Dua Sisi tvOne	4/22/2021	73,583	435	468	www.youtube.com/ watch?v=XVq2a6dylKI
[FULL] Nasib Vaksin Terawan I Dua Sisi tvOne	4/22/2021	701,343	6.7K	3,791	www.youtube.com/ watch?v=5iRSAkGvhuw

This chapter seeks to categorize various topics in which the audience engages by using the computational method, called Latent Dirichlet Allocation (LDA) algorithm (Blei et al., 2003), implemented in a self-developed Python programme. LDA is a supervised machine learning method which does not require any training to classify data. The number of topics obtained from the execution of topic modelling is 34. After closely examining the contents of the comments of each topic, it was found that some topics can be combined due to being semantically similar but using different words. For example, one topic contains comments like "The host directs/interrupts the interviewee's answers", and another topic contains comments like "The host cuts the answers at will", which are combined because they are semantically similar. The combination process results in 17 topics.

5. Evidence-Based Medicine, Reputation and Power

As the fourth most populous country in the world, with almost 270 million inhabitants in 2020 (BPS, 2022) when the COVID-19 pandemic started, Indonesia had to spend a lot of money to get access to vaccines for COVID-19. While non-therapeutic measures, such as controlling and limiting people's mobility, were enforced, it was widely understood that such measures were only to temporarily prevent the pandemic from getting worse. To ultimately end the pandemic was to vaccinate the population which would cost a lot of money. This is also the object of suspicions by many people and of conspiracy theories. This is also the reason why many people and some politicians demand that Indonesia should produce its own vaccine to free it from dependence on foreign providers.

In Indonesia, the state-owned company "PT Bio Farma" has been able to produce vaccines against measles, polio, and hepatitis B. It also has Eijkman Institute, a research institution that is reputable for its research in human genetics and infectious diseases research, covering malaria, hepatitis, and dengue. The public was not aware of the complexity of research and production of the coronavirus vaccine, and the government and the scientific institutions probably could not communicate their lack of capacity for COVID-19 production to the public. Hence, they had to respond to this demand by forming a consortium of various institutions, which included research institutions and universities, to develop the vaccine.

Since the fall of the authoritarian regime in 1998, the Indonesian army, or TNI, has lost its leading role in Indonesian politics (Sebastian & Gindarsah, 2013). But during a crisis, the military has shown that it is the most solid and agile institution. The government regarded the TNI's involvement in distributing vaccine supplies and medical equipment as critical due to its network and facilities across the country, and manpower that is ready to act (Loasana, 2021). Even some high-ranking military officials have played important roles in dealing with the pandemic since it started (Aritonang, 2020). For example, the COVID-19 task force was led by an active army general. The then-health-minister was Terawan Agus Putranto, a military doctor. The Indonesian president even asked Defense Minister Prabowo Subianto to procure medical and personal safety equipment from China to speed up the delivery.

The state intelligence agency (BIN), which used to be led by a military general but is currently being led by a police general, took even more active actions, from creating reports about the development of the COVID-19 cases (Gumelar, 2020) to initiating the development of COVID-19 medicine in collaboration with the University of Airlangga. The proposed medicine was later disapproved by the Agency for Food and Drug Control, or the Indonesian FDA (BPOM).

The focus of this chapter is Vaksin Nusantara (VN), a vaccine unlike conventional vaccines due to a different approach of its development. It is a dendritic cell vaccine therapy in which the vaccine for each patient is individually made from the patient's own blood. The development of VN was claimed to be initiated by Terawan Agus Putranto, popularly known as Terawan, a military doctor who was previously the head of the military hospital RSPAD before being appointed as the health minister in the cabinet of President Joko Widodo's second term. However, it lasted only a year. Prior to his dismissal, a coalition of civil society groups launched an online petition, demanding that

President Joko Widodo dismiss Health Minister Terawan Agus Putranto for his alleged incompetence in managing the COVID-19 pandemic. He was perceived to have underestimated the risk of the pandemic (Oktavianti, 2020). That Terawan is a controversial figure can be seen in the data extracted from Google Trend (Figure 2.1).

There had been more than four times that Terawan attracted public attention. The first one was in April 2018 when the Medical Ethics Council of the Indonesian Doctors Association (IDI) recommended to suspend his membership due to an ethical violation. The reason was practicing a therapy that has not been proven by a clinical trial. It has become a controversy in national media because some people who said they had been treated by Terawan spoke up to defend him. They were high-rank military officials, government officials, and the political elite. The second time, he attracted public attention when he was appointed as the health minister in President Joko Widodo's new cabinet on October 23, 2019. This appointment seems to be political support for him. However, after having problems of communicating with the public, Terawan seldom appeared in front of the public. The government even appointed a spokesperson to communicate about the government's dealing with the COVID-19 pandemic. Ultimately, his position as the health minister was widely questioned after Najwa Shihab, the most popular host of a talk show programme, interviewed an empty chair because Terawan did not respond and come to the programme. And the last public attention on him was when IDI finally dismissed his membership. However, again, many people came to speak up to defend him.

As a medical practitioner, Terawan is a reputable doctor to his former patients, at least to those who defend him on media. Many people, including political and military elites, entrust their health to him. He was regarded as curing his stroke patients through a method called "brainwash", or, in medical terms, intra-arterial cerebral flushing, which sets out

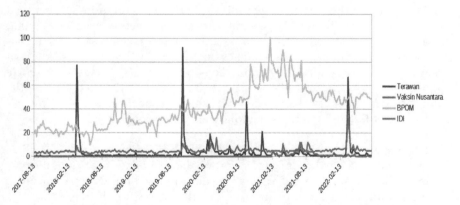

Figure 2.1 Terawan, Vaksin Nusantara, BPOM, and IDI as search terms of Google search engine

24 Ikbal Maulana

to treat stroke patients with a combination of digital subtraction angiography (DSA) and heparin injection. Despite the testimony of his former patients and his own claim that his method was the most effective in curing stroke patients, the ethics board of the Indonesian Medical Association (IDI) asserted that his treatment is violating the Indonesian Doctors Ethics Code and, hence, issued a recommendation to suspend him for a year (The Straits Times, 2018).

After returning back to his position as a medical practitioner in the military hospital, Terawan claimed to initiate the development of VN, a dendritic cell vaccine therapy. Since the vaccine is developed individually for each person using his/her own dendritic cell, Terawan claimed that it is safe. The body would not need to adapt to it, because it is not something foreign but its own blood. Hence, it does not need a pre-clinical trial on animals as required by BPOM. This could be the reason that the VN did not strictly follow the pre-clinical trial as required. Terawan claimed that the result of the trial is good. But this claim was refused by BPOM, which regarded that the trial did not follow the required procedure and did not comply with scientific standards (Bramasta, 2021). This agency does not even give approval for the execution of the second phase of the trial due to the existence of problems in the result of the first phase.

Terawan's claim that VN is an Indonesian-made vaccine has attracted support from the public. Some people have already shown that VN is not an Indonesian-made vaccine. Narasi.tv, a new media corporation cofounded by a respected journalist, Najwa Shihab, released a YouTube video showing that the vaccine is developed by an American company, AIVITA Biomedical. The video shows the highlighted part of the company's web page and its Indonesian translation. The quoted sentence is "AIVITA is evaluating AV-COVID-19 in a 180-participant Phase 2 clinical study in Indonesia, following a successful Phase 1 clinical study showing highly favourable safety and preliminary efficacy" (AIVITA Biomedical, n.d.).

Many people did not pay attention to the above refutation and believed that this vaccine is Terawan's own innovation. Some people even viewed that disapproval of VN by BPOM could be seen as part of a global and local conspiracy to keep Indonesia's dependence on imported vaccines. These kinds of views were not only spread by anonymous social media users, but an article on the website of the People's Consultative Assembly (MPR) containing the objection of the deputy chairman of MPR against the dismissal of Terawan's approach by IDI also contains the following quotation.

It is widely known that the Covid-19 pandemic disaster in the world and Indonesia has become an arena for the exploitation of capitalism in the healthcare sector. Terawan's medical innovation with his Vaksin Nusantara is considered to interfere with the interests of the rent-seekers in the Indonesian health sector.

(MPR, 2022)

More importantly, the argument that a dendritic cell vaccine is safe and does not need a pre-clinical trial on animals is widely received by Terawan's sympathizers, while BPOM still demanded that the phase of the trial must be repeated because there were some problems with the result. The criticism of Terawan was raised by academics. The research has received criticism mostly because it does not follow accepted scientific research and ethical standards, and the data is not accessible to the scientific community.

Once Terawan presented the result of the trial in front of the media and claimed that the result was good, it triggered a medical professor from the University of Diponegoro, Prof. Zainal Muttaqin, to write an open letter, which was uploaded on the blog of Dahlan Iskan (Iskan, 2021), a reputable blogger and also former CEO of a major media corporation, Jawa Pos Group. Dahlan Iskan was a supporter of Terawan and claimed that he has been helped by Terawan through DSA treatment. But, to be fair to every perspective, he uploaded the open letter. In the letter, Muttaqin asserted that any medical research must follow standard research procedures, and the result must be transparent. It must be shown to fellow scientists through publication so that other researchers can assess it. He criticized that VN was not transparent, and the result was shown in parliament rather than in front of a scientific community. The same criticisms were raised by Ines Atmosukarto, an Indonesian scientist who worked at the University of Adelaide, Australia.

Despite the criticism from the academics, Terawan got massive support from the public as well as public figures and some parliamentary members. Terawan was previously the head of the military hospital RSPAD, where he is still working. Some retired generals, who are also public figures or government officials, proactively came to the hospital to be injected with VN to show their support for Terawan. Defense Minister Prabowo Subianto and Presidential Chief of Staff Moeldoko also asked Terawan to get vaccinated with VN. Support was also shown by Aburizal Bakrie, a major businessman and the head of the advisory board of the Golkar party. Some parliamentary members also came to the hospital to get vaccinated by Terawan. One parliamentary member questioned the lack of support from BPOM for the development of VN, whereas BPOM has given the privilege to imported vaccines rather than local innovations (Sari, 2021). During the hearing of the parliament with the head of BPOM and with Terawan, and also during their internal meeting, some parliamentary members showed their discontent with BPOM's lack of support for VN.

During the conflict between BPOM and the team of VN, the government or the ministry of health did not show a clear stance. It was the Indonesian military, TNI, that took the initiative to stop the controversy between BPOM and researchers in the army hospital. The TNI spokesperson asserted that VN, even though its development was carried out in Gatot Subroto Army Hospital (RSPAD), was not a military programme. However, TNI would support any domestic innovation, such as vaccines and medicine, to overcome COVID-19 if it met the criteria and requirements set by BPOM (Tempo,

2021c). The head of the health center of Armed Forces headquarters insisted that VN must have a legal basis for its further development. It must also allow BPOM to monitor and assure that the vaccine would be safe and effective for future use by the public (Tempo, 2021b).

Ultimately, through a memorandum of understanding between Health Minister Budi Gunadi Sadikin, Army Chief of Staff General Andika Perkasa, and Head of the Food and Drugs Monitoring Agency (BPOM) Penny Lukito, it was determined that research on dendritic cell treatment will be conducted in the Gatot Subroto Army Hospital (RSPAD) and that it was not the continuation of Vaksin Nusantara, which its first trial did not pass the requirement of BPOM. It also stated that the research will not produce commercial vaccines. It will be a service to individuals, not for mass production. Hence, it did not require a distribution permit from BPOM (Tempo, 2021a).

6. Public Perception

From the comments on the YouTube videos in Table 2.1, topic distribution is generated using a self-made topic modeling Python application that implements LDA (Figure 2.2). The top five topics were as follows.

1 Attitudes of the host
2 Support and trust in VN
3 Indonesia does not support VN
4 Suspicions against imported vaccines
5 Doubting host's/guests' knowledge

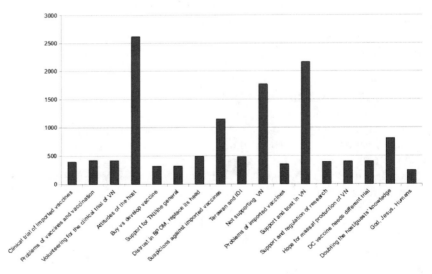

Figure 2.2 The topic distribution of the comments of a YouTube video

The host of the video tried to show fairness toward different perspectives, giving each guest the opportunity to show their opinions. More comments show the support for Terawan or VN than those against him. The comments show that they have their own views and can even disagree and judge the experts' opinions being interviewed in the videos. Their support for Terawan or his team is shown by the highest topic, "Attitudes of the host", which indicates their discontent with the hosts, who they think have been unfair to the persons they support. The starting point of the discussion is that VN did not comply with the research procedure required by BPOM, hence the host questions are directed to reveal the reason for the non-compliance. To the audience, the host has unfairly cornered the supporters. Hence, the following comments emerged:

"Rossi is not fair in questioning, tendentious, and unprofessional."

"Rossi [the host] is not looking for answers for the audience, but for herself. That's why she is just messing around."

"The one who asks is not looking for a definite answer, just keep chasing the interlocutors with questions."

Rossi, the host of Kompas TV, was regarded as unfair in carrying out her investigative interview through a series of questions. The show itself is targeted to understand or investigate the VN by questioning both sides, the proponents and opponents of VN.

VN is still under research and not yet proven, even though Terawan claimed that it was safe and good while imported vaccines were already available and many people had gotten vaccinated with them. As shown in the second highest number of topics, the video viewers tend to show support and trust in VN.

"Support Vaksin Nusantara. Reject imported vaccines."

"It is funny. Previously many people refused vaccines. Now they support vaccine, Vaksin Nusantara."

"It is more morally right if we are proud of our own products, not proud of foreign products.".

"We love domestic production more than foreign production. . . ."

The audience's sentiment is also in line with that of political and military elites. However, they express the same rhetoric of supporting local innovation.

The third highest topic, "Indonesia does not support VN", shows people's discontent with the lack of support from the government or others for the development of VN. They did not pay careful attention to the reasons why VN was not approved to continue to the next phases of the clinical trial. The following criticisms are raised against BPOM and the government.

"Only criticism does not look for solutions let alone support."

"Don't make excuses for banning (VN). Crazy regime. (Initiative) for the people is forbidden."

The controversial attitude of Terawan, which was not for the first time, was not negatively perceived by many viewers. One viewer even made the following comment.

28   Ikbal Maulana

"(His attitude is) the characteristics of a great person who thinks "out of the box". There are those who still think "in the box" . . . there are great persons and there are small persons . . . if you always follow procedures . . . when will there be any innovation?"

All high-tech products that Indonesian people can easily find in their surroundings are imported technologies, even though some of them, such as cars and smartphones, are locally manufactured by the subsidiaries of foreign companies. Only during the era when B.J. Habibie was minister of research and technology did Indonesia make serious attempts to make a technological catch-up, by developing their own aircraft industry and few other manufacturing industries. After his era, there was no more significant technological development being attempted in this country. Therefore, for the admirers of Terawan, a person like him, regardless of his rebellious attitude, must be supported. Otherwise, Indonesia will remain as described in the following comments.

"How can Indonesia progress if its own people's efforts are not appreciated and not supported?"

"The country of Indonesia has been set to become a mere market. Indonesia is a big country, not a slave country!"

To them, the BPOM and scientists' rejection of VN made no sense. But since they were not fools, there must be other reasons besides ignorance. Average people could not challenge them in terms of scientific arguments. The more effective way to counter their arguments is by delegitimizing them, by suspecting that there were evil motives behind their rejection of VN.

The fourth highest topic, "Suspicions against imported vaccines", shows the suspicions about the motivation behind the support for importing vaccines from overseas. The motives can be money or jealousy, such as suspected in the following comments, or even by the mafia.

"Imported vaccines give BPOM a lot of money, which makes it smooth to get licenses."

"Those who block are jealous of Terawan."

"It shows there is a mafia who is unhappy."

A lot of comments also show that the posters feel they are more knowledgeable than the people in the video.

The fifth highest topic, "Doubting the host/guests' knowledge", showed how expertise does not matter when their opinion is against the audience. One comment perceived that asking a series of questions only indicated that the host did not understand the topic.

"We can understand what the doctor means, but Rossi [the host] doesn't. She is also unethical."

Viewers can easily judge an expert, such as the following comments.

"Expert vs expert debate might be more useful. . . . Doctor Tirta, why is he being there?"

"What does Tirta know actually? He just pretends to be smart."

7. Discussion

The case study shows the difficulty of communicating science to the public, even though medical science is something that matters directly to most people, unlike astronomy about millions of light year distant galaxies. It is not due to public doubt of science. What causes confusion to the public is the controversy between BPOM and academics on one side and Terawan and his supporters on the other. While BPOM and the academics should be knowledgeable in medical science, Terawan is also a reputable doctor to his patients. Most importantly, his patients are public figures or elites, people with power, hence it is unlikely that Terawan would take the risk with their health. To the public, the trust of the patients in Terawan is sufficient proof of the efficacy and safety of his treatments. If Terawan's medical treatment is not good, he will not dare to experiment with his vaccines on retired army generals, big businessmen, and members of parliament.

On the contrary, to the public, BPOM and the academics focus too much on Terawan's non-compliance with scientific procedures and transparency. Generally, the public is not aware that medical research should comply with the evidence-based medicine (EBM) framework, which is a universally accepted paradigm in international medical communities, both among practitioners and researchers. Through EBM, any claim can be judged by its level of validation strength (Kaefer et al., 2019). EBM prefers reasoning based on evidence, while reasoning based on intuition or experience of experts is considered inferior (Tonelli, 1998). For the public, the research procedure is only a means to an end, whereas the result is the end. And, for them, the willingness of some elites to get vaccinated from Terawan and their testimony is an obvious result of Terawan's research.

YouTube video viewers may be anonymous users who just express their views without doing research about the issue. They do not face any risk of expressing any inaccurate view. But parliamentary members who are against the rigid procedure of clinical trials are well-educated people. BPOM and the academics failed to communicate the importance of the procedure. Even worse, some members even raised suspicions about the motive of BPOM that favours foreign vaccines, which, in return, triggered public suspicions and adoptions of conspiracy theories about business and foreign interest and even the mafia behind their disapproval of VN.

It is important for BPOM to gain support from the political elites, and the opportunity is there because some members of parliament have a background in medical education. Using the notion of objectivity, it can be persuaded that EBM does not reveal different truths. If the intuition of an expert, such as Terawan, is true, then it will also be true if and when the research was conducted in compliance with EBM. Only, it will cost more money and time.

However, there remains a problem with designing the trial. Terawan, as well as Dahlan Iskan (the former CEO of a major media corporation), questioned the necessity of trial on animals because dendritic cell (DC) vaccine is made of a patient's own blood. Interestingly, this view is also shared by many comments on YouTube. The topic "DC vaccine needs different trial" shows comments that support that view. Some examples of the comments are as follows.

"Why should human cells be tested on animals? It doesn't make sense. What should be tested is the person who is vaccinated, that's logical . . . not the animal. Why are human cells tested on animals? Their cells are different."

"Dendritic cells are personal. No human blood is taken and then put into animals. The sample of Mr. Dahlan's blood taken will be used as a vaccine for Mr. Dahlan only. For testing on animals, yes, the animal's own blood is used as a vaccine/medicine."

"My logic is that in pre-clinical tests, animal blood is taken, and processed and then put back into the animal; not human blood is taken, processed and then put into the animal"

The above comments and others on the same topic show that the public viewed that Terawan's argument that DC vaccine does not require a pre-clinical trial on the animal was a very sound reason. They even accused BPOM and the academics of being unreasonable. Since it could not be concluded that they did not have the knowledge or capacity to understand that, the more reasonable explanation was that there were other motives for the rejection of VN. Such motives could be money, or that they are getting pressured by foreign interests and their local compatriots, or even jealousy of Terawan.

People do make reasoning about any problem that concerns them. During the pandemic, medical science was of growing importance to individuals because it would affect their decisions and survival through the pandemic. They attempted to make justified decisions based on the information they could access, understand, and select. The selection was influenced by their attitude and motivation toward a particular issue (Sinatra et al., 2014). During the pandemic, the sentiment of nationalistic sovereignty in relation to the issue of vaccine production was more easily aroused. It affected the selection of information as a basis for further strengthening the sentiment. Nationalistic sentiment and anti-foreign vaccines, as well as suspicion against the foreign or business interest in imported vaccines, appear in many comments.

The distrust in public institutions was, in large part, caused by populist sentiment, which now can easily spread through social media. The above videos which gave space for academic communities seem to have failed in persuading the audience about the necessity of complying with research standards. Even regarding this matter, popular Twitter users who are also medical doctors did not dare to openly confront the public. That the public and elites do not support EBM, the importance of compliance with a scientific research standard and ethics is a defeat for scientific institutions, not just the organization, such as BPOM, IDI, but more importantly the rules and norms in conducting research. This is a problem of scientific governance, which makes scientific authority lose the public trust and opens the void to be filled by social media influencers (Goldenberg, 2019).

8. Conclusions

This chapter discusses the discourse around vaccine development, which was supposed to be scientific but developed into populist sentiment as it spread beyond the scientific community. Evidence-based medicine, which is embodied in scientific institutions (rules, ethics, and organizations), is being challenged by other ways of thinking. Evidence-based medicine has its own universally agreed-upon criteria of the strength level of evidence, of which a systematic review or meta-analysis of all relevant RCTs (randomized controlled trials) is the highest level, while the opinion of a single expert or the testimony of some patients are not taken into account. Only the opinion of authorities and/or reports of expert committees will be considered and is regarded as relatively low—that is, level VII (Pruka, 2022).

However, in a society that is not familiar with evidence-based medicine, the justification for a valid medicine or vaccine is different. The procedure is regarded as a means to an end, which need not be necessarily followed. The testimony of patients, who are powerful individuals, who dare to take the risk of taking the vaccine, is regarded as sufficient proof of the efficacy of the vaccine. For the public, in this case YouTube users, it is easy to take sides in the controversy. If the vaccine does not do any harm to the people who have taken it (as reported by mainstream media), and the patients feel good after getting vaccinated, the vaccine must be good. They also view BPOM and the academics who opposed VN as unreasonable.

Since it cannot be explained that BPOM and the academics are ignorant people, the public sought to understand it through either a conspiracy theory that there are business interests of global and local businesses or their jealousy of the developer of VN. Public attitude, as well as the elite who also ignored BPOM's recommendation, can weaken scientific institutions, in this case the rules and ethics related to evidence-based medicine.

References

AIVITA Biomedical. (n.d.). *Sars-Cov-2 vaccine*. Retrieved August 11, 2022, from https://aivitabiomedical.com/programs/sars-cov-2/

Aritonang, M. S. (2020, March 26). In COVID-19 response, can Jokowi avoid military "star wars"? *The Jakarta Post*. www.thejakartapost.com/news/2020/03/26/in-covid-19-response-can-jokowi-avoid-military-star-wars.html

Arnoldi, J. (2007). Universities and the public recognition of expertise. *Minerva*, 45(1), 49–61. https://doi.org/10.1007/s11024-006-9028-5

Bergmann, E. (2018). *Conspiracy & populism: The politics of misinformation*. Palgrave Macmillan.

Bhardwaj, A., & Kumar, V. (2022). A framework for enhancing privacy in online collaboration. *International Journal of Electronic Security and Digital Forensics (IJESDF)*, 14(4), 413–432.

Blei, D. M., Ng, A. Y., & Jordan, M. I. (2003). Latent Dirichlet allocation. *Journal of Machine Learning Research*, 3, 993–1022.

32   Ikbal Maulana

BPS. (2022). *Jumlah Penduduk Hasil Proyeksi Menurut Provinsi dan Jenis Kelamin (Ribu Jiwa), 2018–2020.* www.bps.go.id/indicator/12/1886/1/jumlah-penduduk-hasil-proyeksi-menurut-provinsi-dan-jenis-kelamin.html

Bramasta, D. B. (2021, March 13). Riwayat Vaksin Nusantara, Digagas Terawan hingga Dianggap BPOM Tak Sesuai Kaidah Medis. *Kompas.Com.* www.kompas.com/tren/read/2021/03/13/170400365/riwayat-vaksin-nusantara-digagas-terawan-hingga-dianggap-bpom-tak-sesuai?page=all

Goldenberg, M. J. (2019). Antivaccination movement exploits public's distrust in scientific authority. *BMJ,* 367. https://doi.org/10.1136/bmj.l6960

Gumelar, G. (2020, April 3). Indonesia's coronavirus cases may reach more than 106,000 by July, according to spy agency. *The Jakarta Post.* www.thejakartapost.com/news/2020/04/03/indonesias-coronavirus-cases-may-reach-more-than-106000-by-july-according-to-spy-agency.html

Head, B. W., & Banerjee, S. (2020). Policy expertise and use of evidence in a populist era. *Australian Journal of Political Science,* 55(1), 110–121. https://doi.org/10.1080/10361146.2019.1686117

Hopster, J. (2021). Mutual affordances: The dynamics between social media and populism. *Media, Culture & Society,* 43(3), 551–560. https://doi.org/10.1177/0163443720957889

Hustedt, T., & Danken, T. (2017). Institutional logics in inter-departmental coordination: Why actors agree on a joint policy output. *Public Administration,* 95(3), 730–743. https://doi.org/10.1111/padm.12331

Iles, A., & Montenegro de Wit, M. (2020). Who gets to define 'the COVID-19 problem'? Expert politics in a pandemic. *Agriculture and Human Values,* 37(3), 659–660. https://doi.org/10.1007/s10460-020-10118-5

Iskan, D. (2021, April 15). Ical Nusantara. *Disway.Id.* https://disway.id/read/2622/ical-nusantara

Kaefer, M., Castagnetti, M., Herbst, K., Bagli, D., Beckers, G. M. A., Harper, L., Kalfa, N., & Fossum, M. (2019). Evidence-based medicine III: Level of evidence. *Journal of Pediatric Urology,* 15(4), 407–408. https://doi.org/10.1016/j.jpurol.2019.04.012

Kamradt-Scott, A. (2012). Evidence-based medicine and the governance of pandemic influenza. *Global Public Health,* 7(sup2), S111–S126. https://doi.org/10.1080/17441692.2012.728239

Kerridge, I. (2010). Ethics and EBM: Acknowledging bias, accepting difference and embracing politics. *Journal of Evaluation in Clinical Practice,* 16(2), 365–373. https://doi.org/10.1111/j.1365-2753.2010.01412.x

Kovid, R. K., & Kumar, V. (Eds.). (2022). *Cases on emerging markets responses to the COVID-19 pandemic.* IGI Global Publications.

Kumar, K. K., & Geethakumari, G. (2014). A taxonomy for modelling and analysis of diffusion of (mis) information in social networks. *International Journal of Communication Networks and Distributed Systems,* 13(2), 119–143.

Kumar, V., & Gupta, G. (Eds.). (2021). *Strategic management during a pandemic.* Routledge; Taylor & Francis Group.

Kumar, V., & Malhotra, G. (Eds.). (2021). *Stakeholder strategies for reducing the impact of global health crises.* IGI Global Publications.

Kumar, V., & Svensson, J. (Eds.). (2015). *Promoting social change and democracy through information technology.* IGI Global Publications.

Lasco, G. (2020). Medical populism and the COVID-19 pandemic. *Global Public Health*, *15*(10), 1417–1429. https://doi.org/10.1080/17441692.2020.1807581

Loasana, N. A. (2021, August 22). Military involvement necessary in Indonesia's COVID-19 response: President's office. *The Jakarta Post*. www.thejakartapost.com/news/2021/08/22/military-involvement-necessary-in-indonesias-covid-19-response-presidents-office.html

Maulana, I. (2021). The epistemic problem of the COVID-19 pandemic and the necessary information policy. In V. Kumar & G. Malhotra (Eds.), *Stakeholder strategies for reducing the impact of global health crises*. IGI Global Publications.

McKee, M., Gugushvili, A., Koltai, J., & Stuckler, D. (2021). Are populist leaders creating the conditions for the spread of COVID-19? *International Journal of Health Policy and Management*, *10*(8), 511–515. https://doi.org/10.34172/ijhpm.2020.124

Miceli, M., & Castelfranchi, C. (2005). Anxiety as an "epistemic" emotion: An uncertainty theory of anxiety. *Anxiety, Stress, & Coping*, *18*(4), 291–319. https://doi.org/10.1080/10615800500209324

MPR. (2022, March 31). *Terawan Dipecat IDI, Ahmad Basarah Malah Suntik Booster Vaksin Nusantara*. www.mpr.go.id/berita/Terawan-Dipecat-IDI,-Ahmad-Basarah-Malah-Suntik-Booster-Vaksin-Nusantara

Oktavianti, T. I. (2020, October 4). *Civil society coalition starts petition demanding dismissal of Health Minister Terawan*. www.thejakartapost.com/news/2020/10/04/civil-society-coalition-starts-petition-demanding-dismissal-of-health-minister-terawan.html

Park, C. L. (2010). Making sense of the meaning literature: An integrative review of meaning making and its effects on adjustment to stressful life events. *Psychological Bulletin*, *136*(2), 257–301. https://doi.org/10.1037/a0018301

Peters, B. G. (2015). State failure, governance failure and policy failure: Exploring the linkages. *Public Policy and Administration*, *30*(3–4), 261–276. https://doi.org/10.1177/0952076715581540

Pruka, A. (2022). Evidence based practice Toolkit. *Darrell W. Krueger Library*. https://libguides.winona.edu/ebptoolkit/LevelsEvidence#:~:text=Statistics%2C%20Nursing%2C%20Physics-,Levels%20of%20Evidence%20Table,or%20strength)%20of%20recommendation.%22

Saadeldin, M. K., Abdel-Aziz, A. K., & Abdellatif, A. (2021). Dendritic cell vaccine immunotherapy; the beginning of the end of cancer and COVID-19. A hypothesis. *Medical Hypotheses*, *146*, 110365. http://doi.org/10.1016/j.mehy.2020.110365

Sari, H. P. (2021, April 13). Rabu Besok, Komisi IX DPR Akan Disuntik Vaksin Nusantara di RSPAD Gatot Soebroto. *Kompas.Com*. https://nasional.kompas.com/read/2021/04/13/11253681/rabu-besok-komisi-ix-dpr-akan-disuntik-vaksin-nusantara-di-rspad-gatot?page=all

Sebastian, L. C., & Gindarsah, I. (2013). Assessing military reform in Indonesia. *Defense & Security Analysis*, *29*(4), 293–307. https://doi.org/10.1080/14751798.2013.842709

Sinatra, G. M., Kienhues, D., & Hofer, B. K. (2014). Addressing challenges to public understanding of science: Epistemic cognition, motivated reasoning, and conceptual change. *Educational Psychologist*, *49*(2), 123–138. https://doi.org/10.1080/00461520.2014.916216

The Straits Times. (2018, April 10). *"Brain wash" stroke treatment under scrutiny in Indonesia after inquiry*. www.straitstimes.com/asia/se-asia/brain-wash-stroke-treatment-under-scrutiny-in-indonesia-after-inquiry

34 Ikbal Maulana

Taha, S., Matheson, K., Cronin, T., & Anisman, H. (2014). Intolerance of uncertainty, appraisals, coping, and anxiety: The case of the 2009 H1N1 pandemic. *British Journal of Health Psychology, 19*(3), 592–605. https://doi.org/10.1111/bjhp.12058

Tempo. (2021a, April 19). *Army Hospital, BPOM to conduct deindritic cell-based research*. https://en.tempo.co/read/1454276/army-hospital-bpom-to-conduct-deindritic-cell-based-research

Tempo. (2021b, April 19). *Nusantara vaccine must have legal basis: TNI HQ*. https://en.tempo.co/read/1454184/nusantara-vaccine-must-have-legal-basis-tni-hq

Tempo. (2021c, April 19). *TNI asserts nusantara vaccine not military program*. https://en.tempo.co/read/1454087/tni-asserts-nusantara-vaccine-not-military-program

Tonelli, M. R. (1998). The philosophical limits of evidence-based medicine. *Academic Medicine: Journal of the Association of American Medical Colleges, 73*(12), 1234–1240. https://doi.org/10.1097/00001888-199812000-00011

Ylä-Anttila, T. (2018). Populist knowledge: 'Post-truth' repertoires of contesting epistemic authorities. *European Journal of Cultural and Political Sociology, 5*(4), 356–388. https://doi.org/10.1080/23254823.2017.1414620

3 COVID-19 Pandemic and Economic Inequalities

Analysis of the Discourses of Turkish Political Parties on Twitter

Ayşe Fulya Şen

1. Introduction

Social justice theories place a strong emphasis on the idea of inequality, which is the state of not being equal, notably in terms of status, rights, and opportunities (Kumar & Svensson, 2015). The debate over economic inequality has largely come down to two points of view. One's primary worry is the disparity in outcomes in the material aspects of well-being, which can be caused by both ability and effort as well as external factors like race, family background, and gender. Ex-post or achievement-oriented thinking is used in this viewpoint. The second perspective only considers external factors that have an impact on one's prospective outcomes since it is concerned with opportunity disparity (United Nations, 2015). Income inequality refers to the extent to which income is distributed in an uneven manner among a population (Inequality.org, n.d.). From the Marxist perspective, it is argued that inequality and poverty cannot be eradicated without fundamental changes in the mode of production. The Marxist view is that inequality is inherent in the capitalist mode of production. In addition, it is functional to the system, which means that power-holders have a vested interest in preserving social inequality (Peet, 1975). Social inequalities can be the differences in income, resources, power, and status within and between societies (Kumar & Malhotra, 2020). Along with the neoliberal globalization process, it has been claimed that class divisions are dying and are no longer significant (Warwick-Booth, 2013). Inequality is a trending topic in recent economic research as well as public discourse. The distribution of income and wealth and its importance for people's well-being, GDP growth, and other key measures of the economic and social realm now feature as key concerns in (social) science, public debates, and the policy agenda in recent years. From the early 1980s onwards, economic inequality has risen again in many countries and regions around the world. Again, the 1980s mark a decisive shift: the adjusted wage has been relatively stable in the after-war period but started to decrease in the 1980s, with the labour share declining as part of the total national income (Theine & Grabner, 2020).

Unskilled labour saving technological advancement, financial globalization, and less regulated labour markets, especially informal and insecure

DOI: 10.4324/9781003315278-3

employment, are the sources of inequality (Kovid & Kumar, 2022). The danger posed by abroad economic operations reduces the negotiating power of labour, which results in increasing inequality as a result of financial globalization and the increased mobility of capital. In a time of hyper-globalization, rising inequality has given rise to populist politics. It's critical to distinguish between "democracy's" liberal and electoral components. A liberal society is one in which minorities' rights are respected, the government (and legislative) is subject to checks and balances, the judiciary is independent, and the rule of law is upheld. The election process, on the other hand, alludes to a multiparty electoral contest. An electoral "democracy" may elect populist rulers or parties that do not uphold liberalism's values because there is no reason to assume that they will always be present. Because of the largest worldwide recession since the 1930s and the death it is generating, the COVID-19 pandemic is, in this sense, a true human catastrophe (Kumar & Malhotra, 2021). The result is the immiserization of humanity, putting in particular the lives and livelihoods of the weak and marginalized around the world at risk (Murshed, 2020). The pandemic reveals the numerous shortcomings of modern capitalism. While the banking system was the source of the last destructive catastrophe of the twenty-first century, COVID-19 sparked a public health crisis that quickly evolved into an economic and social disaster (Kumar & Gupta, 2021). This immediately affected both daily life and the local and global systems of production, reproduction, and consumption. The COVID-19 situation has also raised the issue of the state's participation and exposed the potential for political action and drastic policy reform (Stevano et al., 2021).

The impact of COVID-19 and Turkey's responses show how the epidemic has altered people's way of life. During the pandemic, indicators like employment levels and unemployment rates have lost their significance; the former is due to the large number of workers on leave, while the latter is due to the unfavourable employment market. Similarly, it is crucial to take into account the number of persons who are awaiting employment while assessing the situation of those who are unemployed. There is a good chance that many people's job-seeking habits have been impacted by COVID-19 and the limits put in place to stop its spread. Along with the unemployment rate, there has been a significant rise in the number of inactive people who are categorized as being too elderly, sick, or disabled to work. The impact of the COVID-19 sanctions, which were announced on November 30, 2020, on the Turkish labour market was predictable. The separation of the December impact led to the conclusion that these measures resulted in the loss of 2.3 million jobs (full time equivalent) from November to December 2020. However, the second wave's effects were not felt equally by all sectors of the economy. While other sectors were largely untouched, the hospitality industry was subject to severe limitations that caused employment losses to return to levels seen in April 2020. Although the government had already devised aid packages to help restaurants and cafes, they probably weren't adequate. Therefore, there was a need for proactive labour market policies and tailored employment services that focus on reskilling and adaptation for a labour market following COVID-19. Additionally, it may be claimed that the current crisis is unique from others in the past. One of the main goals of employment services should be to help affected women get back on the job market as quickly as feasible. In fact, employment initiatives could be designed to produce short-term work right away in order to prevent disadvantaged populations from engaging in excessive economic inactivity (Caro, 2021). When evaluating the Turkish economy during the COVID-19 pandemic, it can be noted that the accommodative policy measures that were adopted by Turkey during the pandemic did generate certain vulnerabilities as a side effect, such as dollarization of the economy, the erosion of central bank reserves, and excessive credit growth (Çakmaklı et al., 2021).

At this point, it is important to discuss and reveal how policymakers frame economic inequalities, how these frames shape policy responses, and whether Twitter is a public sphere for debating economic inequalities. This essay assumes that the inequalities are managed rather than resolved permanently under democratic capitalism. The intertwining of social media and the political arena has made Twitter a more important tool for enhancing participation and the democratic public sphere. There are, on the one hand, more optimistic and, on the other hand, more skeptical views that Twitter constitutes a new public sphere. Social media, according to Fuchs (2014: 206–207), are likely to have a contradictory character in a contradictory society (made up of class conflicts and other conflicts between dominant and dominated groups) and do not necessarily and automatically support/amplify or dampen/limit rebellions, but rather pose contradictory potentials that stand in contradiction with influences by the state, ideology, and capitalism. As a result of decades of neoliberalism, modern societies are currently witnessing severely degraded common goods and services. The end effect has been a global capitalism crisis that gives us the opportunity to consider the idea of enhancing the commons. Shared struggle, which includes, among other things, common communication, is necessary to strengthen the commons.

In order to reveal how the political parties interpret economic inequalities and public interest on the discourse level, I have analyzed the political discourses of the political parties on current economic issues intensifying during the COVID-19 period and discussed the limitations and capacities of the political discourses on Twitter. The aim of this essay is to analyze the political parties' discourses on economic inequality on Twitter during the COVID-19 process. In essence, the key issue of this essay is to examine how the political parties frame and discuss issues related to economic inequality and public policies on Twitter. The reason for the selection of Twitter is that the rise of social media platforms has resulted in public discussions on the implications of these media for the political realm. In this research, I examined the tweets of the political parties covering between 2020–2022 and mapped the political discourses over key themes and users interactivity for investigating issues of economics, economic

38   *Ayşe Fulya Şen*

inequality, and redistribution policies. In addition to the content analysis, by inspiring from Grisold and Silke (2020), I categorized the tweets to the critical discourse analysis (CDA) approach in order to engage in more qualitative understandings of the relevant types of argumentation and legitimization strategies and the ideological aspects of the discourse. Thus, I revealed whether the political parties legitimate and justify official actions and norms in the economy realm and what they suggest to find a solution. The essay aims to answer three key questions:

1 How do the political parties identify and discuss economic inequalities?
2 How do the political parties consider the causes of economic inequality?
3 How do they suggest action plans?

2.   Theoretical Background and Literature Review

Massive wealth and pervasive poverty define the modern world. A number of theoretical assertions based on conventional economic theory support the practice of neoliberalism. Markets are portrayed as social systems that are ideal and self-policing. According to this theory, if markets were allowed to operate freely, they would optimally meet all economic requirements, effectively use all available economic resources, and inevitably create full employment for everyone who genuinely desires a job. According to this perspective, labour unions, the state, and a number of social practices founded in culture and history have all limited markets, which is why there is poverty, unemployment, and periodic economic crises in the modern world (Shaikh, 2005: 41). On the other hand, socialist critics of capitalism have evolved a more radical criticism of capitalism and its enabling ideas since the early nineteenth century. Socialist critiques have analyzed the inequities that capitalism produces as an expression of the unequal distribution of property rather than the failure of markets, and have urged for the equalization or socialization of private property. Generalized commodity production will inevitably lead to the polarization of wealth and poverty, the perpetuation of inequality, and the growing exploitation of the general populace (Clarke, 2005).

One could argue that key political changes have an economic component, and that conventional political discourse and its political communication methods neglect economic disparity in the mediated public domain. Different ways of thinking about inequality and socioeconomic justice are crucial to how these conflicts over the future structure of the social order are fought and how they turn out. Because of this, they are also essential for recognizing and comprehending the unique set of political economic concepts that support journalistic practices and newsgathering discourses in the modern media environment. Long-term trends in economic inequality raise important issues and have ramifications for a number of fundamental beliefs about the nature, outcomes, and political economy of liberal democracy in the advanced capitalist world (Preston & Silke, 2017). As Preston and Silke (2017) highlight, inequality is not merely an economic issue but is also a core political issue in our time. Offe (2018: 75) notes that the vast majority of policymakers are fully aware of the fact that the future of the economy, society, and polity of democratic capitalism is dependent upon the quality of present-day social policies.

Digital democracy, mediated citizenship, network society, and online public sphere are concepts used to describe how social dynamics have changed in the digital age. Skeptics contend that social media's impact on the public sphere, democracy, and civic participation is not always good, despite the possibility that the Internet and social media platforms have created a new setting where influence can be used to raise citizens' social standing and ideologies. According to the public sphere paradigm, political and social involvement demands not only open, unrestricted access for everyone but also effective communication among equal participants (those who are informed, intelligent, and sensible). The public good should take precedence above individual interests, and citizens should be involved in politics and society. In conclusion, the idea of the public sphere is defined as unrestricted rational-critical public discussion on issues of shared interest that is directed toward consensus with the intention of holding nation-state policymaking authorities responsible for their actions. The main issue is whether social media contribute to democracy, revolution, the growth of the public sphere, and citizenship, or if they serve primarily as tools of power and control (Iosifidis & Nicoli, 2021). The debates on the political public sphere focus on the weakening of its critical functions. Before discussing how economic inequalities are framed on Twitter, it is important to briefly explain how capitalist ideology assesses class-based inequalities.

The economic arrangements and "neoliberalism" as a dominating ideological perspective evolved as a result of several social and economic upheavals in the late 1960s and early 1970s. By the early 1980s, neoliberal capitalism had supplanted the "Keynesian compromise" form of capitalism that had existed after World War II. Capitalists formed a collective capitalist class consciousness and mobilized in the 1970s to recapture state authority in reaction to a declining rate of profit in the non-financial and financial sectors as well as challenges to the power and privileges of the rich by various social groups (Volscho, 2017). According to Marxist perspective, the bourgeois state is the capitalist class organized as the ruling class. The propertied capitalist class exploits the property-less working class. The political oppression of ruling class is often under the mask of majority rule to exploit the majority (Das, 2017: 391). Clarke (2005) argues that economic interests dominate cultural and political identities and subjective identifications cannot undermine the fundamental objective character of their opposing class interests.

By the early 1980s, neoliberalism was used to describe the wave of market deregulation, privatization, and welfare state withdrawal. By the early 1990s, neoliberalism had become elevated to an epochal phenomenon. It lives on as a problematic rhetorical device referencing to markets, economics, subjectivities, state authority, globalization, or neocolonialism (Venugopal,

2015). It is commonly asserted that economic liberalization increases income inequality in advanced industrial societies (Kwon, 2018). According to the definition of "neoliberalism," a society's political and economic institutions should be firmly liberal and capitalist, but they should also be reinforced by a constitutionally restrained democracy and a minimal welfare state. In order to safeguard freedom and advance economic success, it supports liberal liberties and the free market. Neoliberalism raises economic inequality, which is harmful in a number of ways and is a major source of worry. There are typically two different types of complaints of inequality. One of them is that it permits the concentration of wealth in a small number of hands, which results in the commercialization of politics. The imbalance of political power between bosses and employees within the company has been mentioned as a risk for neoliberal societies. Neoliberalism is frequently criticized for undermining democracy. The reason for this might be that severe economic disparity threatens democracy. By stressing the preservation of traditional liberal economic liberties, such as the right to private property, neoliberalism risks undermining democracy and restricting the capacity of democratic voters to choose to redistribute wealth (Vallier, 2021).

Neoliberalism is particularly vital for understanding how the problem of poverty and people who live in poverty are governed today. Feldman (2019) has highlighted the ramifications of neoliberalism for the poor and anti-poverty policy, as well as how it relates to social welfare policies that affect the opportunities of the poor. As a result, the effects of neoliberalism on the poor are manifested in a number of interconnected ways, including the welfare state's reorganization, rising inequality, and the manufacture of entrepreneurial subjectivity. Deregulation and welfare state reforms have increased economic inequality, which has been extremely difficult for low-income families. Welfare policies have altered as a result of privatization and pressure placed on social services. Neoliberalism has changed social welfare programmes and what they do by destroying social safety nets that protect the poor and replacing them with market-based antipoverty strategies.

The forms of framing of economic inequalities in a capitalist system by political discourses are important to understand how these socio-economic issues will be discussed in media and the public arena. Since the relationship between the media and politics determines how the media frame the public policies, analyzing how mainstream news media represent economic inequalities contributes to reaching a more democratic public sphere. For instance, Grisold and Preston's (2020) edited book which is about news coverage of economic inequality themes discusses how such storytelling relates to the specific aspects of the economic and public policy factors shaping the onward march of economic inequality and examines how the news media represent economic processes in general and, in particular, the subtheme of economic inequalities, and it reveals significant silences concerning the structural patterns of social power and their actual or potential influence on economic inequalities in the corpus of news media stories.

As Luther et al. (2018: 296) noted, media representations of the poor, the wealthy, and those in between play a major role in forming opinions, showing viewers who these people are and, as a result, what to think about them. Essentially, the media can cultivate impressions about the social classes. Furthermore, Sen and Sen (2016) argue that media contents often reproduce the inequalities that exist in a society based on class, and the working-class identity is not given coverage, and inequality is normalized in the mainstream news media, as in Turkey's case. Şen (2017) also reveals that news coverage of concepts related to class-based rights and social inequalities are not debated sufficiently in the public sphere, these issues are largely ignored by the mainstream news media, and class identity is underrepresented in Turkey. It can be argued that there is an increasing interplay between news and social media coverage of events and issues. Dobson and Knezevic (2017) explored how Internet memes and perceptions about poverty relate to one another. They used critical discourse analysis to examine a collection of frequently used poverty memes and found that memes legitimize and perpetuate power and dominance relationships in society. Neoliberalism therefore approaches poverty as an individual rather than a systemic problem. A large body of work has identified poverty stereotyping in conventional media, including news reporting. This picture of poverty is widely duplicated in a variety of media types. Although social media offers information that conforms to users' world views, it also serves as a useful tool for dispelling myths and presumptions about poverty and a variety of other social justice issues.

Dominant political discussions on poverty and class-based issues determine how these issues would be dealt with in the public sphere. Hence, to what extent the political parties are differentiated from each other in terms of social policies and economic inequalities is an important referent displaying whether they are egalitarian and pluralist. In this context, Twitter is forefront to generate a public debate on economic inequalities. This study has focused on how the political parties depict the inequalities and class-based issues in Turkey's case. How the social welfare rights are depicted in political discourses reflects to the media to build public discourses. In addition, the political discourses on Twitter create an opportunity for the users to express their personal opinions about poverty, inequalities, and social welfare rights. In general, this article is related to the literature over how political actors use Twitter to inform the public and whether Twitter is a public sphere, including responses to the public issues.

Masroor et al. (2019) have analyzed how the political elites use Twitter for the purpose of gaining public acclaim and propagating political ideologies. The analysis reveals the hidden ideological structures and strategies realized through a variety of rhetorical moves in the chosen tweets because the political discourse on Twitter necessitates a critical attention toward linguistic structures and strategies to uncover the relationship between language and social practices. Thus, by influencing public opinion, the cognitive dichotomy of positive self-presentation and negative other-presentation aids in

42 Ayşe Fulya Şen

establishing political dominance and the justification of political activities. Yaqub et al. (2017) have investigated the sentiment of tweets by the two main presidential candidates Hillary Clinton and Donald Trump along with almost 2.9 million tweets by Twitter users during the 2016 US presidential elections, and analyzed these short texts to evaluate how accurately Twitter represented the public opinion and real-world events of significance related with the elections. They have found that Twitter was primarily used for rebroadcasting already-present opinions in the form of retweets, with little communication between users and little original content created by users. The research has also reached the conclusion that of significance was the finding that sentiment and topics expressed on Twitter can be a good proxy of public opinion and important election-related events. In addition, Haman's (2020) study has showed that the global pandemic COVID-19 significantly impacted the discourse on Twitter, and there was a significant growth rate of Twitter users in comparison with pre-pandemic months.

The COVID-19 impacted the Turkish economy hard, exposing the economy's various flaws. One of these flaws, income distribution, had been developing for a long time prior to the pandemic's onset. However, it can be claimed that the epidemic has worsened the economic distribution in Turkish society and increased existing inequities. Additional financial assistance is required for households, especially low-income ones, and business organizations (Bayar et al., 2020). The pandemic, according to Bayar et al. (2020), runs the danger of escalating both the rate and the severity of poverty. It has been observed that macroeconomic policies reviving economic growth must be as inclusive as possible for the communities most likely to be impacted. Therefore, in order to prevent a severe rise in poverty, Turkey needs both measures to boost economic growth and redistributive policies.

In this context, this study seeks to address that how the inequality issues have been framed by the political parties' discourses on Twitter, which is the public sphere. Since Twitter can be acknowledged as a reflection of real-world events and opinions, the messages of the mainstream political parties on economic-based inequalities show how the capitalist viewpoint assesses this issue. The analysis aims to provide an insight into whether the political parties want to solve this problem or articulate it around populist discourses.

3. Method and Research Design

This study's methodology is qualitative content analysis, which places a greater emphasis on hidden material than quantitative content analysis often does. The text's intended meaning is referred to as latent content. Latent content analysis uses statistical methods and coding schemes to determine whether the terms on a website were organized into specific discourses about anything (Ackland, 2013). By allocating successive pieces of the content to the categories of a coding frame, qualitative content analysis describes the meaning of qualitative data. The method's central frame includes all the elements that are included in the description and interpretation of the content. The technique is characterized by three elements: data reduction, systematicity, and adaptability. It necessitates concentrating on a few meaning-related details (Schreier, 2013). Content analysis provides a useful and multifaceted, methodological framework for Twitter analysis. The computer-assisted content analysis of tweets can be organized on two levels. While the first level allows for a word- or phrase-of frequency analyses, second-level analysis means annotating, interpreting, and quantifying text segments (Einspänner et al., 2014). Thematic content analysis is the term for any content analysis in which variables indicate the occurrence (or frequency of occurrence) of particular themes or concepts. The method is useful to reveal the prominence of various themes in texts, reflecting broad cultural shifts (Popping, 2017). An understanding of a communication interaction or process inside a communication event or set of events is provided by a thematic analysis. The results of theme analysis are typically used to further current knowledge, influence policy, and/or enhance communication techniques (Hawkins, 2017). As Hawkins (2017) points out, I have analyzed tweet topics to show political perspectives on economic inequality, recognized patterns that are recurring, and evaluated how those patterns relate to the research issue.

This study presents a critical perspective on economic issues and attempts to explore the political discourses on economic inequalities by using a qualitative research framework. In order to explore the patterns of the political discourse on inequality and poverty, I put together and analyzed the tweets of the political parties by utilizing qualitative data analysis across the research process. I used the different types of digital content analysis and created the sample units by collecting tweets from the political parties' accounts. I pulled out common themes and issues and categorized the responses so that I can compare one group of responses against another. In addition to the keyword frequency, I made the hand coding of tweets and also examined the types of content within tweets (e.g. critics of the government, policy planning and projection, policy proposals, information to citizens, etc.) and conducted a thematic analysis to look for ideas or patterns within the political contents on economic inequalities. Following the methodology adopted for the first stage, I coded tweets in a number of distinct categories and analyzed their treatment of certain key themes related to economic inequality and applied discourse analysis in order to reveal legitimization strategies. As Grisold and Silke noted (2020: 126), legitimation is defined as an aspect of discourse that justifies "official" actions and whereby an institutional actor will claim to respect official norms and remain within the "prevalent moral order". In this context, by adopting Grisold and Silke's (2020: 124–126) model, I tried to identify various "significant silences" in the tweets ignoring issues in the face of growing inequality.

To talk about the features of these political parties, the ruling party, the Justice and Development Party (AK Party), represents a conservative democratic and political-Islamist ideological line, whereas the main opposition

44   Ayşe Fulya Şen

party, the Republican People's Party (CHP), is identified with secularism, center left, social democracy, and Kemalism, also known as Atatürkism, or the founding official ideology of the Republic of Turkey. Neoliberal changes have been enacted in Turkey during the AK Party government. According to Özdemir (2020), AK Party's social policies include some contradictions due to decreasing the power and conditions of labour. Despite its neoliberal policies, the AK Party has gained mostly the votes of the poor of the society. Bahçe and Köse (2017) point out that a new welfare system has formed under the AK Party administration. To lessen poverty and deprivation, this welfare regime is built on voluntary public and private transfers. On the other hand, Emre (2014) contends that the Republican People's Party of the 1960s has fluctuated in a social democratic stance since that time. The growing influence of the left inside the CHP caused the Republican People's Party to reorient itself as "left of center" by the middle of the 1960s.

Since Twitter, as a digital political communication platform, also involves public policy responses in the digital age, analyzing tweets provides insight into the characteristics of political vision on economic inequalities. Thus, this study was limited to a total of 172 tweets of the ruling (AK Party) and main opposition (CHP) parties during the period reflecting the COVID-19 impacts from March 2020–June 2022. The 172 tweets were collected among those that included the keywords related to economic inequalities and subjected to qualitative content analysis. This time frame and the samples formed a framework for the social media discourses on inequalities. As Potter and Levine-Donnerstein (1999) noted, since content analyses need not be limited to theory-based coding schemes and standards, this study is based on manifest and latent content for providing validity and reliability.

4.   Findings and Discussions

Firstly, this chapter provides a summary analysis of the keywords related to economic inequality and analyzes the political parties' stances on what extent economic inequality is problematic for the economy and society. The following table presents coverage of economic policies and problems in the political discourse of the political parties on Twitter. In order to evaluate how the political parties had framed economic-based issues, this chapter discussed the core themes of the political parties' discourses. Table 3.1 shows how the political parties covered economic inequality-related issues by frequency of certain keywords. These keywords were chosen to point out the different aspects of inequality comprehensively. When looking at the political parties' attitude toward economic inequality within the period of analysis, it was seen that the ruling party (AK Party) included low coverage of the economic inequalities in their discourse, but the main opposition party (CHP) highly covered the economic-based issues compared to the ruling party (see Table 3.1). The tweets were counted by using the "Twitter advanced search" application and filtered over the keywords and dates.

COVID-19 Pandemic and Economic Inequalities   45

Table 3.1 Frequency distribution of the keywords on the tweets of the political parties (March 2020–June 2022)

Keywords and Phrases	AK Party @Akparti	CHP @herkesicinCHP	Total
Poverty	—	15	15
Economic crisis	1	1	2
Minimum wage	4	25	29
Unemployment	1	12	13
Inflation	11	25	36
Price increase/increase	1	46	47
Starvation line	—	5	5
COVID–19	4	11	15
Workers' rights	—	—	—
Social policy	—	—	—
Cost of living	—	5	5
Economic issues	1	1	2
Syndicate	—	3	3
Total	23	149	172

Firstly, it is seen that the main opposition party (CHP) had more coverage of the issues related to economic inequality than the ruling party. On the other hand, these findings also revealed that this tweet coverage of the two political parties did not contain any emphasis or proposal for a policy for reducing or reversing the growing economic inequalities. These debates put forward to the public agenda are important to become more visible of growing inequalities and increase awareness among the public. Table 3.1 indicated that the most used words were "price increase", "inflation", and "minimum wage" respectively, and the main opposition party stated them more than the ruling party. Furthermore, not mentioning each of two parties' concepts of workers' rights and social policy means that they disregarded the policies to remove the economic inequalities. Focus Economics report (2022) noted that Turkey's economy will expand at a notably softer pace this year, as domestic demand is dented by pessimistic consumer sentiment, a weak currency, and elevated inflation. Hence, red-hot inflation and deeply pessimistic sentiment have also affected the concept definitions and usages of the political parties. Whereas the keywords referring to social policies and inequality, such as poverty, price increase, the edge of starvation, cost of living, and syndicate, were mentioned in the main opposition party's (CHP) tweets relatively at a low level, and not mentioned in the ruling party's tweets. The "economic crisis", which was an umbrella term citing Turkish economic challenge, was also only once used. Furthermore, social policy topics such as unemployment, minimum wage, cost of living, and the edge of starvation were not emphasized by the political parties adequately, in particular the main opposition party. The ignoring of problematic aspects of inequality or hardly mentioning them can be interpreted as the normalization of the neoliberal regime and seeking a solution within the neoliberal approach. Particularly,

46 Ayşe Fulya Şen

the missing words "workers' rights" and "economic issues" within the main opposition party's discourse meant that there were no differences between the two parties on redistribution policies.

In the second stage, I carried out a thematic analysis to extract meanings from the text. In order to identify how discourses on economy-related problems were framed on Twitter and formed in which context, I coded the tweets in four ways according to the character of the responses of the ruling and main opposition parties and categorized the tweets to the themes. Table 3.2 and Table 3.3 indicate whether tweets were policy-oriented, polemic-oriented, or informative and which one proposed a solution to economic inequality.

Although the main opposition party, CHP, pointed out the negative consequences of growing inequality, it can be said that there was no radical policy proposal. The main opposition party criticized the government due to consumer price jumping and the destructive effects of the price increase. In a market economy, an increase in prices is seen as a "change", and inflation means the rate of increase in prices. Thus, when inflation and price increase concepts, which were the most referred to, are put together, it was seen CHP criticizing the government. On the other hand, the proposal of CHP for the edge of starvation was about giving unemployed people support from unemployment insurance up to the minimum wage. This policy means a tentative solution and poverty reduction strategy. That the CHP did not include "workers' rights" and "social policy" concepts as a social democratic main opposition party can be evaluated as the internalization of neoliberalism.

Table 3.3 displays the characteristics of the ruling party's themes distribution. When the relevant tweets are categorized and the treatment of the key

Table 3.2 Thematic coding of CHP's tweets (@herkesicinCHP)

Themes of the Tweets on Economic Inequality	Critics to the Government	Policy Planning and Policy Proposals	Information to Citizens	Total
Poverty	12	2	1	15
Economic crisis	1	—	—	1
Minimum wage	12	11	2	25
Unemployment	10	2	—	12
Inflation	23	1	1	25
Price increase/increase	46	—	—	46
Starvation line	2	2	1	5
COVID–19	—	—	11	11
Workers' rights	—	—	—	—
Social policy	—	—	—	—
Cost of living	3	2	—	5
Economic issues	1	—	—	1
Syndicate	1	—	2	3
Total	111	20	18	149

COVID-19 Pandemic and Economic Inequalities 47

Table 3.3 Thematic coding of AK Party's tweets (@Akparti)

Themes of the Tweets on Economic Inequality	Critics to the Political Opponents	Policy Planning and Policy Proposals	Information to Citizens	Total
Poverty	—	—	—	—
Economic crisis	1	—	—	1
Minimum wage	—	—	4	4
Unemployment	—	—	1	1
Inflation	—	1	10	11
Price increase/ increase	—	—	1	1
Starvation line	—	—	—	—
COVID–19	—	—	4	4
Workers' rights	—	—	—	—
Social policy	—	—	—	—
Cost of living	—	—	—	—
Economic issues	—	—	1	1
Syndicate	—	—	—	—
Total	1	1	21	23

themes related to economic inequality is evaluated, it was concluded that the ruling party (AK Party) did not touch on the key issues related to the social policies and economic inequalities such as poverty, starvation line, workers' rights, social policy, cost of living, and syndicate but only informed to the citizens on inflation and minimum wage on the basis of new steps and inflation measures by presenting what was done. Instead of debating these topics, the findings revealed that the ruling party (AK Party) did not want to focus on inequality and its negative effects on the citizens.

This thematic analysis proved that the main opposition party highlighted the economic issues leading to inequality but sought solutions to the problems within the capitalist values. On the other hand, it can be claimed that the ruling party did not evaluate economic inequality as a problem and disregarded "poverty" as an umbrella term and a policy; instead, they pointed out raising the minimum wage as a way of reducing poverty. As Johnston (2005) notes, there have been a number of new attempts within neoliberal philosophy as a result of the rising worries about poverty and inequality, and it is thought that liberalization can help to lessen poverty. The reformed neoliberal viewpoint contends that, through enhancing education and training, reducing regulations, and redistributing certain assets, the poor will be better able to engage in markets. According to Johnston (2005: 140), poverty and inequality are unlikely to decrease because continuous supports for liberalization within the reformed approach precludes the implementation of the measures that would best help the poor.

In the third stage, I was inspired by Grisold and Silke's (2020) analysis that focuses on those news media articles that advance discourses that argue or imply that "inequality is a problem or not a problem". Accordingly, I chose the tweets in terms of whether the political parties suggested any action plan, constructed growing inequality as a problem or not as a problem, and had joint keywords in every two parties. Thus, I tried to interpret the approaches of the political parties to reducing or removing inequality via their discourses.

5. Discourses on Reducing Inequality

> With the inflation differentials in July and the new regulations in wages in January, we will further relieve all segments of our nation.
>
> (@Akparti, 13 June 2022)

> The inflation difference will be added to the increase that our workers receive in the collective agreement. We add an additional increase of 2.5 percent.
>
> (@Akparti, 26 January 2022)

> In this minimum wage work, we will protect our workers from inflation and the negative effects of price increases.
>
> (@Akparti, 30 November 2021)

> With the money melted in the first three months, the pensioner could be given a bonus equal to the minimum wage on two holidays. On top of that, the support to the farmers could be increased 3 times and the minimum wage could be increased to 5 thousand liras . . . There is more. Do you see the enormity of the possibilities?
>
> (@herkesicinCHP, 18 May 2022)

> Regardless of where they live in Turkey, every family should and will have an income at least as much as the minimum wage. Every home must have an insured worker. These are not graces. Social state means the state that is on the side of the poor.
>
> (@herkesicinCHP, 9 January 2022)

> No one should despair. Competent cadres that have defeated the inflation monster in the past and will do so in the future are available in the CHP and the Nation Alliance.
>
> (@herkesicinCHP, 7 February 2022)

> Salaries of our citizens called 'stay at home' must be paid from the unemployment insurance fund as the minimum wage for at least 3 months.
>
> (@herkesicinCHP, 3 April 2020)

> Party Spokesperson ÖmerÇelik: We see that there are some crisis beggars. We see that there are those who constantly want the economic crisis to break out and lead to it. As AK Party, we state our theses.
>
> (@Akparti, 18 August 2020)

Deputy Chairman OğuzKaanSalıcı: "Turkey is under a severe economic crisis. You are the cause of the economic crisis, you have been managing it for 18 years!"

(@herkesicinCHP, 17 December 2020)

These statements above implied that issues based on "minimum wage" and "inflation" would or should have been solved and highlighted the reducing inequality. At the beginning of COVID-19, during the quarantine period, many employees had to stay at home. Due to unpaid salaries in some sectors and businesses, CHP prioritized the point of no cuts in wages. When looking at the general discourse framework of the two parties, it was seen that the ruling and main opposition parties were only distinguished from each other in terms of the method. "Economic crisis" was mentioned only one time in the tweets under the research scope and used in the context of two political parties criticizing each other. The findings showed that the ruling party denied the economic crisis and charged the political opponents to want a crisis, but the main opposition party also criticized the ruling party for leading to a severe crisis. These words pointed out a political and populist conflict rather than a rational debate. Another key point in these discourses was that "inequality" had not been mentioned at all. This framework revealed that the discourses were based on a neoliberal approach, reproduced growing inequality as "not a problem", and not toward removing it. As also Munck claims, neoliberalism dominates the political field for both the ruling class and the movements that stand in their way (2005: 60).

6. Conclusion

Mass media play a vital role in the construction and distribution of specific discourses to the public, for example through selecting certain events or stories as newsworthy and then sourcing and framing those news stories in specific ways (Grabner et al., 2020). Similarly, social media has the same function for creating public sphere. Therefore, the political discourses circulating also shape the public discourses and opinions. This paper analyzed how economic inequalities were framed in the political parties' discourse on Twitter. It is important to discuss all aspects of the economic and social inequalities in terms of the development of pluralist democracy in a society. Analyzing political discourses on economic inequality provided insight into whether political parties engaged with economic inequalities and aimed to reach a more democratic society in terms of economic equality. When reviewing the political discourses in this study, it can be argued the political parties confronted with growing inequality did not tend to propose a policy eradicating it. The findings showed that both the ruling and main opposition party assessed raising the minimum wage to ensure economic stability as a strategy to cut poverty. The tweets analyzed here presented the dominant discourses on economic issues in the political arena. Similar to Grisold and

50 Ayşe Fulya Şen

Silke's (2020) research which focuses on news discourses on economic inequality, the analysis of tweets of the political parties on economic inequality also illustrated the silence and blind spots of the ruling and main opposition parties. These discourses were linked to the dominant ideology, neoliberalism, deeply embedded in particular contexts.

When looking at how economic inequality was treated as a problem in the sample of tweets of the political parties, it was seen that economic issues were ignored or tried to be solved by tentative methods. Except for minimum wage and inflation, the keywords related to economic inequalities and issues are hardly mentioned by the AK Party's tweets. Whereas CHP included these keywords more than the ruling party, they framed them superficially and in a populist tone criticizing the ruling party. Whereas the opposition party only focused on criticizing the ruling party instead of proposing a new perspective and debating the issue with the public, the ruling party only presented to the public what they have done instead of what should be done. As a result, the ruling and main opposition parties appeared to aim at only managing poverty. Due to the outbreak of COVID-19 in 2020 and the following financial and economic crisis in Turkey, unemployment and deep poverty were experienced. The political institutions did not propose radical economic policies removing or minimizing economic inequalities and also put forward to the agenda a strong public debate, in particular the main opposition party, CHP. In such context, while it was expected, the main opposition party highlights the economic crisis and inequality by concern of weakening democracy. At the same time, it contented by criticizing the ruling party over inflation and price increase as well. The ruling party, AK Party, also focused on increasing the minimum wage and did not reference the issues stemming from the capitalist economy. Although the two political parties also dealt with poverty-reduction efforts, it was concluded that there was no disagreement on the idea of the free market and the naturalization of economic inequalities. This research revealed the lack of discussions on the fundamental issues within the neoliberal system and that there was a "significant silence" on economic inequality in the political discourse. Hence, it is necessary to aim at reaching a democratic society with a notion of economic equality.

References

Ackland, R. (2013). *Web social science*. Sage.

Bahçe, S., & Köse, A. H. (2017). Social classes and the neoliberal poverty regime in Turkey, 2002–2011. *Journal of Contemporary Asia*, 47(4), 575–595. http://doi.or g/10.1080/00472336.2017.1325919

Bayar, A. A., Günçavdı, Ö., & Levent, H. (2020). Evaluating the impacts of the COVID-19 pandemic on income distribution and poverty in Turkey. *CMI—FEMISE*. www.cmimarseille.org/sites/default/files/newsite/cmi-fem_brief_11.pdf

Çakmaklı, C., Demiralp, S., Yeşiltaş, S., & Yıldırım, M. A. (2021). An evaluation of the Turkish economy during COVID-19. *The Centre for Applied Turkey Studies (CATS)*. www.swp-berlin.org/publications/products/arbeitspapiere/CATS__Working_Paper_ Nr_1_2021_Cakmakli_Demiralp_Yesiltas_Yildirim.pdf

Caro, L. P. (2021, March 16). Impact of the second wave COVID measures on employment in Turkey. *Research Brief*, ILO Office for Turkey. www.ilo.org/ankara/publications/research-papers/WCMS_775757/lang--en/index.htm

Clarke, S. (2005). The neoliberal theory of society. In A. Saad-Filho & D. Johnston (Eds.), *Neoliberalism: A critical reader* (pp. 50–59). Pluto Press.

Das, R. J. (2017). The capitalist state as constitutive of capitalist class relation: Class exploitation and political oppression. In *Marxist class theory for a skeptical world* (pp. 391–414). Brill. https://doi.org/10.1163/9789004337473_010

Dobson, K., & Knezevic, I. (2017). 'Liking and Sharing' the stigmatization of poverty and social welfare: Representations of poverty and welfare through Internet memes on social media. *tripleC, 15*(2), 777–795. www.triple-c.at

Einspänner, J., Dang-Anh, M., &Thimm, C. (2014). Computer-assisted content analysis of Twitter data. In K. Weller, A. Bruns, J. Burgess, M. Mahrt, & C. Puschmann (Eds.), *Twitter and society* (pp. 97–108). P. Lang. https://nbn-resolving.org/urn:nbn:de:0168-ssoar-54492-0

Emre, Y. (2014). *The emergence of social democracy in Turkey: The left and the transformation of the Republican People's party.* I.B. Tauris.

Feldman, G (2019). Neoliberalism and poverty: An unbreakable relationship. In B. Greve (Ed.), *Routledge international handbook of poverty* (pp. 340–350). Routledge. https://doi.org/10.4324/9780429058103

Focus Economics Consensus. (2022, June 7). *Turkey economic outlook.* www.focus-economics.com/countries/turkey

Fuchs, C. (2014). *Social media: A critical introduction.* Sage.

Grabner, D., Grisold, A., & Theine, H. (2020). Stagnation, social tensions, unfairness: Economic inequality as a problem. In A. Grisold & P. Preston (Eds.), *Economic inequality and news media: Discourse, power, and redistribution* (pp. 144–167). Oxford University Press.

Grisold, A., & Preston, P. (2020). *Economic inequality and news media: Discourse, power, and redistribution.* Oxford University Press.

Grisold, A., & Silke, H. (2020). Meritocracy, markets, social mobility: Inequality is not a crucial issue. In A. Grisold & P. Preston (Eds.), *Economic inequality and news media: Discourse, power, and redistribution* (pp. 124–143). Oxford University Press.

Haman, M. (2020). The use of Twitter by state leaders and its impact on the public during the COVID-19 pandemic. *Heliyon, 6*(11). https://doi.org/10.1016/j.heliyon.2020.e05540.

Hawkins, J. M. (2017). Thematic analysis. In M. Allen (Ed.), *The SAGE encyclopedia of communication research methods* (pp. 1757–1760). Sage.

Inequality.org.(n.d.).*Income inequality.*https://inequality.org/facts/income-inequality/#income-inequality

Iosifidis, P., & Nicoli, N. (2021). *Digital democracy, social media and disinformation.* Routledge.

Johnston, D. (2005). Poverty and distribution: Back on the neoliberal agenda? In A. Saad-Filho & D. Johnston (Eds.), *Neoliberalism: A critical reader* (pp. 135–141). Pluto Press.

Kovid, R. K., & Kumar, V. (Eds.). (2022). *Cases on emerging markets responses to the COVID-19 pandemic.* IGI Global Publications.

Kumar, V., & Gupta, G. (Eds.). (2021). *Strategic management during a pandemic.* Routledge; Taylor & Francis Group.

Kumar, V., & Malhotra, G. (Eds.). (2020). *Examining the role of IT and social media in democratic development and social change.* IGI Global Publications.

Kumar, V., & Malhotra, G. (Eds.). (2021). *Stakeholder strategies for reducing the impact of global health crises.* IGI Global Publications.

Kumar, V., & Svensson, J. (Eds.). (2015). *Promoting social change and democracy through information technology.* IGI Global Publications.

Kwon, R. (2018). How do Neoliberal policies affect income inequality? Exploring the link between liberalization, finance, and inequality. *Sociological Forum, 33,* 643–665. https://doi.org/10.1111/socf.12438

Luther, C. A., Lepre, C. R., & Clark, N. (2018). *Diversity in U.S. Mass Media* (2nd ed.). Wiley Blackwell.

Masroor, F., Khan, Q. N., Aib, I., & Ali, Z. (2019). Polarization and ideological weaving in Twitter discourse of politicians. *Social Media+Society.* https://doi.org/10.1177/2056305119891220

Munck, R. (2005). Neoliberalism and politics, and the politics of neoliberalism. In A. Saad-Filho & D. Johnston (Eds.), *Neoliberalism: A critical reader* (pp. 60–69). Pluto Press.

Murshed, S. (2020). Capitalism and COVID-19: Crisis at the crossroads. *Peace Economics, Peace Science and Public Policy, 26*(3), 20200026. https://doi.org/10.1515/peps-2020-0026

Offe, C. (2018). Framing inequality and related policy responses. *Norsksosiologisk-tidsskrift, 2*(1), 74–83. https://doi.org/10.18261/issn.2535-2512-2018-01-006

Özdemir, Y. (2020). AKP's neoliberal populism and contradictions of new social policies in Turkey. *Contemporary Politics, 26*(3), 245–267. https://doi.org/10.1080/13569775.2020.1720891

Peet, R. (1975). Inequality and poverty: A marxist-geographic theory. *Annals of the Association of American Geographers, 65*(4), 564–571. https://doi.org/10.1111/J.1467-8306.1975.Tb01063.X

Popping, R. (2017). Online tools for content analysis. In N. Fielding, R. Lee, & G. Blank (Eds.), *The SAGE handbook of online research methods* (pp. 329–343). SAGE Publications Ltd. https://doi.org/10.4135/9781473957992.n19

Potter, W. J., & Levine-Donnerstein, D. (1999). Rethinking validity and reliability in content analysis. *Journal of Applied Communication Research, 27*(3), 258–284. http://doi.org/10.1080/00909889909365539

Preston, P., & Silke, H. (2017). Economic inequality| contrasting conceptions, discourses and studies of economic inequalities. *International Journal of Communication, 11,* 4324–4349.

Schreier, M. (2013). Qualitative content analysis. In U. Flick (Ed.), *The SAGE handbook of qualitative data analysis* (pp. 170–183). Sage.

Şen, A. F. (2017). Invisibility of class identity in Turkish media: News coverage of class identity and class-based policies. *Palgrave Communications, 3,* Article number: 32. http://doi.org/10.1057/s41599-017-0037-9.

Sen, A. F., & Sen, Y. F. (2016). Media representation of class issues in Turkey: A review on media coverage of work-related rights. In J. Servaes & T. Oyedemi (Eds.), *In social inequalities, media, and communication: Theory and roots* (pp. 125–145). Lexington Books.

Shaikh, A. (2005). The economic mythology of neoliberalism. In A. Saad-Filho & D. Johnston (Eds.), *Neoliberalism: A critical reader* (pp. 41–49). Pluto Press.

Stevano, S., Franz, T., Dafermos, Y., & Waeyenberge, E. V. (2021). COVID-19 and crises of capitalism: Intensifying inequalities and global responses. *Canadian*

Journal of Development Studies/Revue canadienned'études du développement, 42(1–2), 1–17. http://doi.org/10.1080/02255189.2021.1892606

Theine, H., & Grabner, D. (2020). Trends in economic inequality and news media-scape. In A. Grisold & P. Preston (Eds.), *Economic inequality and news media: Discourse, power, and redistribution* (pp. 21–47). Oxford University Press.

United Nations. (2015). *Concepts of inequality, development issues no. 1., Department of economic and social affairs.* www.un.org/en/development/desa/policy/wess/wess_dev_issues/dsp_policy_01.pdf

Vallier, K. (2021). Neoliberalism. In E. N. Zalta (Ed.), *The Stanford encyclopedia of philosophy* (Summer 2021 ed.). https://plato.stanford.edu/archives/sum2021/entries/neoliberalism/

Venugopal, R. (2015). Neoliberalism as concept. *Economy and Society*, 44(2), 165–187. http://doi.org/10.1080/03085147.2015.1013356

Volscho, T. (2017). The revenge of the capitalist class: Crisis, the legitimacy of capitalism and the restoration of finance from the 1970s to present. *Critical Sociology*, 43(2), 249–266. https://doi.org/10.1177/0896920515589003

Warwick-Booth, L. (2013). *Social inequality*. Sage.

Yaqub, U., Ae Chun, S., Atluri, V., & Vaidya, J. (2017). Analysis of political discourse on Twitter in the context of the 2016 US presidential elections. *Government Information Quarterly*, 34(4), 613–626. https://doi.org/10.1016/j.giq.2017.11.001

4 Social Media for Knowledge Sharing and Pandemics

A Systematic Literature Review

Pallavi Vyas and Ujjal Mukherjee

1. Introduction

The COVID-19 epidemic has caused an unparalleled magnitude of societal, financial, and ecological calamity (Bapuji et al., 2020). As a result of widespread lockdowns in February and March of 2020 due to the danger of COVID-19, most employees found themselves working from their home (Anderson & Kelliher, 2020). Government-mandated lockdowns closed numerous non-essential enterprises, while many firms still open reported lower revenues (Afrouzi, 2020). Human resource professionals faced unique difficulties due to the COVID-19 epidemic, needing to quickly explore the "unknown unknowns" in their efforts to aid their employees in adjusting to and thriving in the face of dramatic shifts in the professional and social environments (Carnavale & Hatak, 2020). Supporting the real-time availability of information, disseminating, collecting, and preserving the knowledge that resides inside the individual, the team, and the larger organization were among the many difficulties encountered at the outset of the COVID-19 epidemic (Chernick et al., 2020; Singh & Kumar, 2022). Organizational learning and innovative thinking, propelled by technology-enabled information interchange, became increasingly important for companies to address the escalating worldwide dangers and devastating extra-organizational situations and calamities like the COVID-19 epidemic (Bhardwaj & Kumar, 2022a). The magnitude and speed of the subsequent collapses have been unprecedented. The crisis resulted in several hundred thousands of deaths, tested healthcare systems, and placed the world in a shutdown with the most severe recession since the "Great Depression" (Gopinath, 2020). In addition, people started using SM technologies to expand the depth and breadth of their existing systems and to collect evidence, and now employers are continually looking for methods to incorporate SM into their operations (Kaščelan et al., 2020). Organizations are currently using various information-sharing methods (Baima et al., 2022). For example, social media platforms are used by organizations for citizen awareness, information sharing, and government actions (Platts et al., 2021; Kumar & Nanda, 2022). It is also used as an instrument to produce knowledge within organizations and integrate customers into business activities (Busalim & Hussin, 2016;

DOI: 10.4324/9781003315278-4

Kumar et al., 2022). Higher education institutions exploit SM to motivate students to participate in learning activities (Chatterjee et al., 2020) and for knowledge sharing (KS) in healthcare companies (Wu et al., 2021), to name a few. SM's knowledge-sharing features have drastically altered how we exist, operate, communicate, and learn. It enables sharing of information in the virtual world seamlessly and continuously (Kumar & Nanda, 2020). It is and will be the most potent tool for knowledge transfer among individuals (Bansal et al., 2021). The current paper thus aspires to recognize the development of research surrounding usage of social media for information and knowledge transfer.

The SARS COVID-19 virus had a significant impact on businesses all across the world (Kovid & Kumar, 2022; Kumar & Gupta, 2021). The epidemic has sped up efforts to deploy novel technologies to combat COVID-19's effects (O'Leary, 2020). As the globe embraces the COVID-19 "new normal", businesses are starting to embrace cutting-edge technology to automate corporate processes and carry out virtual activities to improve productivity, efficiency, and overall results (Akpan et al., 2020; Papadopoulos & Balta, 2020; Ting et al., 2020). The coronavirus pandemic has influenced technology design, implementation, and use, and in order to tackle the pandemic, various technologies and apps have been created (He et al., 2021). The epidemic has provided a unique chance to explore technology research and practice, spanning knowledge management, work habits, development, and use (Sein, 2020). The organizations are developing the culture of sharing knowledge in the social media platforms, which enables the employees to access the content from any geographical location (Kumar & Malhotra, 2021). Given the importance of this new development in the business setting, the academic and practitioner world are and will be swamped with literature about working in the virtual world in the next couple of years post-pandemic and thereafter. Thus, it is the right time to consolidate the existing literature on the usage of SM for knowledge and lay a platform to follow for future researchers. Moreover, academicians have underlined the need to understand further the relationship between SM and KS (Hosen et al., 2021; Panahi et al., 2016).

2. Social Media and Knowledge Sharing

SM as defined by Kaplan and Haenlein (2010) is "a group of internet-based applications that are built on the ideological and technological foundations of Web 2.0, and that allow the creation and exchange of user-generated content". "User-generated content" refers to all media content created and produced by the general public instead of hired professionals, eliminating activities like instant messaging, email, and the redistribution of already-existing information (Kasapakis & Gavalas, 2017). Social networking sites, or SNSs, are websites where users can create identity descriptions of themselves and interact with other users (Donath & Boyd, 2004). SM is a blanket term that defines various online platforms like social networking sites, microblogs, photo sharing, collaborative projects, enterprise social networks, video sharing, and bookmarking (Aichner & Jacob, 2015; Kumar & Nanda, 2019). It is useful among the stakeholders who quickly and efficiently transmit their ideas, knowledge content, and other challenges (Chatterjee et al., 2020). Users can share their unique experiences on various SM platforms, which encourages self-reflection, learning, and development and may impact users' happiness (Bosangit & Demangeot, 2016). Such information and learning exchange are fundamental to knowledge-sharing behaviour among individuals.

KS is a process of communication that involves acquiring and disseminating information between two or more people (Ahmed et al., 2019). It is the act of making knowledge available to others within an organization, while the process through which an individual's information is transformed for others' comprehension, absorption, and use is called individual KS (Ipe, 2016). It is a vital aspect of corporate plans, as it helps companies expand and innovate in the market by helping foster an organization's innovation capability and thus acquire a competitive advantage (Ganguly et al., 2019). Enterprise SM platforms make it possible to repost others' content and share their knowledge with a larger audience (Zhang et al., 2010).

SM had been considered an impediment for KS. However, post-Covid, some enterprise networking sites (ENSs) are used extensively to communicate and collaborate with university students (Kazemian & Grant, 2022). The organizational knowledge management systems enable the diffusion, exchange, and retention of experience and ideas via technological innovations competent in quickly gathering and transmitting knowledge within organizations while managing processes and systems collectively (Di Vaio et al., 2020; Mittal & Kumar, 2019).

Before the pandemic, most organizations had realized the importance of SM in disseminating knowledge (Kumar & Ayodeji, 2020). The usage of SM is expectedly to increase further during the pandemic (Lata & Gupta, 2021). The pandemic period provided the organizations the opportunity and reasons to further explore the different resources required to develop their SM platforms for knowledge sharing and to measure their effectiveness. Postpandemic, most organizations continue to use these platforms to enhance the degree of KS among employees. One of the major reasons for this initiative is the rise in the work-from-home workforce. Organizations worldwide are embracing hybrid work models and adjusting their digital transformation strategies. This includes implementing more future of work (FoW) technologies that enable a digital workforce. These improvements are needed to achieve the potential for increased remote work, which is strongest in industrialized economies and digital-output jobs (Sava, 2022). Nearly 80% of U.S., German, U.K., and Chinese employees are happy working remotely during the COVID-19 pandemic; 34% of UK workers adore working from home and could do so indefinitely (StatistaResearchDepartment, 2020). Respondents to a global study of CIOs said that totally remote work will likely evolve into hybrid employment in the future. Prior to the pandemic, approximately 15 to 16% of respondents reported that their companies' personnel worked remotely; 34% of participants expect permanent remote work by 2020. While 42% of survey participants foresee permanent hybrid work by June 2021 (Sava, 2022). According to research, professionals use resources such as blogs, bookmarks, and wikis in a quest for and to uncover organizational knowledge, so the usefulness that a typical worker receives is far more knowledge centric than interpersonal (DiMicco et al., 2008).

According to Leonardi and Neeley (2017), SM is considered a leaky pipe for communication because the directionality and subject matter of different messages is observable by people not involved in it, thus making them useful for KS. Organizations that wish to develop intellectual capital at work should link professionals to different channels so they can adequately reinforce different management information systems. Managers must encourage employees to use SM as a social capital, a by-product created via SM use and helps promote knowledge exchange.

SM may be helpful for KS since they are leaky communication channels, making it possible for outsiders to see the content and direction of a given message. To ensure a wide conversation inside their communities and cultures, SM users organize and support knowledge-sharing initiatives (Ahmed et al., 2019). For digital KS and social learning to be successful, it is essential that employees have the desire, aim, disposition, and behaviour to exchange and co-create knowledge, which is anchored in a positive KS organizational climate (Valk & Planojevic, 2021).

3. Methodology

3.1 Approach to the Systematic Literature Review

The authors conducted a systematic literature review (SLR) of studies on social media for knowledge sharing. An SLR conducted on a topic helps identify, select, and critically analyze to find answers to a predetermined question (Dewey, 2016). In the current study, the authors used the adapted version of "Preferred Reporting Items for Systematic Reviews and Meta-Analyses" (PRISMA) to identify relevant research articles. PRISMA helps increase these reports' clarity, transparency, quality, and value (Liberati et al., 2009). It provides a checklist that encapsulates the fundamental elements under each section of the SLR that future researchers can easily replicate.

3.2 Search

The authors used the Jain University, Bangalore, India (both the authors are associated with this university) library database to identify journals that publish papers related to SM and KS. The authors begin their search by identifying a set of keywords that helped to identify all the possible published papers in

58 Pallavi Vyas and Ujjal Mukherjee

the area of research. The keywords include "knowledge sharing", "information sharing", in association with "social media", "internet", "technology", and "computer-mediated communication". These search strings include "social media for knowledge sharing", "social media for information sharing", "knowledge sharing via social media", "social media for knowledge exchange", "knowledge sharing via social software", "knowledge sharing via Twitter", and "knowledge sharing via Facebook", "knowledge sharing via internet", "knowledge sharing via technology", "knowledge sharing via computer-aided communication", etc. The authors started their search from Google Scholar and subsequently expanded their search to ProQuest and Scopus databases. The duplicate articles were identified and deleted from the list of papers. The last literature review on SM for KS was published by Ahmed et al. (2019) that considered papers published till 2017. The current paper considers the papers published between 2018 and 2022. This period covers the pandemic period between 2020–2021.

3.3 Study Selection Process

Following the initial series of investigation by means of pre-defined keywords, 39 research papers were identified. The authors found eight duplicate papers, and these were deleted. Subsequently, the inclusion and exclusion criteria (refer to table 4.1) were applied to the remaining 31 remaining papers. The researchers focused on every article's title and abstract to apply the criteria. Eight papers were eliminated at this stage. This left a total of 23 papers. The following phase was concerned with examining entire transcript of the 23 selected papers. Three more papers were eliminated at this stage. Twenty studies were considered in the overall figure of the systematic review.

The selected research papers were subsequently arranged in a table and categorized with the researchers' names, titles, years, and a description of

Table 4.1 Inclusion and exclusion criteria

Criteria Type	Criteria
Inclusion	1. The articles had to be focused on social media use by employees for knowledge sharing in organizations. 2. Only English-language publications were considered for this investigation.
Exclusion	1. The learning from the paper does not contribute to the current understanding of the usage of SM for KS. 2. Inaccessibility of the research paper due to a lack of institutional access. 3. A piece of writing not research-based (e.g., editorial note) 4. Abstracts and forewords to different symposia/conferences.

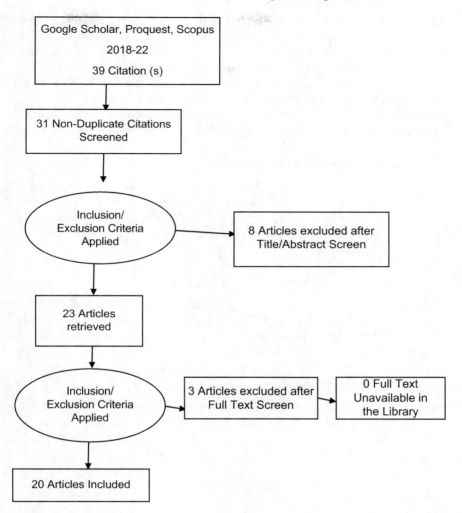

Figure 4.1 PRISMA methodology followed for the selection of research papers

key findings. The key findings and discussions are based on the analysis conducted on this table.

4. Analysis

4.1 Review Structure

This part explores the literature review conducted. The current study's authors examined the publications using Callahan's (2014) four-part review format—what, where, how, and why—to organize the tables. We added the

60   Pallavi Vyas and Ujjal Mukherjee

TCCM framework to Callahan's (2014) study to ensure a thorough examination of the usage of SM using KS. The Theory, Context, Characteristics, and Methodology (TCCM) is a reliable strategy for performing systematic literature reviews through a definite and well-defined arrangement of Concept, Setting, Features, and Methodology. We compared What and Theory Development, What and Characteristics, Where and Context, and How and Methodology. We came up with themes and proposed topics for future research in response to Callahan's fourth question, "Why".

4.2   What Do We Know About KS and SM?

All publications from the resulting pool of research that formed the basis of this literature review are discussed here (refer to Table 4.2). The period covered for this pool was 2018–2022. The table presents the journal name, number of articles published in this journal, the title of the paper, references, citation of the paper in APA, and number of citations.

4.3   Where Is the Actual Study Being Conducted?

The geographic scope of the included journal articles is shown in Table 4.3 As can be seen, the vast majority of KS and SM studies that have been published originate from China, with Scotland coming in second, followed by India, and Indonesia. Continent-wise, most of the studies are conducted in Asia and Europe.

4.4   What Was the Study Methodology?

Table 4.4 depicts the methodology used in the research papers examined in the study. It describes the different methods used in the various papers. Seventy percent of studies (14) are found to be quantitative in nature. The mixed survey was not frequently used and was the least employed (only one).

"Why is it important that researchers, educators, and administrators learn further about KS and SM?"

Table 4.5 represents the findings, limitations, and future scope of the study as acknowledged by studies used in the research. There's a paucity of studies using the mixed method to conduct analysis.

The papers were simultaneously arranged in tabular form and marked with the authors' names, titles, years, and a description of key findings (table 4.5). The results and discussions are based on the analysis conducted on this table.

5.   Discussion and Scope for Future Research

Most studies on the usage of SM for KS during the selected period were in an academic context. Alajmi and Al-Qallaf (2022), Alshahrani and Pennington (2018, 2020), Ansari and Khan (2020), Chatterjee et al. (2020), Hosen et al. (2021), Lin and Wang (2020), Rasheed et al. (2020), Suti and Sari

Table 4.2 List of scientific papers on social media and knowledge sharing used in the current literature review (2018–2022)

Journal Name	No. of Articles in This Journal	Title of the Paper	References	Citation
Journal of Knowledge Management	4	Social media as a tool of knowledge sharing in academia: an empirical study using valance, instrumentality, and expectancy (VIE) approach	(Chatterjee et al., 2020)	38
		How does mobile social media affect knowledge sharing under the "Guanxi" system?	(Zhao et al., 2020)	8
		Enterprise social media usage and knowledge hiding: A motivation theory perspective	(Ma et al., 2020)	33
		How do features of social media influence knowledge sharing? An ambient awareness perspective	(Baima et al., 2022)	30
VINE Journal of Information and Knowledge Management Systems	3	The impact of the COVID-19 pandemic on knowledge sharing in UK higher education	(Laitinen & Sivunen, 2021)	4
		Social network sites (SNS) for knowledge-sharing behaviour among students	(Suti & Sari, 2021)	2
		Does political self-disclosure in social media hamper tacit knowledge sharing in the workplace?	(Yudhistira & Sushandoyo, 2020)	1
Computers & Education	2	Individual motivation and social media influence on student knowledge sharing and learning performance: Evidence from an emerging economy	(Hosen et al., 2021)	48
		Usage of social media, student engagement, and creativity: The role of knowledge sharing behaviour and cyberbullying	(Rasheed et al., 2020)	46
Global Knowledge, Memory and Communication	2	"Maybe we can work together": researchers' outcome expectations for sharing knowledge of social media	(Alshahrani & Pennington, 2020)	3

(Continued)

Table 4.2 (Continued)

Journal Name	No. of Articles in This Journal	Title of the Paper	References	Citation
		Fostering knowledge-sharing behaviour through social capital: The implications of face-to-face and online interactions	(Alajimi & Al-Qallaf, 2022)	0
Architectural Engineering and Design Management	1	The use of social media for work-related knowledge sharing by construction professionals	(Etemadi et al., 2019)	7
Information Technology & People	1	Enablers of and constraints on employees' information sharing on enterprise social media	(Laitinen & Sivunen, 2021)	31
International Journal of Information Management	1	Examining gender differences in people's information-sharing decisions on social networking sites	(Lin & Wang, 2020)	79
International Marketing Review	1	Testing the antecedents of customer knowledge sharing on social media: A quantitative analysis on Italian consumers	(Baima et al., 2022)	2
Journal of Documentation	1	"How to use it more?" Self-efficacy and its sources in the use of social media for knowledge sharing	(Alshahrani & Pennington, 2020)	9
Journal of Global Mobility: The Home of Expatriate Management Research	1	Addressing the knowledge divide: Digital knowledge sharing and social learning of geographically dispersed employees during the COVID-19 pandemic	(Valk & Planojevic, 2021)	2
Kybernetes	1	Social media overload, gender differences, and knowledge withholding	(Wu & Zheng, 2023)	0
Smart Learning Environments	1	Exploring the role of social media in collaborative learning, the new domain of learning	(Ansari & Khan, 2020)	191
Telematics and Informatics	1	Fake news and COVID-19: modeling the predictors of fake news sharing among social media users	(Apuke & Omar, 2021)	367

Social Media for Knowledge Sharing and Pandemics 63

Table 4.3 Geographical focus of the literature

Country	Citation
China	(Zhang et al., 2020); (Ma et al., 2020); (Zhao et al., 2020); (Wu & Zheng, 2023); (Rasheed et al., 2020)
India	(Chatterjee et al., 2020); (Ansari & Khan, 2020)
Scotland	(Alshahrani & Pennington, 2018, 2020)
Indonesia	(Suti & Sari, 2021)
Italy	(Baima et al., 2022)
Nordic Countries	(Laitinen & Sivunen, 2021)
Kuwait	(Alajmi & Al-Qallaf, 2022)
UK	(Kazemian & Grant, 2022)
UAE	(Valk & Planojevic, 2021)
Indonesia	(Yudhistira & Sushandoyo, 2020)
Nigeria	(Apuke & Omar, 2021)
Australia	(Etemadi et al., 2019)
Malaysia	(Hosen et al., 2021)
USA	(Lin & Wang, 2020)

Table 4.4 Methodology-based clustering of the literature

Serial No.	Citation	Methodology	
		Description	Qualitative/ Quantitative/ Mixed
1	(Chatterjee et al., 2020)	Survey method with 320 samples: 82 faculty members and 238 students in higher education institutions.	Quantitative
2	(Zhang et al., 2020)	This research employs Guanxi theory to devise a method for gathering information from NPD groups.	Mixed
3	(Suti & Sari, 2021)	Students in Indonesia were enlisted for a study conducted entirely online.	Quantitative
4	(Baima et al., 2022)	In order to collect data and find an answer, this study takes a quantitative method and relies on participant-administered questionnaires. This study utilized an online data collection tool to poll a sizable sample of the Italian population.	Quantitative
5	(Laitinen & Sivunen, 2021)	Information gathered from semi-structured interviews and an examination of enterprise social media by a major Nordic media company.	Qualitative

(*Continued*)

64 Pallavi Vyas and Ujjal Mukherjee

Table 4.4 (Continued)

Serial No.	Citation	Methodology	
		Description	Qualitative/ Quantitative/ Mixed
6	(Ma et al., 2020)	1. Two hundred eighty-eight valid responses of employees. 2. Created the survey on a Chinese survey site (Soujump.com). Subsequently, this research utilized the website for its paid sample offering.	Quantitative
7	(Zhao et al., 2020)	Researchers created an experiment to boost knowledge work. This experiment builds a knowledge work context to improve knowledge sharing. Researchers created parallel teams to imitate consulting company data analysis teams. They separated 163 graduate students into 13 teams, with 12 or 13 people per team.	Quantitative
8	(Alajmi & Al-Qallaf, 2022)	A set of in-depth interviews were conducted. Twelve educators were approached for participation in the study. Those chosen represent one of Kuwait's 62 educational institutions. The focus group was conducted following the completion of the interviews.	Qualitative
9	(Kazemian & Grant, 2022)	1. A case study method was used. 2. Information was gathered through online chats and in-person discussions to determine what factors influence the adoption of enterprise social networks (ESNs) for the purpose of knowledge sharing. 3. The purpose of the focus group was to determine what aspects of ESN use affect the potential for academics to collaborate and undertake research.	Qualitative
10	(Alshahrani & Pennington, 2020)	Collaborated with scholars at a prominent Scottish university to conduct 30 semi-structured interviews.	Qualitative
11	(Wu & Zheng, 2021b)	Constructed scales for the variables and evaluated data from a sample of 325 social media users at large.	Quantitative

(Continued)

Social Media for Knowledge Sharing and Pandemics 65

Table 4.4 (Continued)

Serial No.	Citation	Methodology	
		Description	Qualitative/ Quantitative/ Mixed
12	(Valk & Planojevic, 2021)	Case study methodology and action research were used to investigate the use of KSPs for the delivery of digital KS and SL within a multinational corporation with its headquarters in the United Arab Emirates.	Qualitative
13	(Alshahrani & Pennington, 2018)	Researchers from the University of Strathclyde (n=144) were asked to fill out a survey online, and their replies were examined using descriptive statistics.	Quantitative
14	(Yudhistira & Sushandoyo, 2020)	1. An online survey combined with the experimental vignette methodology to collect respondent data. 2. Collected 144 responses. 3. Data was gathered from Indonesian government employees.	Quantitative
15	(Apuke & Omar, 2021)	$n = 385$ People in Nigeria were surveyed if they were 18 or older. The concept of Uses and Gratifications was applied to the investigation of this phenomena.	Quantitative
16	(Ansari & Khan, 2020)	Three hundred sixty college students were polled at an Eastern Indian university.	Quantitative
17	(Etemadi et al., 2019)	More than 120 construction industry experts were surveyed.	Quantitative
18	(Hosen et al., 2021)	A total of 407 students attending the best private universities in West Malaysia filled out questionnaires to contribute to the survey.	Quantitative
19	(Lin & Wang, 2020)	Survey administered online at a major US university where 405 college students took part.	Quantitative
20	(Rasheed et al., 2020)	Primary data was collected from 383 research students studying in different universities in eastern China.	Quantitative

Table 4.5 Summary of gap analysis and scope for future research

References	Research Findings	Limitations	Future Research
(Chatterjee et al., 2020)	Importance of knowledge exchange, perceived usefulness of social media, and experience using social media have a positive and significant relationship with the intention to use social media.	1. Respondents have no direct experience relating to the use of social media in knowledge sharing in their respective institutions as this system has not been fully adopted there. 2. Considered some institutions of higher education at the national level. Did not consider other institutions at provincial levels.	The use of other relevant variables as moderators could help improve the relationships.
(Zhang et al., 2020)	The results show that the effect of social media communication function on employees is greater than the impact of collaboration on employees.	First, the research samples in this paper are taken from college students, but the fact is that the NPD team formed by the project is more common among the employees of the enterprise rather than university students. The diversity of the sample is relatively scarce. Secondly, it is limited to the impact of social media collaboration and communication functions.	It is possible to consider the relationship between collaboration and project commitment and trust alone to avoid the influence of communication function on collaboration function and the influence of emotional factors in relationship theory on project commitment. It is possible to evaluate the impact of other functions (such as storage, tracking, and analysis) on KSB. Many factors, such as technology infrastructure, network-related laws (such as copyright), and ethics (such as confidentiality), can be used as research objects for future work. The significant negative impact of feelings on knowledge sharing behaviour (KSB) is worthy of further study.

(Suti & Sari, 2021)	Social capital has a crucial role in increasing cognitive-based trust and affective-based trust.	1. Cross-sectional survey. 2. Collecting data from a single respondent on multiple items that reflect a subjective concept may overestimate it. 3. Study is limited to Indonesian Facebook users.	1. Future research needs to examine specific conditions, situational contexts, and subcultures that may influence social capital, trust, and knowledge-sharing behaviours of Facebook users in other parts of the world. 2. Future research should investigate internal factors (i.e., institution authority, economic and special knowledge, or community) and external factors (i.e., operation ability, organizational comparability, and relationships among users) from the perspective of knowledge-sharing behaviour.
(Baima et al., 2022)	The results of this study reveal that the usage frequency of online reviews (UFORs), social bonds (SBs), subjective happiness (SH), and reciprocity positively impact customer knowledge sharing (CKS). By contrast, the perceived usefulness of online reviews (PUORs), helping others, customer susceptibility to interpersonal influence (CSII) and informational (INFO) do not impact CKS.	Researchers relied on self-reported surveys for collecting data. The study conceptualizes and tests the hypotheses in a single context. The model was tested using data collected only in Italy.	Future research can use objective measures to add validity to the current findings. Future studies could also employ experiments. Future validation of study findings across various contexts, customers, and engagement platforms is required. Given that buying behaviours in Italy may differ from those of other cultures, the model should be tested further in other countries.

(Continued)

Table 4.5 (Continued)

References	Research Findings	Limitations	Future Research
(Laitinen & Sivunen, 2021)	Organizational factors, such as norms, tasks, and media repertoires, are associated with employees' information-sharing decisions.	1. Data based on only one organization. 2. This data sample leaves out some of the younger employees at the organization and may raise questions about those employees' unique social media experience compared to the older generation.	1. Organizational and national culture may play a role. 2. Study technology-mediated communication processes outside the knowledge workers. 3. Further research with more versatile data sets is needed.
(Ma et al., 2020)	The results show that work-related public social media usage has an inhibiting effect on employees' knowledge hiding, whereas the effect of work-related private social media usage on employees' knowledge hiding is not significant; socially related public social media and private social media usage has a promoting effect on employees' knowledge hiding; and job engagement acts in a positive moderating role between socially related private and public social media usage and evasive hiding.	1. Small sample size. 2. The work-related public social media usage was measured only by two items. This study did not consider employees' trust and competitive relationships.	1. Future studies should increase the sample size and combine the objective data to verify the conclusions. 2. Other motivations of enterprise social media usage, types of knowledge, such as explicit and tacit knowledge, and other boundary conditions, such as personal and organizational environmental factors, should also be investigated in the knowledge-hiding process.
(Zhao et al., 2020)	There is a correlation between social media features, ambient awareness, and knowledge sharing.	1. Limited in data size and scope.	1. Further discuss the applicability of this research model in different organizations by enlarging the data size or collecting data from actual management practice. 2. Future research on social media and CVT can try to test their applicability in other organizational environments.

(Alajmi & Al-Qallaf, 2022)	Of all the categories of pedagogical content, knowledge exchanged among teachers; teachers seek knowledge of general pedagogy, representations and strategies, and knowledge of curriculum and media more than any others. When differentiating between online and face-to-face activities, curriculum knowledge, and media are sought more frequently online.	The sample is from schools in Kuwait, hence it can't be generalized.	1. The conceptual framework presented should endorse and stimulate future research from different perspectives. 2. To investigate how the two types of knowledge-sharing processes—knowledge acquisition and knowledge transfer—are differentiated. 3. Future studies should investigate how social ties influence each process, providing tangible examples of professionals' knowledge-sharing behaviours that would strengthen the ties between theory and practice.
(Kazemian & Grant, 2022)	The findings reveal the motivators-outcomes-strategies and the barriers-outcomes-strategies of users. Motivators include feature value, information value, organizational requirement, and adequate organizational and technical support. Barriers include six factors, including resisting engagement on the online platform, emotional anxiety, loss of knowledge, the lack of organizational pressure, lack of content quality, and lack of time. An outcomes framework reveals benefits and disbenefits and strategies for improving user engagement.	1. Conducted in higher education.	1. Future studies could measure the impact of COVID-19 on remote working and research by surveying to generalize results in different higher education communities. 2. Future studies should examine the organizational culture and how it influences the academic staff's use of ESN.

(Continued)

Table 4.5 (Continued)

References	Research Findings	Limitations	Future Research
(Alshahrani & Pennington, 2020)	Social outcome expectations are the social consequences of using social media for knowledge sharing with communities.	1. Based on convenience sampling, participants self-selected. 2. Due to non-response from senior researchers, the majority of participants in this study were PhD students.	Future research could aim for a larger, more diverse sample within the university population or outside.
(Wu & Zheng, 2021b)	1. Three types of social media overload positively affect users' knowledge-withholding behaviour, and that emotional exhaustion significantly mediates the above relationships. 2. Gender differences exist in the decision-making process of knowledge-withholding; for example, females are more likely than males to become emotionally exhausted from social media overload, while males are more likely than females to engage in knowledge-withholding behaviour in the case of emotional exhaustion. 3. Three of four types of social media overload (i.e., communication overload, system feature overload, and social overload) have a significant impact on knowledge-withholding. 4. Significant gender differences in social media overload engendering knowledge-withholding behaviour.	1. Cross-sectional data. 2. Focuses only on the influence of social media overload on knowledge withholding. 3. This study only verified the significant gender differences in social media overload engendering knowledge-withholding; whether other personal differences would exert possible moderating effects remains unknown.	1. Future researchers should collect multiple-wave data and combine more diverse data sets. 2. Can examine whether other stressors would lead to knowledge-withholding behaviour. 3. Recommended to devote more efforts in this field to deepening the understanding of such behaviour.

(Valk & Planojevic, 2021)	1. Implementation of knowledge-sharing platforms customized to employees' needs and preferences within the case study organization facilitated KS and SL.	1. Single case study of one organization within one business sector, encompassing a small sample of 22 employees. 2. A cross-sectional design	1. Use qualitative and quantitative research designs to investigate digital KS and SL using a larger sample of employees across industries and cultures 2. Longitudinal research design to draw inferences about the causal effects of digital KS and SL on individual and organizational outcomes.
(Alshahrani & Pennington, 2018)	1. Participants relied on personal mastery experience, vicarious experience, verbal persuasion, and emotional arousal for social media use.	The convenience sample utilized for this study, which included academic staff, researchers, and PhD students at one university, is small and may not entirely represent the larger population.	1. The study could be replicated at multiple institutions to obtain more understanding and insights. 2. Different methods for collecting and analyzing data could be used for additional triangulation. 3. Empirical studies to investigate these sources and their comparative impact on sharing both tacit and explicit knowledge.
(Yudhistira & Sushandoyo, 2020)	1. Perceived content negativity towards co-workers' political self-disclosure has a weak and significant indirect effect on recipients' willingness to share tacit knowledge, and that perceived value dissimilarity has an insignificant indirect effect on recipients' willingness to share tacit knowledge. 2. Political self-disclosure does not hamper tacit knowledge sharing in the workplace.	1. Cross-sectional research that was conducted at a public organization, with a limited number of samples and non-probabilistic sampling method.	1. Include individual personality and different research contexts. 2. Probing the relationship between political self-disclosure and knowledge sharing in a private organizational setting. 3. Using qualitative methodology.

(Continued)

Table 4.5 (Continued)

References	Research Findings	Limitations	Future Research
	3. Perceived value dissimilarity has no indirect effect on respondents' willingness to share tacit knowledge. 4. Perceived content negativity does have a significant indirect but weak effect on respondents' willingness to share tacit knowledge.		
(Apuke & Omar, 2021)	1. The results showed that altruism was the most significant factor that predicted fake news sharing of COVID-19. 2. Social media users' motivations for information sharing, socialization, information seeking and pastime predicted the sharing of false information about COVID-19. 3. No significant association was found for entertainment motivation.	1. This study was conducted with a focus on the COVID-19 pandemic and drew a sample from the Nigerian society. 2. Failed to test whether cultural background, age, income, and gender would moderate the effect of fake news sharing.	1. Future researchers could add up demographic variables like cultural background, age, income, and gender to test if it has any effect on the outcome of the model. 2. Increase the samples to get a more robust statistical outcome.
(Ansari & Khan, 2020)	1. Online social media used for collaborative learning had a significant impact on interactivity with peers, teachers, and online knowledge-sharing behaviour.	1. Ignores the addiction of social media; excess use may lead to destruction, deviation from the focal point. 2. Confined to only one academic institution. 3. Conducted on university students, ignoring the faculty members.	1. Future research could be possible towards faculty members in different higher education institutions. 2. Have a more diverse sample of institutions/academia

(Etemadi et al., 2019)	1. Facebook and LinkedIn were used by almost half of the survey respondents. Passive KS was the most common type of KS activity. 2. Performance Expectancy (PE) and Knowledge Sharing Self Efficacy (KSSE) had positive impacts on the construction professionals' intention to use (IU) social media. 3. IU and Facilitating Conditions (FC) had positive direct impacts on the use of social media for work-related KS.	1. Sample size (120). 2. Limited to the context of Australia.	Future studies with larger sample sizes can bring more tenable results.
(Hosen et al., 2021)	Social media functions and individual motivation are core factors that HEIs can leverage to encourage knowledge sharing.	1. Includes only private universities in West Malaysia.	1. Study with data obtained from both private and public universities. 2. Investigating student knowledge-sharing behaviour and learning performance in public universities to encourage a comparative analysis.
(Lin & Wang, 2020)	1. Privacy risks, social ties, and commitment were more important in the formation of attitudes toward information sharing for women than men. Gender significantly moderates the relationship between people's perceptions of information sharing and their intention to share information.	1. Respondents: Only college students. 2. Used SNSs as the sole investigation context. 3. Explores a limited set of antecedents of SNS users' information-sharing decision-making.	1. Generalize the research findings to other SNS-user populations in other environments (e.g., the workplace). 2. Employs a cross-platform survey would be useful to validate the proposed comprehensive model of information sharing and generalize the findings to other contexts.
(Rasheed et al., 2020)	1. Students' use of social media is related to their creativity and engagement in graduate research training through knowledge-sharing behaviour.	1. Data is cross-sectional. 2. Model theorized and tested one underlying mechanism in the relationships between graduate research student use of social media and its outcomes.	1. Longitudinal or experimental design to further validate the finding. 2. Explore some more alternative explanations; for instance, student motivation can be investigated other than knowledge-sharing behaviour as a mediating variable in the model.

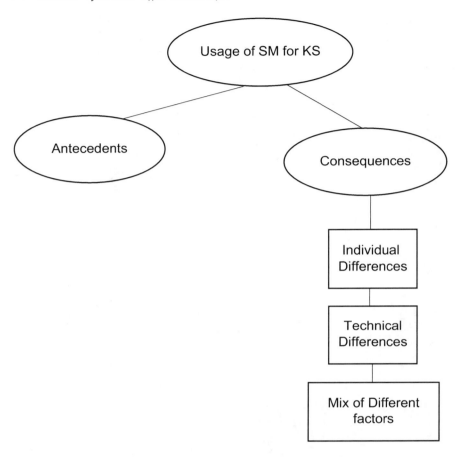

Figure 4.2 Themes developed on the usage of SM on KS

(2021), and Zhao et al. (2020) studied the relation between SM and KS in the academic context. The discussion section is further divided into themes developed by the researcher (refer to figure 4.2). These themes are basically divided into antecedents and consequences of SM on KS. The themes were further divided into sub-themes. The research gaps are extensively discussed under each subsection. Table 4.6 also provides additional inputs for future researchers on research gaps.

5.1 Antecedents

Most research found social media antecedents for knowledge sharing. The antecedents can be categorized into three themes: (i) individual differences, (ii) technical differences, and (iii) a mix of different factors (individual/technical/organizational).

Social Media for Knowledge Sharing and Pandemics 75

Table 4.6 Proposed scope for future research

Thematic Areas	Proposed Topics Based on Identified Research Gaps
Geography	More studies on different countries and continents having different cultures. Need for comparative studies. Testing the relationship between social media, knowledge sharing, and culture.
Methodology	Need for more qualitative studies and mixed methods. A longitudinal research design will help to draw inferences about the causal effects of the studies involving social media usage and knowledge-sharing behaviour.
Types of knowledge sharing	Need to study the behaviour of individuals on both the types of knowledge-sharing processes—knowledge acquisition and knowledge transfer.
Types of social media platforms	Knowledge-sharing behaviour may be different on different platforms. An individual's knowledge-sharing behaviour may be different in one social media platform as compared to any other social media platform.
Influencers and constraints	Study enablers and constraints of the knowledge sharing and social media usage behaviour: internal and external. Studies may focus on internal factors such as emotional factors, psychological aspects, and individual differences such as demography, personality, psychological capital, and self-efficacy that influence their knowledge-sharing behaviour and choice of social media platforms. External factors such as diverse professions, organizational cultures, organizational environmental factors, country's technology infrastructure, network-related laws, and remote working need to be studied. Researchers may identify the influencers of knowledge-hiding behaviour. Influencers and constraints of knowledge-sharing or -hiding or -withholding behaviour among customers/users/clients are worth studying.
Consequences	Identify the negative influence of usage of social media for knowledge sharing. Strength of social relationships. More studies on knowledge-hiding behaviour, especially its positive and negative consequences.

(i) Individual Differences

Chatterjee et al. (2020), Suti and Sari (2021), Baima et al. (2022), Wu and Zheng (2021b), Yudhistira and Sushandoyo (2020), Apuke and Omar (2021), Etemadi et al. (2019), and Hosen et al. (2021) considered individual-level outcomes. Chatterjee et al. (2020) studied faculty members and students in the Indian context and found the positive influence of knowledge exchange, perceived usefulness of SM, and experience using SM on an individual intention to use SM. Knowledge seekers and contributors moderate this relationship. There was a major limitation in this study. The respondents did not have substantial knowledge of KS behaviour in SM.

Moreover, data was collected from institutions where the SM was not fully adopted. Therefore, this result should be accepted with a pinch of salt. There is a need for more studies that can further validate these results using more appropriate respondents. Suti and Sari's (2021) study conducted among the Indonesian SM users explained the importance of social capital on the KS behaviour of individuals. They found the moderating influence of affective and cognitive-based trust in the relationship between social capital and KS behaviour. Zhao et al. (2020) studied the role that ambient awareness plays as a mediator between social media traits and knowledge sharing. A Chinese business school's 156 students were the subjects of the study. They discovered a connection between social media characteristics, general awareness, and knowledge sharing. Strangely, network translucence, which indicates people's awareness of others' ties, had minimal impact on information sharing.

Based on their findings, Baima et al. (2022) conclude that a customer's frequency of online reviews (UFORs), the strength of their social ties (SBs), their level of subjective happiness (SH), and their willingness to reciprocate all contribute positively to customer knowledge sharing (CKS). On the other hand, CKS is unaffected by factors like perceived value of online reviews (PUORs), helping behaviour, customer susceptibility to interpersonal influence (CSII), and informational (INFO).

Wu and Zheng (2021b) found that emotional tiredness considerably affects the interactions between the three social media overload categories that favourably influence users' information-withholding behaviour. They also found that men and women make decisions about knowledge withholding differently. For instance, men are more likely than women to participate in knowledge-withholding behaviour when they experience emotional tiredness from social media use. Knowledge withholding is significantly influenced by three of the four types of social media overload: communication overload, system feature overload, and social overload.

According to Yudhistira and Sushandoyo (2020), perceived content hostility toward political disclosure by co-workers has a minor but substantial indirect impact on the readiness of receivers to disclose tacit knowledge, and is a negligible indirect consequence of perceived value dissimilarity. Altruism is the utmost important predictor of COVID-19 related fraud information dissemination, as per Apuke and Omar (2021). The incentives of social media users in terms of information sharing, socializing, seeking knowledge, and simply passing the time predicted the spread of incorrect information concerning COVID-19. According to Etemadi et al. (2019), performance expectancy (PE) and knowledge sharing self-efficacy (KSSE) had a favourable effect on the intention to use (IU) social media among construction professionals. Alshahrani and Pennington's (2018) qualitative study based on interviews of 30 researchers of a Scottish university revealed the importance of confidential sources such as personal mastery experience, vicarious experience, verbal persuasion, and emotions of the KS behaviour on SM. Participants were found to delve upon one or more of these resources during their KS behaviour.

(ii) Technical Differences

Two studies investigated the influence of technical differences on individual knowledge-sharing behaviour. From a pedagogical standpoint, knowledge-sharing behaviour and social capital were explored in Alajmi and Al-Qallaf's (2022) qualitative study based on individual interviews and focus groups with 12 teachers from Kuwaiti schools. They discovered that media and curricular skills are more in demand online. However, one-on-one interactions are the best way to gain insight into generic instruction. The choice of information sources shows how complicated the types of knowledge needed are and what kinds of social connections are needed to make this exchange possible. Zhao et al. (2020) reported a correlation among social media characteristics, general awareness, and knowledge exchange. Knowledge sharing is unaffected by network translucence, which shows how much each person knows about the relationships of others.

(iii) A Mix of Different Factors (Individual/ Technical/ Organizational)

In a study of 407 students at the top ten private universities in West Malaysia, Hosen et al. (2021) found that some of the most important things that affect tertiary students' online KS are SM functions like documentation, virtual information exchange, and knowledge creation. They also found that individual motivation (reputation) is a key factor that HEIs can use to promote KS and enhance learning outcomes among tertiary students. Additionally, they noted the significance of personal motivations in the previous relationship, such as reputation. Not many studies have identified the influence of external factors on KS behaviour.

Laitinen and Sivunen (2021) studied the influence of external organizational factors on KS behaviour. They found the influence of organizational factors, such as norms, tasks, and media repertoires, on the information-sharing behaviour of employees. The technological affordances of visibility, awareness, endurance, and search ability also influence their behaviour.

Valk and Planojevic's (2021) study during COVID-19 established the positive role of customized KS platforms for employees' KS behaviour. This kind of behaviour also helped people and organizations develop the skills, agility, and flexibility needed in the digital knowledge economy of today. This study was conducted in only one organization as a case study approach. However, future researchers may conduct such experiments in different organizations and contexts. It will be worth studying the type of customization which influences the

KS behaviour of employees most. To find out if there are gender differences in how people choose to share data through social media, Lin and Wang (2020) conducted a study using data from American users of social networking sites (SNSs) from a US-based university. They observed that women's perceptions about information dissemination were more affected by privacy hazards, social relationships, and commitment than for men. People's attitudes toward sharing information and their intention to share information are greatly mediated by gender. There is a need to study more social aspects like peer learning behaviour and peer group influence on KS behaviour.

The users' drivers, outcomes, and strategies, as well as their barriers, outcomes, and strategies, were examined by Kazemian and Grant (2022). Among the motivators are features, information value, organizational requirements, and suitable organizational and technical support (M). Six aspects make up barriers (B), including the inability to participate on the online platform, emotional distress, knowledge loss, absence of organizational burden, poor property of content, and a paucity of time. A framework for outcomes (O) identifies advantages, disadvantages, and solutions (S) for enhancing user involvement.

However, there is a need to identify and study more external factors that may influence the KS behaviour of employees. External influencers such as the role of supervisor, peer, and organization IT infrastructure will be worth studying.

5.2 Consequences

Only four studies researched the consequences of using social media on knowledge-sharing behaviour. Rasheed et al.'s (2020) study among 383 research scholars learning in diverse universities from Eastern China found a positive influence of KS behaviour using SM on students' creativity and engagement. It will be interesting to test the relationships in the workplace context. The practitioners will benefit immensely if similar results are achieved at the workplace.

Zhang et al. (2020) studied the phenomenon in the workplace context. They compared the feeling of sharing on SM with collaboration. They inferred that employees communicating more on the SM platforms develop better feelings, but their KS is lesser. Collaboration had a negative influence on the psychological aspects of employees. Further, they found that extremely close cooperation led to employee differences, which hindered KS. Alshahrani and Pennington (2020) identified social outcome expectation as a social consequence evolving out of this phenomenon.

The social outcomes can be positive or negative. The study revealed the following positive outcomes: appealing individuals, visibility, networking, and social impact. The only adverse outcome was the absence of belief. It will be interesting to identify and test other outcomes such as psychological, psychosocial, etc. Future researchers may also study other types of positive and negative social outcomes. Ma et al. (2020) reported a beneficial moderating role of job engagement among socially related private and public social media usage and employees' knowledge hiding. Socially connected general and personal social media usage encourages employee knowledge conceal-ment. In addition, it is limited by employee's usage of job-related general social media, but this usage has a little influence on employees' knowledge concealment. Ansari and Khan (2020) analyzed the responses of 360 Indian university students to study the interaction effect between interactivity with teachers, peers, and online KS behaviour. The results revealed that social me-dia usage positively improved KS behaviour among students, which further improved their engagement and academic performance. Researchers in the future may consider having objective performance criteria, which will im-prove the credibility of the results.

Most of the studies in the SM and KS literature were found to identify the influencers of this behaviour. Moreover, the studies mainly focused on the individual-level constructs. Only a handful of studies describe the role of external influencers on KS behaviour among individuals.

6. Implications and Conclusion

The current paper is an extensive literature review on the usage of social me-dia for knowledge sharing. The study's results will immensely help academi-cians, particularly future researchers who seek to pursue research in this area. It provides the academicians and industry experts with an opinion on the ex-isting position of affairs in this important area of research. The current study provides valuable inputs on the antecedents, consequences, and importance of knowledge sharing on SM. It provides the answers to the practitioners on the questions like "How to improve knowledge sharing behaviour among the employees in the social media platform?" and "What are the technical and organizational support systems which help in improving such behaviour?"

The authors employed the PRISMA technique to identify relevant research papers on the topic under discussion from Google Scholar, SCOPUS, and ProQuest. The review of the paper was conducted using the TCCM and 4W framework. These frameworks helped list and discuss the theoretical, con-ceptual, characteristics, and methodology of each research paper selected for the study. The data analysis helped to identify the qualitative (type of papers) and quantitative status (number of papers under each theme and sub-theme) of the "Social Media for Knowledge Sharing" literature. The study helped characterize the varied business domains where the studies are conducted.

Further analysis revealed that most studies were directed toward un-derstanding the antecedents of knowledge-sharing behaviour on the SM platform. There was a lack of studies focussing on the negative aspects of knowledge sharing on SM. Some studies considered knowledge hiding and knowledge withholding as research variables.

The organizations are increasingly using the SM platform for KS. This creates immense opportunities for future research to study individual, team, and organizational variables that influence KS behaviour. The positive and negative outcomes will also be worth studying.

References

Afrouzi, H. (2020). Strategic inattention, inflation dynamics, and the non-neutrality of money. *CESifo working paper no. 8218*. Retrieved May 30, 2023, from https://afrouzi.com/strategic_inattention.pdf

Ahmed, Y. A., Ahmad, M. N., Ahmad, N., & Zakaria, N. H. (2019). Social media for knowledge-sharing: A systematic literature review. *Telematics and Informatics, 37,* 72–112. https://doi.org/10.1016/J.TELE.2018.01.015

Aichner, T., & Jacob, F. (2015). Measuring the degree of corporate social media use. *International Journal of Market Research, 57*(2), 257–275. https://doi.org/10.2501/IJMR-2015-018

Akpan, I. J., Soopramanien, D., & Kwak, D. H. (2020). Cutting-edge technologies for small business and innovation in the era of COVID-19 global health pandemic. *Journal of Small Business & Entrepreneurship*, 1–11. http://doi.org/10.1080/08276331.2020.1799294.

Alajmi, B. M., & Al-Qallaf, C. L. (2022). Fostering knowledge-sharing behavior through social capital: The implications of face-to-face and online interactions. *Global Knowledge, Memory and Communication, 71*(4–5), 274–292. https://doi.org/10.1108/GKMC-01-2021-0007

Alshahrani, H., & Pennington, D. (2018). "Why not use it more?" Sources of self-efficacy in researchers' use of social media for knowledge sharing. *Journal of Documentation, 74*(6), 1274–1292. https://doi.org/10.1108/JD-04-2018-0051

Alshahrani, H., & Pennington, D. (2020). "How to use it more?" Self-efficacy and its sources in the use of social media for knowledge sharing. *Journal of Documentation, 76*(1), 231–257. https://doi.org/10.1108/JD-02-2019-0026/FULL/PDF

Anderson, D., & Kelliher, C. (2020). Enforced remote working and the work-life interface during lockdown. *Gender in Management: An International Journal, 35*(7/8), 677–683.

Ansari, J. A. N., & Khan, N. A. (2020). Exploring the role of social media in collaborative learning the new domain of learning. *Smart Learning Environments, 7*(1), 1–16. https://doi.org/10.1186/S40561-020-00118-7/TABLES/5

Apuke, O. D., & Omar, B. (2021). Fake news and COVID-19: Modelling the predictors of fake news sharing among social media users. *Telematics and Informatics, 56,* 101475. https://doi.org/10.1016/J.TELE.2020.101475

Baima, G., Santoro, G., Pellicelli, A. C., & Mitręga, M. (2022). Testing the antecedents of customer knowledge sharing on social media: A quantitative analysis on Italian consumers. *International Marketing Review, 39*(3), 682–705. https://doi.org/10.1108/IMR-03-2021-0122

Bansal, R., Mittal, R., & Kumar, V. (2021). Popularity and usage analytics of social media platforms in higher education. In *2021 international conference on computational performance evaluation (ComPE)* (pp. 631–635). IEEE. https://doi.org/10.1109/ComPE53109.2021.9752143

Bapuji, H., de Bakker, F., Brown, J., Higgins, C., Rehbein, K., & Spicer, A. (2020). Business and society research in times of the corona crisis. *Business & Society, 59,* 1067–1078.

Bhardwaj, A., & Kumar, V. (2022a). A framework for enhancing privacy in online collaboration. *International Journal of Electronic Security and Digital Forensics (IJESDF), 14*(4), 413–432.

Bosangit, C., & Demangeot, C. (2016). Exploring reflective learning during the extended consumption of life experiences. *Journal of Business Research, 69*(1), 208–215. https://doi.org/10.1016/J.JBUSRES.2015.07.033

Busalim, A. H., & Hussin, A. R. C. (2016). Understanding social commerce: A systematic literature review and directions for further research. *International Journal of Information Management*, 36(6), 1075–1088. https://doi.org/10.1016/j.ijinfomgt.2016.06.005

Callahan, J. L. (2014). Writing literature reviews: A reprise and update. *Human Resource Development Review*, 13(3), 271–275. https://doi.org/10.1177/1534484314536705

Carnavale, J. B., & Hatak, I. (2020). Employee adjustment and well-being in the era of COVID-19: Implications for human resource management. *Journal of Business Research*, 116, 183–187.

Chatterjee, S., Rana, N. P., & Dwivedi, Y. K. (2020). Social media as a tool of knowledge sharing in academia: An empirical study using valance, instrumentality and expectancy (VIE) approach. *Journal of Knowledge Management*, 24(10), 2531–2552. https://doi.org/10.1108/JKM-04-2020-0252/FULL/PDF

Chernick, H., Copeland, D., & Reschovsky, A. (2020). The fiscal effects of the COVID-19 pandemic on cities: An initial assessment. *National Tax Journal*, 73(3), 699–732. https://doi.org/10.17310/NTJ.2020.3.04

Dewey, A. D. (2016). Module 1: Introduction to conducting systematic reviews. *Cochrane Training*. Retrieved July 31, 2022, from https://training.cochrane.org/interactivelearning/module-1-introduction-conducting-systematic-reviews

DiMicco, J., Millen, D. R., Geyer, W., Dugan, C., Brownholtz, B., & Muller, M. (2008). Motivations for social networking at work. In *Proceedings of the ACM conference on computer supported cooperative work* (pp. 711–720). CSCW. https://doi.org/10.1145/1460563.1460674

Di Vaio, A., Palladino, R., Hassan, R., & Escobar, O. (2020). Artificial intelligence and business models in the sustainable development goals perspective: A systematic literature review. *Journal of Business Research*, 121, 283–314. https://doi.org/10.1016/J.JBUSRES.2020.08.019

Donath, J., & Boyd, D. (2004). Public displays of connection. *BT Technology Journal*, 22(4), 71–82. https://doi.org/10.1023/B:BTTJ.0000047585.06264.CC

Etemadi, R., Hon, C. K. H., Murphy, G., & Manley, K. (2019). The use of social media for work-related knowledge sharing by construction professionals. *Architectural Engineering and Design Management*, 16(6), 426–440. https://doi.org/10.1080/17452007.2019.1688637

Ganguly, A., Talukdar, A., & Chatterjee, D. (2019). Evaluating the role of social capital, tacit knowledge sharing, knowledge quality and reciprocity in determining innovation capability of an organization. *Journal of Knowledge Management*, 23. https://doi.org/10.1108/JKM-03-2018-0190

Gopinath, G. (2020, April 14). The great lockdown: Worst economic downturn since the great depression. *IMFBlog*. https://blogs.imf.org/2020/04/14/the-great-lockdown-worst-economic-downturn-since-the-great-depression/

He, W., Zhang, Z. J., & Li, W. (2021). Information technology solutions, challenges, and suggestions for tackling the COVID-19 pandemic. *International Journal of Information Management*, 57, 1–8. https://doi.org/10.1016/j.ijinfomgt.2020.102287

Hosen, M., Ogbeibu, S., Giridharan, B., Cham, T. H., Lim, W. M., & Paul, J. (2021). Individual motivation and social media influence on student knowledge sharing and learning performance: Evidence from an emerging economy. *Computers and Education*, 172. https://doi.org/10.1016/J.COMPEDU.2021.104262

Ipe, M. (2016). Knowledge sharing in organizations: A conceptual framework. *Human Resource Development Review*, 2(4), 337–359. https://doi.org/10.1177/1534484303257985

Kaplan, A. M., & Haenlein, M. (2010). Users of the world, unite! The challenges and opportunities of Social Media. *Business Horizons*, 53(1), 59–68. https://doi.org/10.1016/J.BUSHOR.2009.09.003

Kasapakis, V., & Gavalas, D. (2017). User-generated content in Pervasive games. *Computers in Entertainment*, 16(1). https://doi.org/10.1145/3161570

Kašcelan, L., Bach, M. P., Rondovic, B., & Durickovic, T. (2020). The interaction between social media, knowledge management and service quality: A decision tree analysis. *PLoS ONE*, 15(8). https://doi.org/10.1371/JOURNAL.PONE.0236735

Kazemian, S., & Grant, S. B. (2022). The impact of the COVID-19 pandemic on knowledge sharing in UK higher education. *VINE Journal of Information and Knowledge Management Systems*, ahead-of-print (ahead-of-print). https://doi.org/10.1108/VJIKMS-06-2021-0096/FULL/PDF

Kovid, R. K., & Kumar, V. (Eds.). (2022). *Cases on emerging markets responses to the COVID-19 pandemic*. IGI Global Publications.

Kumar, V., & Ayodeji, O. G. (2020). Web analytics for knowledge creation: A systematic review of tools, techniques and practices. *International Journal of Cyber Behavior, Psychology and Learning (IJCBPL)*, 10(1), 1–14.

Kumar, V., & Gupta, G. (Eds.). (2021). *Strategic management during a pandemic*. Routledge; Taylor & Francis Group.

Kumar, V., & Malhotra, G. (Eds.). (2021). *Stakeholder strategies for reducing the impact of global health crises*. IGI Global Publications.

Kumar, V., & Nanda, P. (2019). Social media to social media analytics: Ethical challenges. *International Journal of Technoethics (IJT)*, 10(2), 57–70.

Kumar, V., & Nanda, P. (2020). Social media as a tool in higher education: A pedagogical perspective. In *Handbook of research on diverse teaching strategies for the technology-rich classroom* (pp. 239–253). IGI Global Publications.

Kumar, V., & Nanda, P. (2022). Approaching the Porter's five forces through social media analytics. *International Journal of Services Operations and Informatics (IJSOI)*, 12(2), 184–200.

Kumar, V., Nanda, P., & Tawangar, S. (2022). Social media in business decisions of MSMES: Practices and challenges. *International Journal of Decision Support System Technology (IJDSST)*, 14(1), 1–12.

Laitinen, K., & Sivunen, A. (2021). Enablers of and constraints on employees' information sharing on enterprise social media. *Information Technology and People*, 34(2), 642–665. https://doi.org/10.1108/ITP-04-2019-0186/FULL/PDF

Lata, M., & Gupta, A. (2021). Education during the pandemic: Technology-based solutions. In *Stakeholder strategies for reducing the impact of global health crises* (pp. 209–224). IGI Global Publications.

Leonardi, P., & Neeley, T. (2017). *What managers need to know about Slack, Yammer, and Chatter*. Retrieved July 31, 2022, from Harvard Business Review website https://hbr.org/2017/11/what-managers-need-to-know-about-social-tools

Liberati, A., Altman, D. G., Tetzlaff, J., Mulrow, C., Gøtzsche, P. C., Ioannidis, J. P., Clarke, M., Devereaux, P. J., Kleijnen, J., & Moher, D. (2009). The PRISMA statement for reporting systematic reviews and meta-analyses of studies that evaluate healthcare interventions: explanation and elaboration. *BMJ (Clinical Research Ed.)*, 339, b2700. https://doi.org/10.1136/bmj.b2700

Lin, X., & Wang, X. (2020). Examining gender differences in people's information-sharing decisions on social networking sites. *International Journal of Information Management*, *50*(May 2019), 45–56. https://doi.org/10.1016/j.ijinfomgt.2019.05.004

Ma, L., Zhang, X., & Ding, X. (2020). Enterprise social media usage and knowledge hiding: A motivation theory perspective. *Journal of Knowledge Management*, *24*(9), 2149–2169. https://doi.org/10.1108/JKM-03-2020-0234

Mittal, S., & Kumar, V. (2019). Study of knowledge management models and their relevance in organisations. *International Journal of Knowledge Management Studies*, *10*(3), 322–335.

O'Leary, D. (2020). Evolving information systems and technology research issues for COVID-19 and other pandemics. *Journal of Organizational Computing and Electronic Commerce*, *30*(1), 1–8. http://doi.org/10.1080/10919392.2020.1755790

Panahi, S., Watson, J., & Partridge, H. (2016). Conceptualising social media support for tacit knowledge sharing: Physicians' perspectives and experiences. *Journal of Knowledge Management*, *20*(2), 344–363. https://doi.org/10.1108/JKM-06-2015-0229

Papadopoulos, T. B., & Balta, M. E. (2020). The use of digital technologies by small and medium enterprises during COVID-19: Implications for theory and practice. *International Journal of Information Management*, 1–4. http://doi.org/10.1016/j.ijinfomgt.2020.102192

Platts, K., Breckon, J., & Marshall, E. (2021). Enforced home-working under lockdown and its impact on employee wellbeing : A cross-sectional study conceptualization of wellbeing at work wellbeing in a home-working context. *BMC Public Health*, *22*, 1–15.

Rasheed, M. I., Malik, J., Pitafi, A. H., Iqbal, J., Anser, M. K., & Abbas, M. (2020). Usage of social media, student engagement, and creativity: The role of knowledge sharing behavior and cyberbullying. *Computers and Education*, *159*(February), 104002. https://doi.org/10.1016/j.compedu.2020.104002

Sava, J. A. (2022, April 7). *Future trends in remote work worldwide from 2020 to 2021*. Statista. www.statista.com/statistics/1199110/remote-work-trends-covid-survey-september-december/

Sein, M. (2020). The serendipitous impact of COVID-19 pandemic: A rare opportunity for research and practice. *International Journal of Information Management*, 55.

Singh, J., & Kumar, V. (2022). Combating the pandemic with ICT based learning tools and applications: A case of Indian higher education. *International Journal of Virtual and Personal Learning Environments (IJVPLE) Platforms (IJVPLE)*, *12*(1), 1–21.

StatistaResearchDepartment. (2020, June 13). *Opinion on home office due to coronavirus (COVID-19) 2020, selected countries*. Statista. www.statista.com/statistics/1132948/opinion-on-remote-work-due-to-covid-19-selected-countries/

Suti, M., & Sari, H. (2021). Social network sites (SNS) for knowledge-sharing behavior among students. *VINE Journal of Information and Knowledge Management Systems*. https://doi.org/10.1108/VJIKMS-04-2021-0043

Ting, D. S., Carin, L., Dzau, V., & Wong, T. Y. (2020). Digital technology and COVID- 19. *Nature Medicine*, *26*(4), 459–461.

Valk, R., & Planojevic, G. (2021). Addressing the knowledge divide: Digital knowledge sharing and social learning of geographically dispersed employees during the COVID-19 pandemic. *Journal of Global Mobility*, *9*(4), 591–621. https://doi.org/10.1108/JGM-02-2021-0019/FULL/PDF

Wu, D., & Zheng, J. (2023). Social media overload, gender differences and knowledge withholding. *Kybernetes*, *52*(1), 24–43.

Wu, S. Y., Wang, W. T., & Hsiao, M. H. (2021). Knowledge sharing among healthcare practitioners: Identifying the psychological and motivational facilitating factors. *Frontiers in Psychology*, 12. https://doi.org/10.3389/FPSYG.2021.736277/FULL

Yudhistira, D. S., & Sushandoyo, D. (2020). Does political self-disclosure in social media hamper tacit knowledge sharing in the workplace? *VINE Journal of Information and Knowledge Management Systems*, *50*(3), 513–530. https://doi.org/10.1108/VJIKMS-08-2019-0128

Zhang, J., Qu, Y., Cody, J., & Wu, Y. (2010). A case study of micro-blogging in the enterprise: Use, value, and related issues. *Conference on Human Factors in Computing Systems—Proceedings*, *1*, 123–132. https://doi.org/10.1145/1753326.1753346

Zhao, Y., Zhang, X., Wang, J., Zhang, K., & Ordóñez de Pablos, P. (2020). How do features of social media influence knowledge sharing? An ambient awareness perspective. *Journal of Knowledge Management*, *24*(2), 439–462. https://doi.org/10.1108/JKM-10-2019-0543

5 Infodemic Management in India

A Social Media Perspective

Ritu Bajaj, Maitri, and Sangeeta Gupta

1. Introduction

Man being a social animal needs to interact with family members, colleagues, and friends, but with the fast spreading of the novel coronavirus (COVID-19) declared as a pandemic by WHO across the world (Cucinotta & Vanelli, 2019), overnight governments across the globe declared lockdowns and made restrictions for people to stay at home for their own well-being (Kumar & Gupta, 2021; Kumar & Malhotra, 2021). Even in India, being the second most populous nation of the world, people overnight were restricted to sit in the four walls of their houses. Physical interactions got banned, social distancing became a new normal (Kovid & Kumar, 2022). Even family members at home had to maintain social distancing; as a result, people across the globe changed, and people became completely dependent on the internet for social interactions by using their gadgets at home (Singh & Kumar, 2022). For social interactions, the average time in the US in the year 2020 increased from 54 minutes to 65 minutes (Dixon, 2022). Sharing of information was through social media such as Facebook, where people could at least tentatively escape their negative emotions (Abbas et al., 2021). Along with Facebook (Marino, 2018), the positive experience at other media platforms and online experiences led to developing a close emotional bonding to social media use, leading to a strong desire to stay online permanently (Brailovskaia, 2018).

On one hand, dependency on social media became a natural phenomenon across the globe; on the other hand, COVID-19 spread caused tremendous challenges and crisis management issues, such as economic crisis, social stigma, environmental effects, and health emergency worldwide (Salamatbakhsh, 2019). Initially, there was lots of confusion among people about how the virus was being spread. By that time, it was known by the medical fraternity that the virus was being spread by not only the touch of humans but also by the droplets of human beings in the air, dust, and fumes (Wang & Du, 2020; Asadi, 2020). One infected person could spread the virus to many. There were two main routes of infection—through direct and indirect contact by sneezing coughing and talking too (Ningthoujam, 2020). Healthcare systems across the globe were not prepared to fight the spread of virus in such a fast way

DOI: 10.4324/9781003315278-5

86 *Ritu Bajaj, Maitri, and Sangeeta Gupta*

(Bhardwaj & Kumar, 2022). This situation led to the pandemic, and the intensity at which it was spreading led to shortage of medicines, beds, and medical equipment in many countries. There were no vaccines to even stop further spread and control. It was not only the severity of virus but rather the high degree of uncertainty about its symptoms that was building up panic globally.

It was not only the virus but also a lot of misinformation, amplified on social media, that started spreading through various social media platforms that was as much a threat to global public health as the virus itself (WHO, 2020a). The COVID-19 pandemic has brought an insight on how a prodigious biological event can cause a socio-economic disturbance, not only through its severity but also through misinformation and social media (Bansal et al., 2021).

1.1 *Infodemic and COVID-19*

Infodemic is a situation of excessive dependence on social media resulting in false or misleading information in digital and physical environments during a disease outbreak (Tangcharoensathien et al., 2020). Social media provides positive and negative data, and COVID-19 has resulted in a worldwide infodemic (Abbas et al., 2021). An infodemic is too much information causing confusion and risk-taking behaviour of individuals that can harm their health. Infodemic leads to mistrust in health authorities and undermines the public health response. An infodemic can further escalate when people are not sure what steps they need to do to protect their own health and health of their nears and dears around them. The term "infodemiology" is a "new emerging research discipline and methodology" comprising "the study of the determinants and distribution of health information and misinformation—which may be useful in guiding health professionals and patients to quality health information on the Internet" (Eysenbach, 2020).

The spread of misinformation about COVID-19 diagnosis as well as treatment was excruciating. On one hand, there was risk and panic among people of physical health and mental health issues and no physical interactions. On the other hand, social media was spreading these issues, and deaths were taking place like a fire. Moreover, people were not taking positive and appropriate action that would help protect their health; they were taking actions that may have spread the illness or engaging in other problematic behaviours (Ahmed et al., 2020). As a result, through media and social media, the news of the virus was spreading rigorously, and people starting hoarding medications and oxygen required for treatment.

1.2 *Appeal of Infodemic Management by WHO*

The World Health Organization (WHO) had a very important role to play, and it took a quick action call. They started an awareness campaign about the risks of incorrect and false information regarding the coronavirus pandemic. "Stop the Spread" was a global campaign started by WHO to raise awareness about the risks of misinformation around COVID-19. It encouraged people to double-check information with trusted sources (i.e. WHO and national health authorities) before believing them. WHO itself used social media to promote the campaign across the world to countries like Africa, Asia, Europe, Middle East, and Latin America, etc. As per (WHO, 2020 b), newsletter on infodemic, infodemic management is the systematic use of risk and evidence-based analysis and approaches to reduce the impact of infodemic during health emergencies. WHO emphasized on four activities: (i) listening to the concerns of the community and queries of questions they have, (ii) not reacting to misinformation and ability to withstand adversity and bounce back from difficult life events, (iii) promoting and understanding of healthcare advice, and (iv) engaging and empowering communities to take positive action.

1.3 Use of Social Media for Engaging and Empowering Communities to Take Positive Action During the Pandemic in India

India was not fortunate enough to be left aside during the pandemic; rather, its people also became carriers of the COVID-19 virus. As per WHO 2020, India had 360 confirmed cases, including seven deaths in 23 states and nine union territories, while Southeast Asia had 979 confirmed cases, including 38 deaths, which was quite low as compared to the global effect of the coronavirus having 2,66,073 confirmed cases, including 11,184 deaths till March 31, 2020. On March 19, 2020, Sh. Narendra Modi, the prime minister of India, addressed the nation through media and social media. It was his first address with reference to this crisis, where he requested the people of the country for a day-long lockdown which was named as "Janta Curfew". But still the spread was increasing, and the number of infected cases got accelerated to 1,000 by the end of March 2020 (Nguyen & Chauhan, 2020). Keeping the uncontrolled situation in mind, PM addressed the nation again and imposed a 21-day lockdown from March 25, 2020 till April 14, 2020 to restrain the spread of the coronavirus in the country (Hebbar, 2020).

Apart from announcing lockdown, measures sped up to practice social distancing. To scale down the community spread, all stringent measures were taken and enforced to be practiced by citizens of India. India was trying to emerge as a leader to fight against corona. The Indian government announced a series of rigorous measures and was continuously spreading information through social media. People were using social media more than usual because they relied on news sources to seek health information for themselves and their loved ones (de Calheiros Velozo & Stauder, 2018).

Social media platforms' usage became a welcome relief in the health disaster and global crisis during the ongoing COVID-19 pandemic (Zhong, 2021;

Lata & Gupta, 2021). Social media was aptly used by the government to spread the message of social distancing, use of face masks, hand sanitizers, and frequent hand washing. The Indian PM made an appeal to the citizens to follow all measures of prevention. Exhaustive and extensive efforts were taken to combat this corona crisis. Further, schools, offices, malls, cinema halls, and even places of worship like temples were closed. All events and activities were cancelled to avoid public gatherings. But still there was panic among people, and social media was used for searching of hospital beds, oxygen cylinder, and meditation for loved ones. Social media become a helpline during COVID-19 (Bhasin, 2021; Fang et al., 2020). Keeping the outburst of panic, the central and state administrative authorities were communicated to strictly monitor the successful executions of government orders. Overall, peer support through social media to retain social connection was helping reduce the social isolation and became necessary to manage mental health disorders, depression, anxiety, and secondary trauma (Lin & Kishore, 2021; Yang et al., 2021).

The way the virus was disseminating from one individual to another and all sorts of measures to stop its spread were being adopted by the Indian government. Further, the Indian government immediately planned and started research and development activity at war foot for the development of a vaccine. This resulted in a lot of initiatives by doctors and researchers, along with commitment by the pharma companies to invent and bring the vaccines to market. Covaxin, India's indigenous COVID-19 vaccine by Bharat Biotech, was developed in collaboration with the Indian Council of Medical Research (ICMR)—National Institute of Virology (NIV). COVISHIELD was manufactured by Serum Institute of India Pvt Ltd along with AstraZeneca. As per Ananth (2020), an appeal by the government to install and usage of Aarogya Setu app was also introduced, the Prime Minister also made an appeal to the people of the country to use the Indian vaccine. He used social media platforms to reach large number of mobile phone users in India.

Government had not only put efforts towards physical well-being through social distancing, mask wearing, etc. Efforts for mental and spiritual well-being were also initiated by the government. Infodemic management played an important role to carry the core value systems embedded in Indian culture, which were reinforced through the initiatives taken by India. With the COVID-19 pandemic's adverse effects on global public health, the government was trying to reinforce positivism all around and the indispensable role of social media to provide the correct information in the COVID-19 health crisis (Abbas et al., 2021). Social media was used for spreading positive campaigns too. Indian government initiatives announced by Prime Shri Minister Narendra Modiji to combat COVID-19: Time duration from March 19 to April 14, 2020. Table 5.1 represents the major initiatives taken for the well-being of people and spread of initiatives by the people.

The purpose of this chapter is to study the initiatives taken by the government to stimulate the mental well-being and boost the morale of people during the pandemic through social media for infodemic management.

Table 5.1 Indian government initiatives for the people and by the people

Serial No.	Government Initiative	Announcement Date	Execution Date	Purpose
1	Janta Curfew	19th March 2020	22nd March 2020	Self-isolation at home for one day
2	Lockdown 1	24th March 2020	24th March 2020	**Draw lakshman rekha at doorstep**
3	Taali Bajao, Thaali Bajao'	19th March 2020	22nd March 2020	To pay tribute to the corona warriors, to propagate "Seva Parmo Dharma"—that is, service being the highest duty for five minutes at 5:00 pm
4	Ek Diya Desh Ke Nam	24th March 2020	5th April 2020	To pay gratitude by to switching off lights and lighting of candles, Diya flashlights of mobile to show solidarity to all essential service providers from at 9:00 pm for nine minutes
5	Relief Packages	26th March 2020	26th March2020	Relief packages were announced by the finance minister for financial support during COVID-19

90 Ritu Bajaj, Maitri, and Sangeeta Gupta

2. Opinion Survey from Indian Citizens for the Initiatives by the Indian Government

Social media was showing a mix review (Abbas et al., 2021) about these initiatives on its different platforms like the PM's personal Facebook post, Twitter, Instagram, and WhatsApp, etc. On social media, some people were giving very positive views; on the other hand, some were criticizing the way the Indian government was dealing with the COVID-19 pandemic. So in order to know the opinion of Indian citizens on these initiatives made by the Indian government, an opinion survey was conducted.

2.1 Research Methods

The present study is a primary, observational, and cross-sectional study conducted transversely in India. A convenience or purposive sampling technique was used. A structured questionnaire was developed in Google form. A questionnaire was developed with three sections; first section is related to demographic profile of the respondents, second sections pertains to constructs in which we are asking the impact of COVID-19 on mental health, physical health, and work-life balance. The third section was devoted to know the opinion of respondents on government initiatives taken by the Indian government during the pandemic. The survey was conducted online by sending a link of the Google form on emails and various WhatsApp groups of researchers' contacts. Researchers used the contacts of their friends and colleagues to motivate as many people as possible to respond to this questionnaire. Being an online study, people who had internet connection participated. After receiving and clicking the link, the participants came across auto-directed information related to the study and their consent to be a part of the study. Participants who were at least graduates, understood English, were technology savvy, and who accepted to be part of the study were included in this research. Researchers initiated data collection on April 1, 2020 and closed on April 30, 2020. In this study, responses were received across India. The survey includes socio-demographic variables such as gender, occupation, years of experience, qualification, job type, and location. Then respondents answered on the initiatives taken by the Indian government on a five-point Likert scale of strongly disagree (1) to strongly agree (5). There are five items included in studying government initiatives. Percentages have been used in the study to analyze the findings.

2.2 Respondents' Profile

The sample size for the study was calculated with the help of G power software, and it suggested 89 as the appropriate sample size. However, 300 responses were received, out of which 228 responses were complete and used for the study. All the participants were of Indian origin. There was almost an equal divide between male, 49.5%, and female, 50.4%, respondents.

Infodemic Management in India 91

Table 5.2 Demographic profile of the respondents

Variable	Values	Percentage
Gender	Male	49.5
	Female	50.4
Organization	Government	18.4
	Private	75.0
	PSU	1.3
	Corporate	5.3
Job Type	Faculty	64.0
	Government Employees	2.2
	Corporate Professionals	14.0
	Entrepreneur	5.7
	Researcher	4.4
	Non-Teaching Staff	7.0
	Student Cum Employee	2.6
Years of Experience	0–10	54.8
	11–20	32.5
	20	12.7
Qualification	Doctorate	29.8
	Postgraduate	54.8
	Graduate	09.6
	Others	05.7
Location	North India	61.0
	Central India	17.1
	West India	12.3
	South India	09.6

Seventy-five per cent of the respondents were working in private organizations. More than 60% of the population was from the teaching profession (64%). Most of the respondents (54.8%) had ten years of experience at their workplace. Education level of 54.8% respondents was up to post-graduation; however, 29.8% respondents were PhD holders. Majority of the respondents, 61%, belonged to north Indian states like Haryana, Punjab, and Delhi. A summarized view of the demographic profile of respondents is given in Table 5.2.

2.3 Data Analysis and Results

Opinion Regarding Janta Curfew

This was the first initiative by the Indian government. PM announced a social curfew named "Janta Curfew" on March 22, 2020 from 7:00 am to 9:00 pm. People of our country were requested to stay at their homes for the initial 14 hours. Only essential service providers were allowed to go outside of their homes. It was a curfew by the janta and for the janta. Only 28% of the respondents agreed to this initiative. Like the government, they also wanted to know that the nation was ready for lockdown and precaution measures.

On the other hand, 58.4% respondents disagreed to this way of dealing with the pandemic crisis. Maybe in the beginning people were not aware that this medical emergency needed precaution through social distancing rather than medicine.

Opinion About Thali & Tali Initiative

The Indian Express reported on March 22, 2020 that the PM appeals to the citizens to pray for warriors and pay gratitude to them. Indians gave a standing ovation on March 22 at 5:00 pm by clinging thali/metal plates, clapping, bell ringing, and blowing conchies. It was an acknowledgment to all the service professionals and corona warriors who were sweating, sacrificing their lives in keeping the public safe. The air reverberated with a medley of sounds to appreciate all, especially the frontline workers. It was melodious to the ear to listen to the reverberations and feel thankful. People from all classes, creeds, and cultures enthusiastically participated in this initiative, which also reflected the value system of a democratic country like India (Express Web Desk, 2020).

More than 50% of the respondents (55.7%) were against "Thali & Tali" movement. They thought the whole world would laugh and make fun of Indians because of how they fought with a pandemic which is a medical emergency. They took it as a kind of Indian orthodox. However, 32% of the respondents took it as the spiritual way of Indians to overcome such a panicky situation. Moreover, this was a request made by our PM, and we have a long history of following our national leaders. Although intellectuals were not in favour, practically all segments of people took keen participation in this drive.

Opinion About Lockdown 1

PM, with all humility and folded hands, urged citizens to stay at home. To adhere to the call of the nation's lockdown, he requested the citizens of India to not to cross Lakshman Rekha. He appealed to the citizens to save their lives by not stepping out of their doorsteps as it was of paramount importance. "If these 21 days will not be handled properly our family and country may go 21 years backward" was quoted in the PM's speech. It had a huge economic cost but was still important. Many people of India followed it too. Citizens were appealed to live patiently and follow the 21-day lockdown (The Times of India, 2020).

There was not a clear mandate of the sample regarding lockdown of 21 days, but 43.4% strongly agreed with this government call. According to them, this is not the solution to handle the situation. On other hand, 32% of the respondents disagreed with the 21-day lockdown, as in this period of time central and state governments got sufficient time for preparation to fight with the pandemic. Many people were strongly against this and termed it as premature. Rather, they suggested going for phase-wise lockdown.

Opinion About Relief Packages Announcement

In 2014, the Rangarajan Committee announced the population below the poverty line was *454 million*, that is, 38.2% of the population (Press Bureau of India, 2014). When government announced lockdown due to COVID-19, everyone had to stay at their home (Singh, 2020). Daily wage workers had no way of earning their bread and butter. Relief packages were announced to provide real-time help to the needy and poor people. This crisis must not hit anybody so badly that they may not be able to feed themselves and their family. So financial packages were planned intelligently to help the needy and the poor. The finance minister announced the Rs 1.70 Lakh Crore relief package under Pradhan Mantri Garib Kalyan Yojana for the poor to help them fight the battle against the coronavirus (Ministry of Finance, 2020). Thirty-one per cent of the respondents agreed that this was a good step taken by the government. However, 28% of the respondents strongly disagreed with the announcement of economic packages to the needy. Social media further helped spread the message about food and clothing distribution.

Opinion Regarding Ek Diya Desh Ke Naam

All citizens were requested to switch off lights and light diyas, candles, flashlights of mobile phones, or torchlights for nine minutes at 9:00 pm on April 5, 2020 to show unity in the fight again COVID-19 pandemic. Indians showed comradeship and strength. Lighting diyas was a collective display of solidarity and peace. It was really a show of unity for dispelling the darkness spread by the coronavirus. Indians have showcased a communal display. Diyas were displayed in different forms to manifest spirituality.

The lighting of a lamp or diya to pay gratitude towards COVID-19 warriors was another call of the Indian government. Almost 30% of the respondents from all over India agreed with this call. According to them, this is the way we made them or their families feel proud. The COVID-19 or pandemic warriors were serving the society even at the cost of their own lives. On the other hand, 32% of the respondents disagreed with this call. They were of the view that, instead of wasting money on this kind of movement, the government should create more quarantine centers and run awareness campaigns (Best Media Info Bureau, 2020).

3. Discussion

At the initial stage of the spread of COVID-19, a lot of rumours and misinformation started spreading through various social media platforms, which was worsening the pandemic. However, the government of India strategically used the positive side of social media to spread information and manage the information by infodemic management, then the same social media became a life-rescuing platform. For the study, an opinion survey and information available on various social media platforms, government websites, and the

94   *Ritu Bajaj, Maitri, and Sangeeta Gupta*

PM's Facebook account were studied and analyzed. In the opinion survey, people across India participated and shared their views. It was found that vaccination was not ready by the time the janta curfew was announced by the government. The pandemic was spread by touch and interaction with infected humans, and the government had no other way to control it except through social distancing, so they announced the janta curfew and the first lockdown. But initially people were not aware about the severity of this medical emergency which was spreading panic on social media. However, the government strategically made the use of media and social media for spreading the message of social distancing as the only rescue. Further in the chapter, various initiatives taken by the government for masses were involved like Tali Thali. It was the communication strategy adopted by the government of India spread through social media (Mody, 2022). The sound of beating of Thali added positivism in the environment and human well-being, so the Indian government requested to common man to sit on the walls of their own homes and show gesture of gratitude towards the COVID-19 warriors like healthcare workers, police, cleaning staff, etc., by clinging thali or clapping hands through social media. This initiative by the government became a Tali Thali campaign of beating utensils for five minutes in March 2020. Nearly 55–60 million people could be reached (Safi, 2022).

Participation from all cross sections of society was witnessed and also got reported by media. Surprisingly, our research suggests diverse opinions about these initiatives. India, a democratic country, obeyed the prime minister's order, so they observed the curfew, clapped for warriors, and lit candles enthusiastically. Indians supported all calls by giving positive remarks in media interviews. They also sent their photos and videos to the media channels, and all these were a clear reflection of showing unity and solidarity at this difficult time of the COVID-19 crisis. But since different countries of the world were facing this crisis more intensely and taking different measures to reduce and curb corona, most of the people were thinking of more scientific, intellectual, and sincere approaches which could meet the need of the people and country in crisis. This research presents the data from working professionals, educated class who are well aware about all the strategies being employed for health, safety, and well-being of citizens of developing and developed countries. This research highlights that policymakers used a fine mix of public engagement activities along with emphasis on development of vaccination and health facilities during the pandemic.

4. Conclusion

COVID-19 is a big threat for lives and livelihood of human beings across the globe and in India too. It is the first time a pandemic of this magnitude was faced globally, and misinformation spread around further worsened the situation. Infodemic management was the need of the hour as a lot of misleading news was getting circulated through social media. Staying at home during janta curfew and lockdown 1.0 became a new normal because maintaining social distancing was the only way to minimize risk of COVID-19. People across the globe became dependent on mobile phones and the internet. This chapter concludes that Government of India successfully handled the situation of individuals staying at home. Which otherwise, would have led to negative thoughts from misinformation spreading across, through social media. Many countries, like the U.K., the U.S., and China, showed the negative role of social media and misinformation about COVID-19, which created panic among social media users. However, the Indian government learned from other countries and used social media for engaging the public and informing them about janta curfew, lockdown 1.0, and distribution of relief packages, and for thanking all the COVID-19 warriors by adopting a communication strategy of tali thali and ek diya desh ke naam. This study, gave an insight into infodemic management. The study shows a mix response of government initiatives during the pandemic. India became the role model to combat the crisis with resilience and bounce back to a normal, healthy life and sound economy. Leadership through the continuous government initiatives shown during the COVID-19 crisis paved the way for other leaders across the world. India worked on both the scientific and emotional fronts to balance the citizens of the nation and made them come out of a panicky situation. Organizations should take the leadership lessons from this crisis to handle situations proactively. The unequivocal compliance of the people/employee is also mandatory to successfully navigate and go ahead with plans. Media and social media had played a vital role by circulating initiatives on time. Reinforcement got increased by watching effective implementations of all initiatives through different channels. Social media acted as a mirror and enabler of effective initiative implementations. India has proven that sensible and right use of media and social media can be a morale booster and change-maker. Hence, government initiatives and the use of social media played a significant role for managing the infodemic about COVID-19 in India.

References

Abbas, J., Wang, D., Su, Z., & Ziapour, A. (2021). The role of social media in the advent of COVID-19 pandemic: Crisis management, mental health challenges and implications. *Risk Management and Healthcare Policy*, *14*, 1917–1932. https://doi.org/10.2147/rmhp.s284313

Ahmed, W., Vidal-Alaball, J., Downing, J., & López Seguí, F. (2020). COVID-19 and the 5G conspiracy theory: Social network analysis of Twitter data. *Journal of Medical Internet Research*, *22*(5), e19458. https://doi.org/10.2196/19458

Ananth, V. (2020). *Government requests social media platforms to promote Aarogya Setu*. Retrieved December 31, 2022, from https://economictimes.indiatimes.com/tech/software/government-requests-social-media-platforms-to-promote-aarogya-setu/articleshow/75080073.cms?utm_source=contentofinterest&utm_medium=text&utm_campaign=cppst

Asadi, S., Bouvier, N., Wexler, A. S., & Ristenpart, W. D. (2020). The coronavirus pandemic and aerosols: Does COVID-19 transmit via expiratory particles?

Aerosol Science and Technology: The Journal of the American Association for Aerosol Research, 54(6), 635–638. https://doi.org/10.1080/02786826.2020.17 49229

Bansal, R., Mittal, R., & Kumar, V. (2021). Popularity and usage analytics of social media platforms in higher education. In *2021 international conference on computational performance evaluation (ComPE)* (pp. 631–635). IEEE. https://doi.org/10.1109/ComPE53109.2021.9752143

Best Media Info Bureau. (2020). *News18 India urges viewers to join PM Modi's appeal to dispel darkness with 'Ek Diya Desh ke Naam'*. Retrieved October 31, 2022, from https://bestmediainfo.com/2020/04/news18-india-urges-viewers-to-join-pm-modi-s-appeal-to-dispel-darkness-with-ek-diya-desh-ke-naam

Bhardwaj, A., & Kumar, V. (2022). Privacy and healthcare during COVID-19. In *Cybersecurity crisis management and lessons learned from the COVID-19 pandemic* (pp. 82–96). IGI Global Publications.

Bhasin, R. (2021). *How Indians turned social media into COVID-19 helpline to battle pandemic*. Retrieved October 31, 2022, from www.newsclick.in/How-Indians-Turned-Social-Media-Into-COVID-19-Helpline-Battle-Pandemic

Brailovskaia, J., Schillack, H., & Margraf, J. (2018). Facebook addiction disorder in Germany. *Cyberpsychology, Behavior and Social Networking*, 21(7), 450–456. https://doi.org/10.1089/cyber.2018.0140

Cucinotta, D., & Vanelli, M. (2019). WHO declares COVID-19 a pandemic. *Acta Biomed*, 91(1), 157–160. https://doi.org/10.23750/abm.v91i1.9397

de Calheiros Velozo, J., & Stauder, J. E. A. (2018). Exploring social media use as a composite construct to understand its relation to mental health: A pilot study on adolescents. *Children and Youth Services Review*, 91, 398–402. https://doi.org/10.1016/j.childyouth.2018.06.039

Dixon, S. (2022). *Social media use during COVID 19-worldwide- Statistics and facts*. Statista. Retrieved November 14, 2022, from www.statista.com/topics/7863/social-media-use-during-coronavirus-covid-19-worldwide/#topicHeader__wrapper

Express Web Desk. (2020, March 22). Watch: From clapping to beating thalis, how people responded to PM Modi's call on "janata curfew". *The Indian Express*. https://indianexpress.com/article/coronavirus/watch-janata-curfew-claps-ringing-bells-pm-modi-6326761/

Eysenbach, G. (2020). How to fight an infodemic: The four pillars of infodemic management. *Journal of Medical Internet Research*, 22(6), e21820. https://doi.org/10.2196/21820

Fang, J., Wang, X., Wen, Z., & Zhou, J. (2020). Fear of missing out and problematic social media use as mediators between emotional support from social media and phubbing behavior. *Addictive Behaviors*, 107(106430), 106430. https://doi.org/10.1016/j.addbeh.2020.106430

Hebbar, N. (2020, March 24). PM Modi announces 21-day lockdown as COVID-19 toll touches 12. *Thehindu.com*. www.thehindu.com/news/national/pm-announces-21-day-lockdown-as-covid-19-toll-touches-10/article61958513.ece.

Kovid, R. K., & Kumar, V. (Eds.). (2022). *Cases on emerging markets responses to the COVID-19 pandemic*. IGI Global Publications.

Kumar, V., & Gupta, G. (Eds.). (2021). *Strategic management during a pandemic*. Routledge; Taylor & Francis Group.

Kumar, V., & Malhotra, G. (Eds.). (2021). *Stakeholder strategies for reducing the impact of global health crises*. IGI Global Publications.

Lata, M., & Gupta, A. (2021). Education during the pandemic: Technology-based solutions. In *Stakeholder strategies for reducing the impact of global health crises* (pp. 209–224). IGI Global Publications.

Lin, X., & Kishore, R. (2021). Social media-enabled healthcare: A conceptual model of social media affordances, online social support, and health behaviors and outcomes. *Technological Forecasting and Social Change*, 166(120574), 120574. https://doi.org/10.1016/j.techfore.2021.120574

Marino, C., Gini, G., Vieno, A., & Spada, M. M. (2018). A comprehensive meta-analysis on problematic Facebook use. *Computers in Human Behavior*, 83, 262–277. https://doi.org/10.1016/j.chb.2018.02.009

Ministry of Finance. (2020). Finance Minister announces Rs 1.70 Lakh Crore relief package under Pradhan Mantri Garib Kalyan Yojana for the poor to help them fight the battle against Corona Virus. *Press Information Bureau, Government of India Ministry of Finance*. Retrieved November 14, from https://pib.gov.in/Pressreleaseshare.aspx?PRID=1608345

Mody, P. G. (2022). *A nation to protect: Leading India through the Covid crisis*. Rupa Publications.

Nguyen, T. M. N., & Chauhan. R. (2020). *Noval coronavirus disease (COVID 19): Situation update report-8* (pp. 1–6). Retrieved November 20, 2022, from www.who.int/docs/default-source/wrindia/situation-report/india-situation-report8bc9aca340f91408b9efbedb3917565fc.pdf?sfvrsn=5e0b8a43_2

Ningthoujam, R. (2020). COVID-19 can spread through breathing, talking, study estimates. *Current Medicine Research and Practice*, 10(3), 132–133. https://doi.org/10.1016/j.cmrp.2020.05.003

Press Information Burea. (2014). *Rangrajan report on poverty*. Retrieved November 20, 2022, from bhttps://pib.gov.in/newsite/printrelease.aspx?relid=108291

Safi, S. M. (2022). *Tali-Thali in first lockdown was PM's communication strategy, DHNS, Kolkata*. Retrieved November 20, 2022, from www.deccanherald.com/national/tali-thali-in-first-lockdown-was-pm-s-communication-strategy-1113036.html

Salamatbakhsh, M., Mobaraki, K., Sadeghimohammadi, S., & Ahmadzadeh, J. (2019). The global burden of premature mortality due to the Middle East respiratory syndrome (MERS) using standard expected years of life lost, 2012 to 2019. *BMC Public Health*, 19(1), 1523. https://doi.org/10.1186/s12889-019-7899-2

Singh, J., & Kumar, V. (2022). Combating the pandemic with ICT based learning tools and applications: A case of Indian higher education. *International Journal of Virtual and Personal Learning Environments (IJVPLE) Platforms (IJVPLE)*, 12 (1), 1–21.

Singh, S. G. (2020, July 2). Covid-19: Here's a timeline of events since lockdown was imposed in India. *Business Standard*. www.business-standard.com/article/current-affairs/here-s-a-timeline-of-events-since-lockdown-was-imposed-in-in-dia-120070201413_1.html

Tangcharoensathien, V., Calleja, N., Nguyen, T., Purnat, T., D'Agostino, M., Garcia-Saiso, S., Landry, M., Rashidian, A., Hamilton, C., AbdAllah, A., Ghiga, I., Hill, A., Hougendobler, D., van Andel, J., Nunn, M., Brooks, I., Sacco, P. L., De Domenico, M., Mai, P., . . . & Briand, S. (2020). Framework for managing the COVID-19 infodemic: Methods and results of an online, crowdsourced WHO technical consultation. *Journal of Medical Internet Research*, 22(6), e19659. https://doi.org/10.2196/19659

The Times of India. (2020). *Don't cross' Lakshman Rekha' of social distancing: PM Modi urges countrymen*. Retrieved December 25, 2022, from https://timesofindia. indiatimes.com/india/dont-cross-lakshman-rekha-of-social-distancing-pm-modi-urges-countrymen/articleshow/74960581.cms

Wang, J., & Du, G. (2020). COVID-19 may transmit through aerosol. *Irish Journal of Medical Science, 189*(4), 1143–1144. https://doi.org/10.1007/s11845-020-02218-2

WHO. (2020a). *Infodemic*. Retrieved December 25, 2022, from www.who.int/health-topics/infodemic#tab=tab_1

WHO. (2020b). *Non-communicable diseases in the South East Asia*. Retrieved December 25, 2022, from www.who.int/southeastasia/health-topics/noncommunicable-diseases.

WHO. (2020c). *Situation in numbers: Covid report*. Retrieved December 25, 2022, from www.who.int/docs/default-source/wrindia/situation-report/india-situation-report-8.pdf?sfvrsn=cd671813_2

WHO. (2020d). *Coronavirus disease (COVID-19): Weekly epidemiological update, 31 August 2020*. Retrieved December 25, 2022, from www.who.int/docs/default-source/coronaviruse/situation-reports/20200831-weekly-epi-update-3.pdf

Yang, E., Kim, J., & Pennington-Gray, L. (2021). Social media information and peer-to-peer accommodation during an infectious disease outbreak. *Journal of Destination Marketing & Management, 19*(100538), 100538. https://doi.org/10.1016/j.jdmm.2020.100538

Zhong, B., Huang, Y., & Liu, Q. (2021). Mental health toll from the coronavirus: Social media usage reveals Wuhan residents' depression and secondary trauma in the COVID-19 outbreak. *Computers in Human Behavior, 114*(106524), 106524. https://doi.org/10.1016/j.chb.2020.106524

6 The Role of Trust in Disaster Management Using Social Media

COVID-19 Perspective

Gabriel Ayodeji Ogunmola and Ujjwal Das

1. Introduction

The 2019 coronavirus disease (COVID-19) pandemic has caused unparalleled damage to human society, with over two million confirmed cases worldwide (Kovid & Kumar, 2022). World leaders have gone from hesitant acceptance to full-blown emergency. Unlike other pandemics, including 1918's H1N1 flu, COVID-19 is spreading throughout a global community that is incredibly connected because everyone is carrying a cell phone. Due to quarantine regulations, people are increasingly dependent on global digital social platforms like Facebook and Twitter to stay in touch with one another and share information about the virus (Kumar & Malhotra, 2021). Some of the ways that social media has hampered efficient replies to COVID-19 are discussed below. We discuss potential responses from government officials, social media firms, and healthcare providers. In the end, all of these parties play a part in proving that social media could serve its critical civic duty of promoting honest public expression and dialogue, also preventing it from being weaponized to spread doubt and further damage public health. In the context of online social networks, the concept of legitimacy has shifted. Users are increasingly viewing peers as credible authorities on topics because of their contributions to the creation and dissemination of high-quality content. When information spreads, it usually gains credibility as it reaches more people. When compared to other methods of information dissemination and validation, such as those more directly governed by intermediaries (such as traditional media), who have specialized knowledge and specific obligations in terms of verification and dissemination, this approach has some distinct advantages. There has been a significant shift toward using this type of collaboration in the dissemination of health and medical information to the general population. Naturally, those seeking information about the COVID-19 pandemic are turning to the Internet and other forms of virtual reality (Kumar & Gupta, 2021). Misinformation is a new sort of viral content that has spread rapidly because of digital social networks (Bhardwaj & Kumar, 2022c). There has been deliberate dissemination of scientifically baseless material in an effort to undermine public confidence in institutions and as

DOI: 10.4324/9781003315278-6

a sociopolitical tool (Moral, 2022). Within the few months after the first COVID-19 cases were reported, a wide variety of incorrect information had spread through traditional media as well as social media in what the World Health Organization has dubbed an infodemic (Bhardwaj & Kumar, 2022a). In this case, the premature evidence showing chloroquine as a good treatment for COVID-19 shows how dangerous incorrect information may be. As the number of people infected with COVID-19 continued to skyrocket, the unchecked and rapid spread of misleading information, primarily driven by social media, presented an urgent public health crisis for COVID-19 control and containment measures. This is because the confusion sown by misinformation impedes public trust, consensus, and subsequent action.

Despite efforts by social media firms to curb the transmission of COVID-19 misinformation and disinformation, it has continued to proliferate unabated in the media. The World Health Organization (WHO) called the rapid dissemination of incorrect, erroneous, and misleading information about COVID-19 an "infodemic," and the UN issued a warning against it. This included harmful misconceptions and questionable so-called prevention approaches and cures that opposed global mitigation efforts and put people's lives in danger (Diseases, 2020). The ability to effectively communicate is still essential in the fight against pandemics. Media coverage that is both factual and persistent can help people learn more about and prepare for a pandemic. According to Vivian (2022), information overload in the media ecosystem means that social media can have as much of an impact as traditional media on how the public perceives the infection and how they respond to it. Since social media platforms lack the standard methods for vetting content quality, they pose a challenge. Scholars can use them to distribute scientific results and advice efficiently, while millions of others spread vast amounts of misleading information that minimizes the severity of the disease, raises public mistrust about prevention and mitigation techniques, and encourages risky methods and behaviours, especially in cultures with high rates of illiteracy as well as low rates of media literacy. At the 2020 Munich Security Conference, WHO Director-General Tedros Adhanom Ghebreyesus, stated, "We're not just fighting a pandemic; we're fighting an infodemic" (Diseases, 2020). Since the COVID-19 pandemic began, the prevalence of false information, conspiracy theories, and misinformation has soared in the age of social media. Consequently, social media users need to be able to differentiate between correct and incorrect information. Knowing what to believe or not to believe is a function which will go a long way in guiding the actions of the public when responding to the pandemic. This is where the trust becomes important. Trust is a key component of risk and crisis management because, in the context of natural catastrophes, it serves as a significant precursor to both the perception of danger and the acceptance of risk (Houston et al., 2015).

In this work, we study the convergence between the management of COVID-19 pandemics, trust, and social media in order to gain a better understanding of how trust may be verified online. We do this by relying on

The unique context that is offered by pandemics. This method expands on previous research (Hagar, 2006; Jennings et al., 2021) that classifies the usefulness of social media by evaluating the validation of information during the pandemic utilizing a guardianship of trust model. This method draws attention to the mechanisms that influence and assure confidence in interactions between persons and organizations that provide emergency services and impact power in those relationships. In order to accomplish this goal, this study attempts to define trust from both a theoretical and an epidemiological point of view simultaneously (Kumar & Pradhan, 2020). The following section provides an overview of the technique that was utilized to conduct an analysis of the three primary approaches that are utilized by emergency management organizations to validate content shared on social media platforms during times of crisis. After that, three different models relating to trust in social media are given and discussed. In its final section, the article discusses the consequences for the management of social media during the pandemic.

2. Review of Literature

There is currently a dearth of scholarship on the role of social media and online communities in times of crisis and disaster. Moreover, it emphasizes the urgent measures necessary for dealing with crises and quickly recovering from them. Since both social media and this type of study are still relatively novel, it is unsurprising that no long-term studies have been conducted as of yet. The academic community has been interested in "new media" for at least a decade, including the Internet, but the vast majority of studies on social networking sites were conducted after 2007 (Kumar & Svensson, 2015). The number of published papers, however, appears to be rising quickly. It is important to distinguish between the literature on "social media" and that on the "social dimensions of mass media," a considerably broader topic that includes more traditional and long-standing ways of disseminating information, such as radio and television (Jung & Moro, 2014). As part of a larger trend toward investigating the efficacy of social contact via the web and mobile devices, research of social media in crises have been done. Torous et al. (2021) mentioned numerous utilizations of social networks:

- Development and utilizing algorithms to improve social networking or monitor it.
- The degree to which individuals use social networks, how people perceive them, and people's communication preferences are the primary foci of both bodies of literature.
- The widespread availability of smart phones and the number of people they have enabled to join social networks. Furthermore, those interested in risk, crisis, and disaster studies have looked at.
- The role of social media during an emergency.
- How social media interact with traditional channels of information.

102 Gabriel Ayodeji Ogunmola and Ujjwal Das

- The perspectives and comments of emergency officials and journalists on social media and the degree to which the media content is integrated with more traditional means of communication.

The study of the technical and the study of the social aspects of contemporary media are two quite different things. The former involves the development of new platforms and algorithms (Kottmann et al., 2021; Karizat et al., 2021), while the latter involves research into different types of communication and their outcomes (Jung & Moro, 2014; Torous et al., 2021). As for the nuts and bolts, there's research into things like message-spreading rates and channels. Jing et al. (2021) proposed a more systematic method to the utilization of social networking application in crisis situations, beginning with a classification of uses and potentials, even as researchers work to develop tools for the effective dissemination of messages via social networks during emergency situations (Ayodeji & Kumar, 2019). The benefits and cons of social media are a point of contention among researchers (see further later), but they agree on the technology's many applications. The constant stream of information and the ease of access across platforms are two key benefits of social media. Locational and geographical information can supplement the situational updates. To adapt to changing circumstances, you can get information right when you need it. In addition, journalists' reporting and public discourse have a structure thanks to the prevalence of social media platforms.

2.1 Social Media in the COVID-19 Pandemic

The function of social media in today's society is crucial. Services like Facebook, TikTok, Twitter, LinkedIn, Instagram, YouTube, Telegram, etc. allow users to connect with one another and build virtual communities where they may discuss and exchange information on any issue that matters to them (Nanda & Kumar, 2021). Banerjee and Meena (2021) found that people, particularly young adults, are constantly or often checking their social media accounts. This consumption skyrocketed during the COVID-19 epidemic. In the aftermath of tragedies, people often make contact with loved ones in the region to find out how they are doing. They inquire about or pass on data pertaining to necessities such as food, transportation, healthcare, and preventative medicine. Online social media such as Facebook and Twitter can serve the public, whereas many phone networks are unable to handle a sudden rush in calls (many individuals trying to call simultaneously). These media can act as a communication medium, endure heavy traffic loads, and remain accessible online. Also, unlike television and radio, it allows for two-way conversations. During times of natural disaster, when power is interrupted, so are these means of communication (radio and television). Then consumers can access social media via smartphones, tablets, and other devices.

Family and friends can check in on how they are doing and where they currently are. In a crisis, every person can be a vital source of data collection

The Role of Trust in Disaster Management Using Social Media   103

and dissemination. As a result, online social media can play a crucial role in times of disaster and emergency, and their use is really on the rise. It's widely acknowledged that the proliferation of smartphones is a key enabler of people's ability to use social networking sites. Twitter has been widely used in recent years to disseminate real-time information such as the number of victims and damages, information about donation drives and alerts, and even multimedia content like videos and images. Web-based manual crisis mapping sites have been set up by the network of health organizations and government officials in response to recent emergency situations such as the 2010 Haiti earthquake, the 2010 Russian wildfire, Hurricane Sandy in New York in 2012, the Oklahoma tornado in 2013, and the COVID-19 pandemic (Li, 2021). Social media is a constant source of new information that can be useful to emergency responders. Researchers have begun focusing on network components as a result of the proliferation of network technologies, with the goals of mitigating the effects of network elements and speeding up recovery times following catastrophic occurrences. The capacity, dependability, and interactivity of social media make it a promising candidate for improved emergency communication as a new and developing form of communication technology. While there are some literature reviews on the issue of disaster and/or crisis management, they tend to focus on a narrow aspect of administration or management, such as public health, social media use during catastrophes, or case studies relating to a specific event. Research has been done on the information processing challenges presented by social media data. The fact that some of these studies were conducted as far back as 2007 also makes them a touch stale. Botelho (2021) is one of the most current studies to explore the use of crowdsourcing by volunteers in the fields of disaster response, marketing, and communication. Participatory crowdsourcing was studied by Wang et al. (2023) to determine its potential for use in the planning, design, and construction of emergency management infrastructure in urban areas. Both studies examine the issue from a managerial and policy-making perspective, with scant attention paid to the computational methods and tools at play.

2.2 Social Media Function in Covid Pandemic Management

Social media has been used during the COVID-19 outbreak to help prevent the further spread of the virus while also meeting the demands of the general people for their social and emotional needs during the period of quarantine. Researches (Banerjee & Meena, 2021; Wang et al., 2023) have identified the following function of social media during the pandemic:

- **Listening function:** One that involves listening. It is the power of social media to offer those who would otherwise not have a platform a chance to speak up. They also make it easier to share ideas and information with others, allowing for a surprisingly democratic type of public discourse

involvement. Social media can shed light on a nation's psyche and emotions in times of crisis by helping people come to consensus on solutions to problems (or by encouraging them to donate money). Despite the fact that this may sound far-fetched, it is worth noting that Wang et al. (2023) suggested that the introduction of current information and communications systems entails changes that are as deep as those that happened after the creation of printing. The vast majority of people are now feeling the effects of these shifts or will do so shortly.

- **Situation monitoring**: In contrast to the more passive nature of the listening function, the goal of monitoring is to gain insight into how the public as a whole is thinking and behaving so that appropriate action can be taken. According to a recent study, Yue et al. (2022), the usage of social media does nothing to promote damaging and incorrect rumours. The explanation for this is that once a large number of individuals get involved, any untrue rumours that start to spread can be quickly debunked by those who know better. As a result, there was minimal evidence that the widespread use of social media by the populace contributed to the successful dissemination of rumour and outrageously false information about COVID-19 (Houston et al., 2015).
- **Emergency response and crisis management using social media integration**: According to a study conducted by Moral (2022), 80% of the US general population and 69% of Internet users agreed that it would be helpful for Covid emergency response organizers to constantly monitor social networking sites. However, this is not the case worldwide. Agencies worry that information sourced from social networks may be unreliable (Vivian, 2022). Furthermore, many of them would have to alter their methods of operation in order to fully incorporate social networks into disaster management, as "command-and-control models do not easily adapt to the expanding data-generating and data-seeking activities by the public," to quote Jennings et al. (2021). The potential for data transmission to become a two-way street, in which information is both received from and provided to the public, is, however, enormous (Hagar, 2006; Jung & Moro, 2014; Torous et al., 2021).
- **Collaboration and crowdsourcing in software development**: The public typically acts as the initial responders in crisis situations. In addition, social capital is at play, which takes the shape of the mobilization of resources such as expertise, leadership, networks, support structures (Kottmann et al., 2021; Kumar & Nanda, 2020; Bhardwaj & Kumar, 2022b). Connecting with others and participating in group activities is central to this idea since it has been shown to boost efficiency and provide value to results. The unique talents of their members are an asset to the social networks. Crowdsourcing is one way in which social capital is built through social media. One such site is called Ushahidi (Karizat et al., 2021), and it is used to facilitate crowdsourced disaster mapping. These efforts can only succeed with the help of unforeseen individuals. Because of this, they receive

The Role of Trust in Disaster Management Using Social Media 105

positive reinforcement; the more people who utilize them, the more enthusiastic they become about contributing to them.

- **Facilitating therapeutic efforts and fostering social cohesion**: Using social media, you can get more people involved in your causes and campaigns. They can help people feel more connected to their neighborhoods or online groups. A number of studies (Jing et al., 2021; Ayodeji & Kumar, 2019) have found that when social media are heavily involved, those affected by a disaster report feeling more encouraged and hopeful. In addition, the visibility and accessibility of nonprofits can be elevated through the use of social media to encourage more people to volunteer. They can boost morale and camaraderie in the group this way.
- **Advancing a worthy cause or causes**: Launching a contribution drive on social media like Twitter is a great option. Regarding COVID-19, while television was proven to have a considerably larger impact in this regard, Botelho (2021) observed that a Twitter campaign did elicit a significant reaction from public donations. The World Health Organization (WHO) earned $8 million in just 48 hours thanks to text message donations, according to research by Yue et al. (2022). Wang et al. (2023) found that donations spiked sharply in the immediate aftermath of the tragedy, when media attention was at its peak, and then steadily declined as coverage of the event faded.

3. COVID-19 Crisis Informatics

The study of crisis informatics spans many different academic disciplines. Hagar (2006) popularized the term, which refers to the interdependence of individuals, groups, and systems in the face of emergency situations where communication and coordination are paramount. It investigates the complete cycle of a crisis, from pre-crisis planning to post-crisis recovery, by looking at how social, technical, and informational issues all intertwine. An increase in interaction and the complexity of the information environment are common results of crises. Trusted information within this intricate information ecosystem is more important than ever during an emergency.

3.1 Infodemic

As a kind of meaning-seeking in the face of ambiguity, rumour spreads swiftly and is often based on a kernel of truth (Chiou et al., 2022). When individuals are unable to get the facts they need to deal with a crisis, they turn to rumours and try to piece together a story to explain what's happening. Word-of-mouth news tends to be inflated as it travels from person to person, making it more likely that its subject will be investigated. People had many questions during the COVID-19 pandemic, including Who was infected? Where did the COVID-19 virus come from? How did it spread? How many people would get it? Who would get priority for vaccination?

and questions about government involvement, such as whether or not the virus was just a big rumour to get people to spend on the health sector, thus boosting the economy. How can we tell the difference between gossip and fact? And how can we evaluate the reliability of the data presented? To what extent is truth reflected in rumours, and who determines this, exactly? Efforts to correct misinformation on COVID-19 and highlight reliable sources are much appreciated in light of the critical situation. It is important that content standards be created in a way that allows for a variety of viewpoints, including those that are critical of government policies, while yet enforcing controls over the veracity of statements and the soundness of advice given. Complicating factors make this goal difficult to achieve. It is crucial that these guidelines be established so that social media can continue to serve as a forum for honest public debate about public issues, including genuine disagreements regarding the response of governments and international health organizations to the pandemic. As people start to question the broader benefits, such as those of physical separation, criticism is expected to grow louder. As these conflicts between public health officials and the public escalate, the likelihood that false information may spread also rises. To ensure that citizens are heard and to increase public confidence in the openness and accountability of policy-making, social media platforms are invaluable. It is the responsibility of public health professionals to ensure that any measures taken strike a fair and just balance between the competing values of free expression and public health protection and promotion.

Finally, as more people go to social media for guidance, it becomes more challenging to tell armchair epidemiologists from those with the expertise to deliver useful information online. The general population may seek to choose the most credible person in their inner circle to use as a fact-checker. These people may worry that they lack the resources to successfully counteract the spread of disinformation on social media. The general public and reliable information sources (like epidemiologists) can use inoculation as a tactic for debunking falsehoods. In this context, "inoculation" refers to the process of fostering a person's pre-existing beliefs and values in order to fortify them against the spread of false information. For instance, the notion that COVID-19 was artificially created is widely disseminated on social media. Conspiracy theory language can be validated by confirming the spread of false information about COVID-19. This kind of language frequently alludes to connections that haven't been proven and brings up ideas like hidden criminal networks that are behind the pandemic's spread. Due to the widespread nature of COVID-19-related disinformation, all participants in these extensive digital social networks (including government agencies, social media companies, healthcare providers, and consumers or propagators of information themselves) have a responsibility to help resolve the broader implications of this pandemic and the underlying infodemic in order to strengthen community resilience.

3.2 Trust

A high level of trust is essential for successful communication, and it is a fundamental part of everyday life (Zhang et al., 2022). Better conversations and exchanges of ideas are the result (Singh et al., 2020). Knowledge sharing relies on trust (Łukasiewicz & Werenowska, 2022) to facilitate communication, boost collaboration and coordination, and strengthen interpersonal bonds inside and between organizations. Trust (and the ability to gauge trustworthiness) is always important, but its importance increases dramatically in times of emergencies (Williams et al., 2018). The influence of ambiguity on people's experiences is often highlighted in definitions of trust. People's information-gathering strategies change depending on their level of trust in those providing it during times of crisis. The ambiguity of one's own understanding is a hallmark of crisis situations, as identified by Zhang et al. (2022). Those directly impacted by the crisis sometimes lack the information necessary to cope with it. Because it determines how one acts and what one expects from others, trust is crucial in social interactions. As individuals grow more reliant on one another during times of crisis, as mentioned by Singh et al. (2020), the value of their social connections increases. According to Liu and Mehta (2021), an individual's level of confidence in other individuals or institutions determines how much they will reveal about themselves. In times of crisis, relying on others to make judgements regarding reliable information and contacts is frequently glaringly obvious. Two major issues are discussed further: Exactly what do individuals believe when they say they trust a source? Who are the most reliable sources of news and information? Relationships with those who offer information can significantly affect which sources are relied upon. Because taking action based on credible information can significantly shape and affect the character of a crisis, knowing which sources and information sources to trust is crucial. The absence of trust in times of crisis or calamity contributes to the proliferation of rumours, as will be shown in the following section.

4. Trust Management During Disasters

It is well acknowledged that trust in the aftermath of disasters is a crucial factor in the development of perception of risk and risk acceptance (Yue et al., 2022), making it an integral part of risk as well as crisis communication. Many things can be said about trust, but one general definition is "the conviction that in the absence of evidence, things will balance out" (Wang et al., 2023). A more precise definition is provided by Chiou et al. (2022):

> The readiness of a party to be vulnerable to the acts of another party based on the expectation that the other will perform a certain activity significant to the trustor, irrespective of the trustor's ability to monitor or control that other party.

This definition, taken from the field of management studies, highlights the fact that trust is typically viewed as a dyadic process involving two entities: a trustor (the person doing the trusting) and a trustee (the party receiving the trust). However, trust also serves a purpose in more intricate relationship models with several partners and distinct power dynamics. Beliefs in the reliability of another person or organization are founded on three factors: their competence, their kindness, and their honesty (Singh, 2020; Łukasiewicz & Werenowska, 2022). A person's perceived ability can be described as the set of abilities and knowledge that allows them to exert influence in a given context (Williams et al., 2018; Liu & Mehta, 2021). The degree to which the "trustee is regarded to want to do good to the trustor" is the measure of perceived kindness (Xie et al., 2022). Whether or not the trustor believes that the trustee is honest and trustworthy depends on whether or not the trustee is seen to be following norms, beliefs, and values that are important to the trustor (Jennings et al., 2021; Park, 2022). Perceptions of competence, kindness, and honesty all contribute to an individual's trustworthiness (Park, 2022). Expertise, self-interest, and scepticism are all identified by disaster researchers as factors that contribute to trust and so affect related judgements and behaviours (Gu et al., 2022).

4.1 Trust Amid Time Pressures and Uncertainty

Over time, when people, groups, and governments work together, learn from one another, and grow to trust one another, trust will naturally grow (Kumar & Pradhan, 2018). It's easy to take trust in business and financial dealings for granted until it's put to the test by something like a natural calamity. Disasters' combined elements of unpredictability and urgency can both test people's faith in one another and open up new channels for it. Despite the fact that emergency management services enjoy widespread public trust, the complexities of disasters often leave people questioning the reliability of their information and increasing their preference for alternate resources (Banerjee & Meena, 2021).

Some of the fundamental assumptions of principal-agent interactions are put to the test by social media communication during crisis, opening up space for the evaluation and generation of continuous trust (Kumar & Malhotra, 2020). Through two-way contacts with other people on social media, crowdsourced information, self-regulation, and debunking of posts, principals are able to keep tabs on the information posted by their organization's agents thanks to the transparency afforded by social media (Williams et al., 2018; Chiou et al., 2022). Because of the difficulty in establishing reliable connections with users across large regions where disasters may occur, this can be a serious issue for emergency management agencies. In addition, the inability to verify the accuracy of content posted online limits the effectiveness of emergency management organizations.

Concurrently, the credibility and experience of emergency management agencies can help establish a bond of trust between both social media users and the relevant agencies. Sharing a company's history with its online communities has the potential to further bolster trust between the two (Chu, 2022). For instance, the Queensland Police Service's engagement with its online community in the wake of the pandemic that hit the north-eastern state of Australia (Wang et al., 2023) fostered sufficient impersonal confidence to support the expansion of the network and the maintenance of two-way contact throughout following crises and day-to-day operations. As a result of a company's shared history, ongoing social media contacts, and the reputation it eventually forges with the online community, social media provides a mechanism via which impersonal trust can be transformed into interpersonal trust.

5. Trust Models for Social Media Use

There are three overarching models for the placement of social media use in emergency management organizations that have emerged from this research. These models each lead to a unique method of establishing and confirming confidence in netizens and the pandemic-related information supplied. The three described models are ideal kinds; in emergency management, a variety of hybrids of these models are used (see Figure 6.1 and Table 6.1). In addition, the models' divergent views on social media's involvement in pandemic management and communication call for a rethinking of where personnel responsible for managing these platforms should be housed within the larger organization. Although this study focuses on social media's role during the pandemic, it's not hard to imagine that the same models may be applied to future man-made emergencies and crises. These examples should be useful for regulatory agencies in other developed countries as well.

Figure 6.1 Intelligence gathering model

110   Gabriel Ayodeji Ogunmola and Ujjwal Das

Table 6.1 Quasi-journalistic verification model

Social Media Trust Model	Verification Procedure	Trust Relationships
The authenticity of individual communications' contents and senders is verified in a manner like that of the news media.	Users and emergency service providers evaluate content and sources to ensure accuracy; manual, low-volume data processing.	Interpersonal trust principles in multiple dyadic relationships; emergency services taking over while retaining some control over the situation; people's ability to keep tabs on developments.

5.1   Intelligence Gathering Model

The first method relies on social media to gather information about the disaster zone. This model aims to do two things:

- Find unanticipated crises by monitoring for sudden increases in activity on social media involving key crisis-related terms like "death," "cough," "shortness of breath," and "vaccines."
- Keep tabs on already-known events by monitoring for the emergence of recognizable markers, like Twitter hashtags.

Real-time social media analytics evaluate volumetric, sentiment analysis, and network in the incoming data stream, making them a primary tool for identification and tracking (Kumar et al., 2022). Borah et al. (2022) have presented a comprehensive discussion of the notion of social media analytics as a whole. These are sometimes paired with additional manual examination and oversight, particularly if signs of a possible crisis have been detected (Kumar & Nanda, 2022). This method of intelligence collecting is then used to cross-reference the social media information detected with other data sources at the disposal of the emergency management organization, such as reports from emergency personnel on the ground and historical data on the areas affected by the crisis. This means that the information gleaned from social media platforms as a whole, and the veracity of individual posts on the local situation, are not taken into account. Instead, they are used as part of a larger data set and associated with other sources of data, which also typically only exist in aggregate form. By analyzing data in terms of patterns rather than single data points, direct interaction with social media users as the providers of these data is unnecessary (update clarification). This intelligence gathering model is the quickest and least resource-intensive method of extracting information via social media feeds because it is based solely on observation and is mostly automated, at least once the underlying infrastructure for the real-time surveillance and analysis of such feeds has been developed.

As shown in figure 6.1, In this model, the main people in the process of verifying information are the people who work for the emergency management organization and use the tools for gathering intelligence from social media. People who use social media are regarded as agents, but they are looked at from an overall, bird's-eye view rather than as trusted collaborators in the process of verifying information. In fact, their updates are never checked to make sure they are what they say they are. Confidence in the situational patterns that emerge from social media feeds is only based on the correlation of these patterns with other information sources. Even though this use of social media to gather intelligence is still in its early stages, emergency management groups are starting to make plans for how to find and verify information on social media platforms. During the pandemic, tools that use data mining and natural language processes to look at social media messages can give authorities a better idea of what's going on. This on-the-ground and almost-real-time information is very important for emergency management organizations to be able to make good decisions about how to respond and how to help people recover (Yang et al., 2022). For the time being, though, it gets around the problem of building trust in groups and individuals of users of social media by focusing on patterns of activity among very sizeable numbers of users. Even then, these patterns are often only used as early warning signs of an upcoming crisis. Any further and more fine-grained interaction with the social media content behind large increases in activity needs different, less automated approaches and, as a result, builds on different mechanisms for developing trust in the user's information provided.

5.2 Quasi-Journalistic Verification Model

The second major model, quasi-journalistic verification, has some similarities to the intelligence gathering approach and can be used to validate information gleaned from social media in emergency management situations like pandemics. On the other hand, it is much more limited in scope and is managed by the organization's social media staff on a much more hands-on basis. This model is predicated on the standard journalistic practice of verifying sources, which, in its most canonical form, states that any piece of information must be corroborated by two separate sources before it is considered publishable. Consequently, under this model, emergency management organizations' social media teams take a more hands-on approach to monitoring social media feeds and focus less on the raw patterns of relevant social media activity and more on individual iterated responses. They, like journalists, must rely on their own discretion when determining which news items can be trusted and which ones should be ignored. As shown in Table 6.1, information obtained from social media platforms during disasters has been slow to gain the trust of user's data unless it has been independently confirmed by another emergency response organization or credible source (Fröhlich, 2018). However, emergency management agencies must now consider how to incorporate information collection and verification strategies during times of crisis due to the rising use of social media during such events (Scott et al., 2022).

In this second trust approach, social media staff adhere to the journalistic principle of independent verification by checking with at least two social media users in the crisis area who have reported the situation independently (for example, in original tweets that do not retweet or reply to each other) in order to confirm the veracity of the information. They may interact with users via public replies or private direct messages on Twitter or their equivalents on other channels, rather than merely passively monitoring information streams. Active verification boosts trust in social media data, even when it isn't correlated with other sources used by emergency management organizations, and, over time, helps institutions learn which users can be relied on to update the situation in a given area during future crises. Social media users become more active agents and are invited to engage in more direct two-way conversations with the emergency management organization's social media staff, who remain principals in the information evaluation process. Unfortunately, during an emergency, it would take too much time and manpower to manually verify all the social media updates that are being posted. It is possible that a combination of automated intelligence gathering and human verification will be required to overcome these limitations.

5.3 Crowdsourcing Model

Crowdsourcing is the third method that has been shown to increase trust. In acute crisis circumstances, it is rarely possible for emergency management employees to create interpersonal trust connections with social media users beyond a limited number of clearly essential social media users functioning as vital information sources because of the time and effort required to do so. However, a sizeable and complex network of interpersonal trust relationships among users predates the emergence of any disaster requiring the attention of emergency management organizations, and this is precisely why social media, which is by definition designed around the creation and maintenance of relationships (social) between users, is so important (Morrow et al., 2022). Instead of trying to build trust with a large number of people in a short amount of time, emergency management organizations might take advantage of the natural and ongoing processes of information verification that occur amongst users in social media platforms. This model therefore differs more significantly from the other two in how it collects and verifies social media information during a crisis, as shown in Table 6.2. Here, instead of only acting as sources of information about the present situation in the crisis region, social media (or more generally the Internet) users are more actively engaged during the verification process themselves. As a result, the verification procedure may be completed more quickly as there may be more people willing to help with it than even in a fully staffed emergency management agency. According to Yigitcanlar et al. (2022), a larger number of volunteer participants

Table 6.2 Crowdsourcing model

Social Media Trust Model	Verification Procedure	Trust Relationships
Crowdsourcing of verification procedures.	Verification of the content and sources based on ratings provided by communities of volunteer users; rapid processing of information across a distributed network.	Networked relationships rely on both personal and interpersonal trust; power and monitoring capability are shared among users; the correctness of the results may vary depending on the intents of the users.

with varying degrees of experience in analyzing situational information is now involved in the endeavor, which can raise doubts about the dependability of this verification procedure.

Despite its potential benefits, the crowdsourcing concept has only been tested in a limited number of crises so far, and usually without the direct involvement of official emergency management agencies. Depending on the results of these experiments, emergency management groups may begin to more widely adopt crowdsourcing strategies. The crowdsourcing method takes elements from both of these other models. To begin, it expands upon the automated intelligence collection technique by employing comparable techniques to detect and capture social media updates that are relevant to the situation in real time. It may also engage in some aggregation and preselection to identify the updates that are most essential and likely to be reviewed further by the crowdsourcing community. Secondly, it follows up this first stage of finding and filtering by asking volunteers to use their own common sense to decide how trustworthy and reliable each social media update might be. Then it compiles these various assessments for each update (and in more advanced systems, also for each distinct user in the data set, when the person has provided several situational update) to arrive at confidence scores that indicate which updates are most important and trustworthy. The evaluated social media feeds may then be sent back into the internal procedures of the emergency management organization, where they can be connected with situational and background information gleaned from other sources and ranked in order of confidence.

6. Social Media Ethical Usage During Pandemic

The ethical challenges posed by social media have not been missed by scholars (Kumar & Nanda, 2019). Researchers in the fields of law and medicine were the first to look at this. Associations in the United States that represent medical professionals have warned against unrestrained social media use because

114 *Gabriel Ayodeji Ogunmola and Ujjwal Das*

it might create conflicts of interest, such as if a doctor befriends a patient online. As Tsoy et al. (2021) pointed out, situations like this constitute a legal quagmire, and lawyers are increasingly keeping an eye on them for potential lawsuits. Managers in charge of emergencies often have to strike a balance between taking unnecessary risks and appearing negligent. Ethical considerations will need to be revisited frequently, as noted by Dow et al. (2021): "The changing architecture of technology, and the relatively recent usage of social media in research, implies that ethical concerns will have to be evaluated periodically." The same will hold true for safeguards against unlawful state surveillance of private lives (Ali et al., 2021). Abbas et al. (2021) argue that the disclosure of private information is governed by culturally specific norms regarding what is appropriate and how it should be communicated. Contextual integrity theory describes this idea. An invasion of privacy results from breaking the rules. Norms set or respected by one player, such as the author of a personal blog, can be easily violated by republishing the content in a different context, such as a public blog, as noted by Borah et al. (2022).

As mentioned before, there are dangers linked with the completely unregulated public mass communication infrastructure that the Internet provides. In short, bad actors may use social media to persecute or smear the reputations of others, to spread malicious rumours, to incite violence at protests, or to coordinate terrorist attacks (Dow et al., 2021; Abbas et al., 2021). Invasion of privacy and unauthorized disclosure of personal information are examples of less severe forms of damage. Furthermore, any disaster response or risk reduction system that relies on social network for access to its services risks not including individuals who do not have access to the essential tools. No amount of bragging about the widespread availability of "smart" mobile phones can change the fact that some people still do not have access to them and do not know how to utilize them, whether because of financial hardship, physical limitation, or personal preference. In addition, it is evident that the more a person is well off, young, physically active, and self-conscious, the more likely they are to be completely aware of the services provided through social media and its usefulness in varying conditions. In a society increasingly reliant on electronic means of communication, a lack of computer skills might be seen as a significant disadvantage. The fact that individuals are able to assist a disadvantaged person cope through word of mouth is just a partial compensation for this. But complete fairness cannot be required for social media to work because social exclusion will always be an issue.

Now more than ever, platforms like Facebook, Instagram, Twitter, YouTube, Snapchat, and WhatsApp play a crucial role in disseminating information and news to the public. However, in developing nations like Pakistan, these platforms can also contribute to the spread of fear and false information. Many people may panic if they read false information regarding COVID-19 online because they may believe it to be true. Individuals living in Pakistan are prone to spreading false information and fanning the flames of unfounded panic. Panic can result from false reports, especially

The Role of Trust in Disaster Management Using Social Media   115

those related to the COVID-19 pandemic. In some cases, people may take false information they read online as fact. There is a notion circulating online that the coronavirus was created to wage biological war on China in retaliation for the country's rapid economic development. Threatening the collaboration amongst Chinese and Western experts in the creation of a vaccine against COVID-19, allegations arose via social media inside China and elsewhere that the coronavirus had been genetically altered in a bioweapons laboratory in Wuhan and then unleashed worldwide. Twitter was also used to spread false information in Iran, claiming that COVID-19 could be cured with unproven therapies such mint-flavored drinks, herbal cures, and spices like saffron. Questions arise in the midst of an emergency or disaster that must be answered quickly. In developing countries, bureaucrats may take too long to give the necessary information. A sad reality of modern life is that social media and mass media are more likely to spread unsubstantiated assertions and personal opinions than hard scientific or biomedical evidence. As it is, there is no solid framework for holding people accountable for their online behaviour. Because of the potential for misinterpretation and exaggeration in the wake of the COVID-19 outbreak, public leaders are hesitant to make hasty declarations. Paradoxically, this cautious approach may help create a data void that can be easily filled by fabricated claims. Governments can use mass media campaigns to urge the public not to share content on social media that mocks or trivializes the impact of the COVID-19 pandemic. Members of the public health community, as well as educators, religious leaders, and elected officials, have a responsibility to notify their followers about the current COVID-19 situation on social media.

7. Conclusion

The global pandemic of COVID-19 has altered the way we live. The rapidity with which the virus was spreading and the ways in which it was being transmitted posed a threat to our sense of safety, but the preventative measures used to contain it necessitated isolating ourselves from others in order to keep from succumbing to our most basic human need. Traditional media and social media perform a significant role in the lives of individuals, groups, and communities in this climate of physical danger, social isolation, and physical distance. The ability of social media (Internet) to bring together massive audiences is undeniable. Discrimination and false information can easily spread on social media. The public's adherence to the COVID-19 prevention measures recommended by global health organizations can be facilitated through social media. Appropriate health attitudes as well as prevention are promoted via adaptive responses in a variety of media industries and platforms. During the current COVID-19 epidemic, social media can help individuals deal with physical and social distance and lessen stigma, prejudice, discrimination, and injustices. This brief investigation of three methods for the validation of social media information verified by health organizations has shown a nuanced web of trust relationships. These decide how much and how such data can be used into crisis response activities. Even though this instance of an emergency organization actively leveraging the trust of its current social media community to refute information spread by untrustworthy sources is an outlier, it serves to illustrate the tremendous potential of strong trust connections between public and government organizations. While there are many intriguing models and processes for the examination and verification of user-generated content, emergency management organizations often lack the time to build such long-lasting, mutually beneficial trust relationships. These can be used in the moment to put at least some faith in the status updates people post on social media.

References

Abbas, J., Wang, D., Su, Z., & Ziapour, A. (2021). The role of social media in the advent of COVID-19 pandemic: Crisis management, mental health challenges and implications. *Risk Management and Healthcare Policy*, *14*, 1917.

Ali Taha, V., Pencarelli, T., Škerháková, V., Fedorko, R., & Košíková, M. (2021). The use of social media and its impact on shopping behavior of Slovak and Italian consumers during COVID-19 pandemic. *Sustainability*, *13*(4), 1710.

Ayodeji, O. G., & Kumar, V. (2019) Social media analytics: A tool for the success of online retail industry. *International Journal of Services Operations and Informatics*, *10*(1), 79–95.

Banerjee, D., & Meena, K. S. (2021). COVID-19 as an "infodemic" in public health: Critical role of the social media. *Frontiers in Public Health*, *9*, 610623.

Bhardwaj, A., & Kumar, V. (2022a). A framework for enhancing privacy in online collaboration. *International Journal of Electronic Security and Digital Forensics (IJESDF)*, *14*(4), 413–432.

Bhardwaj, A., & Kumar, V. (2022b). Web and social media approach to marketing of engineering courses in India. *International Journal of Business Innovation and Research (IJBIR)*, *27*(4), 541–555.

Bhardwaj, A., & Kumar, V. (2022c). Privacy and healthcare during COVID-19. In *Cybersecurity crisis management and lessons learned from the COVID-19 pandemic* (pp. 82–96). IGI Global Publications.

Borah, P., Austin, E., & Su, Y. (2022). Injecting disinfectants to kill the virus: Media literacy, information gathering sources, and the moderating role of political ideology on misperceptions about COVID-19. *Mass Communication and Society*, 1–27.

Botelho, F. H. (2021). Accessibility to digital technology: Virtual barriers, real opportunities. *Assistive Technology*, *33*(sup1), 27–34.

Chiou, H., Voegeli, C., Wilhelm, E., Kolis, J., Brookmeyer, K., & Prybylski, D. (2022). The future of infodemic surveillance as public health surveillance. *Emerging Infectious Diseases*, *28*(Suppl 1), S121.

Chu, T. L. A. (2022). Applying positive psychology to foster student engagement and classroom community amid the COVID-19 pandemic and beyond. *Scholarship of Teaching and Learning in Psychology*, *8*(2), 154.

Diseases, T. L. I. (2020). The COVID-19 infodemic. *The Lancet. Infectious Diseases*, *20*(8), 875.

The Role of Trust in Disaster Management Using Social Media   117

Dow, B. J., Johnson, A. L., Wang, C. S., Whitson, J., & Menon, T. (2021). The COVID-19 pandemic and the search for structure: Social media and conspiracy theories. *Social and Personality Psychology Compass*, 15(9), e12636.

Fröhlich, R. (2018). The integration of findings: Consequences of empirical results for the advancement of theory building. In *Media in war and armed conflict* (pp. 287–309). Routledge.

Gu, M., Guo, H., Zhuang, J., Du, Y., & Qian, L. (2022). Social media user behavior and emotions during crisis events. *International Journal of Environmental Research and Public Health*, 19(9), 5197.

Hagar, C. (2006). Using research to aid the design of a crisis information management course. In *Paper presented at ALISE annual conference SIG Multicultural, Ethnic & Humanistic concerns (MEH). Information seeking and service delivery for communities in disaster/crisis*. San Antonio.

Houston, J. B., Hawthorne, J., Perreault, M. F., Park, E. H., Hode, M. G., Halliwell, M. R., Turner McGowen, S. E., Davis, R., Vaid, S., McElderry, J. A., & Griffith, S. A. (2015). Social media and disasters: A functional framework for social media use in disaster planning, response, and research. *Disasters*, 39(1), 1–22. https://doi.org/10.1111/disa.12092

Jennings, W., Stoker, G., Bunting, H., Valgarðsson, V. O., Gaskell, J., Devine, D., McKay, L., & Mills, M. C. (2021). Lack of trust, conspiracy beliefs, and social media use predict COVID-19 vaccine hesitancy. *Vaccines*, 9(6), 593. https://doi.org/10.3390/vaccines9060593

Jing, L., Guo, G., Ogunmola, G. A., & Shibly, F. (2021). Digital learning for students and its impact on the present system of education. *Journal of Multiple-Valued Logic and Soft Computing*, 36(1–3), 117–134.

Jung, J. Y., & Moro, M. (2014) Multi-level functionality of social media in the aftermath ofthe Great East Japan Earthquake. *Disasters*, 38(S2), S123–S143.

Karizat, N., Delmonaco, D., Eslami, M., & Andalibi, N. (2021). Algorithmic folk theories and identity: How TikTok users co-produce knowledge of identity and engage in algorithmic resistance. *Proceedings of the ACM on Human-Computer Interaction*, 5(CSCW2), 1–44.

Kottmann, J. S., Alperin-Lea, S., Tamayo-Mendoza, T., Cervera-Lierta, A., Lavigne, C., Yen, T. C., Verteletsky, V., Schleich, P., Anand, A., Degroote, M., Chaney, S., Kesibo, M., Curnow, N., Solo, B., Tsilimigkounakis, G., Zendejas-Morales, C., Izmaylov, A., & Aspuru-Guzik, A., (2021). Tequila: A platform for rapid development of quantum algorithms. *Quantum Science and Technology*, 6(2), 024009.

Kovid, R. K., & Kumar, V. (Eds.). (2022). *Cases on emerging markets responses to the COVID-19 pandemic*. IGI Global Publications.

Kumar, V., & Gupta, G. (Eds.). (2021). *Strategic management during a pandemic*. Routledge; Taylor & Francis Group.

Kumar, V., & Malhotra, G. (Eds.). (2020). *Examining the role of IT and social media in democratic development and social change*. IGI Global Publications.

Kumar, V., & Malhotra, G. (Eds.). (2021). *Stakeholder strategies for reducing the impact of global health crises*. IGI Global Publications.

Kumar, V., & Nanda, P. (2019). Social media to social media analytics: Ethical challenges. *International Journal of Technoethics (IJT)*, 10(2), 57–70.

Kumar, V., & Nanda, P. (2020). Social media as a tool in higher education: A pedagogical perspective. In *Handbook of research on diverse teaching strategies for the technology-rich classroom* (pp. 239–253). IGI Global Publications.

Kumar, V., & Nanda, P. (2022). Approaching the Porter's five forces through social media analytics. *International Journal of Services Operations and Informatics (IJSOI), 12*(2), 184–200.

Kumar, V., Nanda, P., & Tawangar, S. (2022). Social media in business decisions of MSMES: Practices and challenges. *International Journal of Decision Support System Technology (IJDSST), 14*(1), 1–12.

Kumar, V., & Pradhan, P. (2018). Comprehensive three-layer trust management model for public cloud environment. *International Journal of Business Information Systems, 28*(3), 371–339.

Kumar, V., & Pradhan, P. (2020). Trust management: Social vs digital identity. *International Journal of Service Science Management, Engineering and Technology* (IJSSMET), *11*(4), 26–44.

Kumar, V., & Svensson, J. (Eds.). (2015). *Promoting social change and democracy through information technology*. IGI Global Publications.

Li, L., Bensi, M., Cui, Q., Baecher, G. B., & Huang, Y. (2021). Social media crowdsourcing for rapid damage assessment following a sudden-onset natural hazard event. *International Journal of Information Management, 60*, 102378.

Liu, B. F., & Mehta, A. M. (2021). From the periphery and toward a centralized model for trust in government risk and disaster communication. *Journal of Risk Research, 24*(7), 853–869.

Łukasiewicz, K., & Werenowska, A. (2022). The importance of trust in social media. In *Trust, digital business and technology* (pp. 84–95). Routledge.

Moral, P. (2022). The challenge of disinformation for national security. In *Security and defence: Ethical and legal challenges in the face of current conflicts* (pp. 103–119). Springer.

Morrow, G., Swire-Thompson, B., Polny, J. M., Kopec, M., & Wihbey, J. P. (2022). The emerging science of content labeling: Contextualizing social media content moderation. *Journal of the Association for Information Science and Technology, 73*(10), 1365–1386.

Nanda, P., & Kumar, V. (2021). Social media analytics: Tools, techniques and present day practices. *International Journal of Services Operations and Informatics (IJSOI), 11*(4), 422–436.

Park, Y. E. (2022). Developing a COVID-19 crisis management strategy using news media and social media in big data analytics. *Social Science Computer Review, 40*(6), 1358–1375.

Scott, M., Wright, K., & Bunce, M. (2022). *Humanitarian journalists: Covering crises from a boundary zone*. Taylor & Francis.

Singh, J., Crisafulli, B., & Xue, M. T. (2020). "To trust or not to trust": The impact of social media influencers on the reputation of corporate brands in crisis. *Journal of Business Research, 119*, 464–480.

Torous, J., Bucci, S., Bell, I. H., Kessing, L. V., Faurholt-Jepsen, M., Whelan, P., Carvalho, A. F., Keshavan, M., Linardon, J., & Firth, J. (2021). The growing field of digital psychiatry: Current evidence and the future of apps, social media, chatbots, and virtual reality. *World Psychiatry: Official Journal of the World Psychiatric Association (WPA), 20*(3), 318–335. https://doi.org/10.1002/wps.20883

Tsoy, D., Tirasawasdichai, T., & Kurpayanidi, K. I. (2021). Role of social media in shaping public risk perception during COVID-19 pandemic: A theoretical review. *International Journal of Management Science and Business Administration, 7*(2), 35–41.

Vivian, D. T. (2022). Media literacy and fake news: Evaluating the roles and responsibilities of radio stations in combating fake news in the COVID-19 era. *International Journal of Information Management Sciences*, 6(1), 33–49.

Wang, S., Huang, X., Hu, T., She, B., Zhang, M., Wang, R., Gruebner, O., Imran, M., Corcoran, J., Liu, Y., & Bao, S. (2023). A global portrait of expressed mental health signals towards COVID-19 in social media space. *International Journal of Applied Earth Observation and Geoinformation*, 116, 103160.

Williams, B. D., Valero, J. N., & Kim, K. (2018). Social media, trust, and disaster: Does trust in public and nonprofit organizations explain social media use during a disaster? *Quality & Quantity*, 52(2), 537–550.

Xie, L., Pinto, J., & Zhong, B. (2022). Building community resilience on social media to help recover from the COVID-19 pandemic. *Computers in Human Behavior*, 134, 107294.

Yang, J. Z., Dong, X., & Liu, Z. (2022). Systematic processing of COVID-19 information: Relevant channel beliefs and perceived information gathering capacity as moderators. *Science Communication*, 44(1), 60–85.

Yigitcanlar, T., Regona, M., Kankanamge, N., Mehmood, R., D'Costa, J., Lindsay, S., Nelson, S., & Brhane, A. (2022). Detecting natural hazard-related disaster impacts with social media analytics: The case of Australian states and territories. *Sustainability*, 14(2), 810.

Yue, Z., Zhang, R., & Xiao, J. (2022). Passive social media use and psychological well-being during the COVID-19 pandemic: The role of social comparison and emotion regulation. *Computers in Human Behavior*, 127, 107050.

Zhang, M., Xu, P., & Ye, Y. (2022). Trust in social media brands and perceived media values: A survey study in China. *Computers in Human Behavior*, 127, 107024.

7 Social Media and Trust Management During the Pandemic

Manju Lata and Saurabh Mittal

1. Introduction

Unlike past pandemics, for example, the H1N1 pandemic of 1918, Covid-19 spread much faster across the world due to more connectivity and movement of people. The people across the world were connected via cell phones in virtual mode (Kumar & Mittal, 2020) and sharing information about pandemic as well as personal matters with others using social media platforms such as Twitter, Facebook, Instagram, etc. However, social media was found to be responsible for diluting the actual reactions to Covid-19. Social media might influence healthcare providers, common citizens, as well as policymakers (Lata & Gupta, 2020). Ultimately, these entities have a significant role in preventing social media from becoming a weapon to sow mistrust and further threaten public health.

Generally, people observe trusted persons within their peer networks who sustain the creation and exchange of valuable information as trusted sources of info. As this information is further distributed, its perceived legitimacy regularly increases. The information sharing method has become the driving force behind public health and medical information being produced and distributed. The distribution and authentication of information depends on mediators like media channels, who have specialized skills for accurate information creation and distribution.

Social media networks enabled the rise of various virus-related disinformation entities. The scientific disinformation is widely disseminated as a means of undermining faith in governments (Guess et al., 2018). WHO quoted the term 'infodemic' for the variety of misinformation, including rumours, falsehood and excessive misinformation which was spread in the conventional media and social networks, making it difficult to identify credible sources of information (Garrett, 2020). Falsehood can have irreversible significance, as demonstrated via the proliferation of previous proof proposing that chloroquine is an operational and actual cure for Covid-19 (Egan, 2020). With millions of cases worldwide, the Covid-19 epidemic led to unparalleled public disruption (Limaye et al., 2020), and according to World Health Organization, confirmed cases of COVID-19 stood at 755,116,409

DOI: 10.4324/9781003315278-7

Social Media and Trust Management During the Pandemic 121

as of February 9, 2023, including 6,831,681 deaths (https://covid19.who.int/). The quick increase of the Covid-19 pandemic led to unfettered and quick spread of disinformation largely fuelled over social media (Vigdor, 2020). Falsehood and disinformation have been found to obstruct public trust, agreement and consequent action. With the exponential spread of pandemics, it was important to develop mechanisms to efficiently distribute the correct and updated information and to rapidly identify and remove misinformation or invalid guidance. Government organizations utilized social media giants like Instagram, Twitter and Facebook to flag, fact-check and even eliminate incorrect or obsolete information from these networks. Social media companies have addressed content regulation in light of the pandemic (Shu & Shieber, 2020). Destroying misinformation could encourage social media customers to collect and distribute correct information, assisting them to stay safe and decreasing the threat to others.

2. Growth of Social Media and Its Users

The term social media explains communication technologies that enable the formation or sharing of information, notions, occupation interests and additional procedures of communication using networks and virtual groups (Sneep et al., 2020; Lata & Gupta, 2020). There are a wide variety of popular platforms including FacebookTM, TwitterTM, InstagramTM, and blogging platforms, LinkedinTM, WhatsAppTM and WeChat. The growth of social media has been fuelled by the developments in technology and the social desire to communicate. The foremost reason for social media usage is that mobile opportunities for customers are constantly refining and making it progressively easier to access social media no matter where you are (Mittal & Kumar, 2018). Most social media networks are also accessible as mobile apps or have been enhanced on behalf of mobile browsing, creating an easy way for customers to access their desired sites. The rapid and massive adoption of technology has changed the way news broadcast is accessed. As of 2022, the number of global Internet users has risen to 5.3 billion (Petrosyan, 2023), with internet penetrations now accounting for 62.5% of the total world population. The data shows that the number of Internet users increased by 192 million (+4.0%) compared to the earlier period. The average annual growth rate of the social media users from 2023 to 2025 is estimated at 3.7% (www.oberlo.in/statistics/how-many-people-use-social-media). Following are the most important social media statistics that define the current state of digital world. Over 67.1%, or two-third of world population, currently use a mobile phone, with individual users reaching 5.31 billion in early 2022. Globally, it grew as a result of a 1.8% increase over the past year, with 95 million different operators of mobile users since this time the previous year.

According to a review of CMOs, social media marketing budget expenses were greater than before, from 13.3% in February 2020 to 23.2%

in June 2020 (Moorman & McCarthy, 2021). According to the survey, companies are seeing significant returns on their social media investments. The actual involvement of social media in worldwide corporation activities has been enhanced by up to 24% in the same time period. CMOs expected investment in social media marketing budgets to increase by 23.4% in 2021 (https://cmosurvey.org/results/). Thus, it is obvious that social media continues to perform a significant role in motivating people toward digital offerings (Lata & Kumar, 2021b).

Facebook remains the utmost commonly used social media platform in the world (https://datareportal.com/social-media-users). Even though there is another social media platform, each platform reports more than 1 billion monthly active users. Additionally, 17 social media platforms contain at least 300 million active users as of January 2022. Messaging family and friends is the most popular activity on Facebook, while TikTok users mostly visit the platform to look for entertaining and funny videos. The users on Snapchat and Instagram are interested in publishing their content, but this action is considerably less popular on LinkedIn, Reddit and TikTok. Furthermore, marketers may like to know that Pinterest users are mostly interested in researching or following brand-related content on the globe's most trendy online pinboard.

3. Social Media and Communication During Pandemic

Throughout the Covid-19 pandemic, the use of social media has accelerated to such an extent that it has become a ubiquitous part of awareness, contact tracing, medical advice, psychological assistance, news updates and modern healthcare systems (Wong et al., 2021). In the year 2020 and 2021, which had the maximum impact of the coronavirus, billions of users worldwide were spending more time on social media. In a big trend of 2020, TikTok saw the biggest increase in monthly users by 38% over the rated phase, Pinterest came in second, followed by Reddit. Meanwhile, Twitter and Facebook had also seen significant growth rates in the year 2020 (Dixon, 2022).

Regardless of the discussion about the usage of medical advice on social media, it has recognized itself at medical seminars and as a platform for distribution of information (Venkataraman et al., 2016). For controlling the spread of the coronavirus, several nations announced physical distancing plans that involved limiting physical interaction. This restriction increased the usage and requirement on social media platforms to stay connected for the task, learning, training and social resolutions (Anwar et al., 2020; Lata & Gupta, 2021, Mittal & Kumar, 2022). Such tough procedures were required to control the spread of the virus, and social media was important to have quick and vast awareness among medical workers as well as masses. Mobile phone features like tracking location and contact tracing was found to be very important in the fight against the pandemic (Anwar et al., 2020).

Social media platforms were used as a communication tool during the pandemic, such as the following:

3.1 Source of Information on Covid-19

Covid-19 quickly became a global pandemic in the times of social media. Government departments and medical professionals also utilized social media to help citizens better understand actions and their impacts. People could share their views and knowledge about the epidemic using social media platforms. Individuals, businesses as well as government departments used social media to spread awareness about the virus through public or actionable events.

3.2 News Update

In all the panic and chaos due to the virus, news channels played no small part in the distribution panic. Several news outlets began to provide conflicting information about the virus, with many cases and deaths around the world. In this difficult time, the plan prepared by the John Hopkins Center of Systems Science and Engineering proved to be excellent. It created record-type data on valuable citizens and deaths. Professor Lauren Gardner and her researcher created a dashboard that offered technical tools (SARS-COV-2 Surveillance Tools) for the public health system, the general public and researchers to track reported cases and deaths in a friendly manner (Kamel Boulos & Geraghty, 2020). The SARS-COV-2 tracking tool was published online on January 22, 2020, to promote its utilization. Highlighting the spread of the virus around the world reduced the insecurity about its geographical distribution and helped the nations to implement and initiate early measure. Worldometer was also another platform to provide the latest statistics and updated news regarding Covid-19 (www.worldometers.info/coronavirus/). Additionally, on January 26, 2020, the World Health Organization (WHO) revealed its Arc Geographic Information System (ArcGIS) operational control panel to support the Covid-19 pandemic, which reports and maps the number of cases and deaths as of the date of reporting (Yao et al., 2020).

3.3 Guiding People to Follow Covid-Appropriate Behaviour

Prior to the Covid-19 pandemic, most people were not aware about social distancing, maintaining a minimum of six feet from others to stop the virus spread. As the world went into lockdown, the social media users, celebrities and governments motivated citizens to stay fearless throughout but maintain social distancing and stay at home. Social media effortlessly distributed the information to a large audience. Quarantine or work from home became a trend as people had moved from dealing with lockdown to embracing it. Many organizations also came up with fun activities to connect with people

124 *Manju Lata and Saurabh Mittal*

on social media, for example, the Getty Museum requested people to restore artwork with items created in homes (Kushner, 2020; Van Dijck & Alinejad, 2020).

3.4 Psychological Support

During the lockdown, people began to gather information posted on social media or new websites and then share it with their network. Spiritual sites also attracted people amid Covid-19 emergencies by spreading intuitive information about the treatment and prevention of the infection. Stress is a common physiological reaction of a person to various adverse situations that occur in the life cycle. Those who can't be able to control it suffer nervousness or stages of depression. Depression can manifest in psychological as well as physical actions that differ from person to person. In addition, virtual mental health facilities also worked to combat mental illness, and psychologists and psychiatrists on social media delivered free debates. The fundamental role of the of social media is to keep the people connected, entertained and well-versed. The encouraging influence of social media has been revealed during the pandemic emergency in endorsing sensitive solidity among the public. Groups as well as pages on social media platforms such as Instagram or Facebook were in progress to post videos regarding physical as well as mental health. Several relaxation workouts were promoted, and books became available for free. People connected to the educational groups utilized online learning tools without a fee to support children of different ages. Many institutes sprung up to encourage people to homeschool by posting daily worksheets designed for kids. During road and air travel, advertisements such as "Face covering mandatory in public", "Stay at home, stay safe", "Avoid gatherings", "Keep your distance from each other and on the road" as well as "Wash the hands, stay healthy, stay away from pandemic'. Psychologically, this recurrence is key to cementing its role in stopping the spread of the virus (Van Dijck & Alinejad, 2020). This operation was run amazingly by social media via all essential resources.

3.5 Medical Advice

E-health is a facility that is also offered via online mode to patients for well-being or medical information, disease monitoring and query resolution using a safe connection, preserving patient and doctor privacy. It uses a large number of technical tools such as integrated clinical information systems, telephone discussions and audio-video sessions to solve difficulties faced by sick persons in society (Anwar et al., 2020). During the Covid-19 period, e-medicine has developed for the support of medical practice and the treatment of online patients. People were afraid to go to hospitals even for major complications, correspondingly a number of online customer services were set up to allow public to analyze whether their indications are appropriate for

Social Media and Trust Management During the Pandemic 125

testing for the coronavirus. Social media was used to support it and therefore followed the lockdown norms.

However, there is no medicine for Covid-19 so far, and some possible remedy has been given to the patients without an authentic medicinal study. The use of vitamin C to boost immunity as well as make it stronger as a protective measure in contrast to the virus has been widely emphasized. A meta-analysis demonstrated the role of prophylactic vitamin C ingestion in decreasing the viral load, but no result on protection and incidence have been established (Ströhle & Hahn, 2009). Currently, quite a few large pharmaceutical companies are dedicated to the prevention and treatment of the Covid-19 virus. Although, apart from Genentech's Remdesivir, no one has a promising drug to support the treatment of Covid-19. Therefore, when chloroquine emerged as hope, it spurred media attention as a probable treatment. Several political figures have formed the publicity and encouraged chloroquine by claiming it to be operational in contrast to the Covid-19 virus and calling it the prime change in the world (Anwar et al., 2020).

3.6 Spreading Positivity

Certainly, no platform is made faultless. But along with the misinformation and anxiety on social media, there has also been much life-saving information, correlation with others and overall consensus. Social media provides the facility to share understandings with friends and family, which helps combat emotional and exact isolation while prompting a person that they are all in this together. There are many other ways social media has positively impacted the entire epidemic. A number of fundraising events were organized on social media to help raise money for those in need. People posted pictures and videos to share their experiences on social media, which further built confidence in people in facing the coronavirus infection.

4. Challenges Created on Social Media

4.1 Untrusted Social Media Sources

Unfortunately, some people used social media to spread falsehoods as well as sensationalist precautions, false claims of martial law, conspiracy concepts, etc., resulting in the lack of reliable sources of information about Covid-19 (Van Dijck & Alinejad, 2020). During the pandemic, the public was looking for maximum information, but they became more vulnerable to untrue and risky claims. The initial claim about infection being more severe for the aged population were found misplaced as it also affected several young people. This type of unconfirmed fact or rumour spread similarly to wildfire in the media as well as affected the seniors to suffer a lot of mental and physical distress. Rumours of old persons being separated from children or domestic people increased the sensitivity of abuse among them. These rumours have

126 *Manju Lata and Saurabh Mittal*

changed people's observation of geriatric people and caused them to become increasingly depressed depending on society's quick responses. In addition, distractions in daily life and overdependence on social media resulted in intolerance and injustice in society too. Several cases of domestic violence have also been reported (Lata & Gupta, 2020; Kushner, 2020; Van Dijck & Alinejad, 2020). This also includes the already-growing depression caused by the quarantine.

4.2 Unverified Users Sharing Information

On the other hand, several fake 'doctors' also came up on the well-known social media platforms to spread misinformation about the virus and home-cure methods. For example, steam inhalation as a way to kill the virus was shared on social media, and it made its way to the other news channels too. Many rumours or claims concerning the virus circulated on social media like how it could be spread by houseflies or mosquito bites, remedies like hot water and cow urine to cure Covid-19. Social media accounts have spread the rumour that alcohol can also be a remedy of Covid-19 virus (Naeem et al., 2021; Trew, 2020). There was also fake news of Tunisian and Israeli scientists developing a remedy for the Covid-19 virus. Even a group of people from a certain ethnicity or religion was blamed for the spread of the virus. The rumour was first referring to a story written in a British tabloid that claimed that an institute instructor as well as others in the UK were capable of treating themselves using honey and whiskey. All stories were false. Simultaneously, unlimited health specialists and various doctors have promoted untested pills, remedies, stories, therapies as well as advice as a process to strengthen the immune system (Naeem et al., 2021; Caulfield, 2020).

4.3 Fake Products or Treatments

With the spread of the virus, social media has arisen as a significant means of socialization along with a way to find and share information about the disease. A fake Covid-19 test kit has become riskier than a fake Chanel handbag (Murphy, 2007). A false test could lead someone to believe they are negative when they have been infected. A fake medicine could leave someone worse off than before and possibly lead to death. Even a fake N95 mask could lead to more spread of the virus (www.vox.com/recode/2020/4/1/21196941/coronavirus-n95-mask-respirator-shortage-trump).

4.4 Panic Buying

In the initial phase of lockdown, several persons bought large quantities of sanitization products, household items and food in a panic, just like what people do during other natural disasters. Such excessive buying became so popular that social media users invented a new phrase 'panic buying'

(Kushner, 2020). Panic buying was discussed on social media in two different procedures: sharing pictures of shopping trolleys with frozen food, water bottles and toilet paper, or pictures of empty shelves or carts as a way to humiliate would-be panic shoppers.

5. Responsible Social Media Usage During Pandemic

5.1 Source Tracking

When searching for facts or data on social networks, people want to confirm whether the data uploaded on social media is truthful or trustworthy, and whether the jeopardy related to acting on or receiving untruthful data is bearable. As great influences of news flood the shores of social media every day, people produce such type of decisions hastily to escape being distressed. Users were advised to remain careful and not to use absolute or alarmist language to stop the spread of misinformation and fearmongering on social media throughout the pandemic (Kushner, 2020). Trusted data can allow people to meet the demand for right information, create great resolutions and attach them with trusted persons. In contrast, incorrect data can lead to a deficit, security, privacy, currency and further damage. Some e-commerce organizations' work have considered aspects that affect social media performance, for example, trust, jeopardy and social ties (Chen & Sharma, 2013; Cheung et al., 2015; Assensoh-Kodua, 2016; Warner-Søderholm et al., 2018; Lata & Kumar, 2021a). The threat of harassment or intimidation on social media, falsifications of a person's profiles, the problem of validating data on social media as well as the difficulty in getting trustworthy data due to the speed and amount of material distributed on social media are also key concerns.

5.2 Developing Trust

Some researchers have recognized danger and trust as two main causes prompting how persons share personal information, experiences and knowledge on social networks; and the phase of trust is correlated to risk tolerance as well as evaluation (Wang et al., 2016). It was found that trust is multidimensional and can be controlled by three concepts: integrity, capability and benevolence (Svare et al., 2020). Integrity is the certainty that a reliable party is true and trustworthy and also will define what is exact. In this sensibleness, integrity is slightly equal to the measure of reliability procedure by librarians and data professionals (McKnight et al., 2002). Capability is the certainty that a reliable party has the abilities as well as understanding to do their measures fine. This certainty is correlated to observed capability and proficiency. In this sensibleness, certainty in capability is related to the expert measure practiced to assess the web and academic resources (McKnight et al., 2002). Benevolence is the certainty that the reliable party cares about people's attention, has welfare and emphasizes the persons more than the party's profit (McKnight et al., 2002).

5.3 Responsible Sharing

In 2021, the world was in very bad conditions, and democracies were constantly under attack, with many attributing the risks to fake data on social media, explaining the fear of destruction of certainty in society (Auxier, 2020; Hsieh-Ano, 2021). According to Gorman's debate (Chronicle of Higher Education, 2007), users were unsystematically consigned to groups on behalf of discussion. Two groups were assigned to proceed with the levels of support for social media as a trusted source of data, although another two groups were assigned to proceed the opposite way on social media and risks caused by fake data (Hsieh-Yee, 2021). Social media was found to have a large impact on the public, which became important all through the epidemic. Social media allows agencies as well as institutions, for instance, educational institutions and libraries, along with governments to share data with the public in an appropriate manner, particularly in crises (Lata & Gupta, 2021). Social media is a self-governing and a level playing field, as platforms allow the expressive public to speak their opinions, insights or anxieties, and foster the greater consideration of gratitude towards each other.

5.4 Content Monitoring

Several questions are still being debated, such as whether we can expect tech companies to police content on social networks. Could the technology-based resolutions become actual in keeping secure people from risky communications? Can the local news of media become encouraged to deliver trustworthy evidence to the people, or is it losing combat due to the big media enterprises that have taken control of local media? Is fact proving the resolution? How many people check the facts that they come across on social networks? The discussion also included who can report the issues of misinformation on social media and how information professionals, as well as libraries, can support people who utilized social media.

5.5 Social Media Ethical Code

The ethical codes and basic ethics of the data professions offer motivation to provoke incorrect data on social networks and make people live, and be active, but aware from time to time of confusing data surroundings (Mittal & Kumar, 2020). People must be well-informed about why and how to avoid sharing wrong information on social media and threats created by it. Data and fact literacy that begins at an early stage is possible to advance in people who are adept at evaluating the quality of information on any platform. This process allows the detonation of uncontrolled information and the expansion of disinformation. Social media usage increased by 20–87% worldwide during the emergency (Stewart, 2020). According to the Bruno Kessler Foundation in Italy, approximately 46,000 news posted on Twitter each day in

Social Media and Trust Management During the Pandemic 129

March 2020 were incorrect as well as associated with falsification about the emergency (De et al., 2021; Choden, 2022).

6. Trust Management Mechanism

Social media became serious about marketing at the time of the Covid-19 epidemic. A social media strategy on behalf of the pandemic world and trust management mechanism sets compulsory rules for public interaction, which became the key to its success deal with falsehoods and attaining public trust (OECD, 2020; Moorman & McCarthy, 2021).

6.1 Communicating With Timeliness and Consistency

Through public communication, the government can decrease the likelihood of falsehood or misinformation taking hold by circulating information promptly when it becomes available. Throughout the Covid-19 period, governments held regular briefings to keep the public updated; for example, Korea held these briefings even twice per day. Simultaneously, deflating misinformation requires regular monitoring and assessment of emerging content to guide an understanding of which information poses more risks to be refuted. This activity can be sustained by supporting official narratives constantly and by maintaining the focus of the government.

6.2 Making Communication Participatory

Communication can allow for shared dialogue with citizens that replies more openly to requirements and provides governments with better visions. This progressively happened on messaging platforms like Telegram and WhatsApp, or dedicated chatbots and channels being set up in Australia, Italy, Latvia and France, among other nations. The US state of Kansas collected citizens' knowledge on the effects of the Covid-19 epidemic through an online story bank and with automated replies. Open government data on the epidemic, for example, that circulated through an online platform in Korea, and on Canada's open government portal, is also making it probable for people to contribute to visualizing and circulating truthful information.

6.3 Pre-empting and Correcting Falsehood/Misinformation

Emerging research also advises pre-emptively or pre-bunking exposing the citizens to small doses of falsehood or misinformation in a way that highlights their faulty or weak reasoning. It can protect audiences from incorrect content when adopting a similar approach in its communications, where it informs the citizens on scientific advances and other specialists. Conversely, the effectiveness of contradicting individual rumours or deflating is increasingly thrown into question via findings that it may attract more attention to the rumours themselves. Therefore, it may be more suitable in cases where a part of falsehood or misinformation is properly wide-ranging and poses a significant threat if it has extended to over 10% of the public, as stated by one estimate.

6.4 Basing Interference on Evidence

Strategic communication is made on a strong consideration of the information challenges of audiences' attitudes and their progress of activities on information. Such as, public attitudes concerning messengers carry implications on behalf of communication on the virus, and 85% of study respondents in ten countries claimed to select hearing from scientists instead of from politicians (Organization for Economic Co-operation and Development, 2020).

6.5 Get the Right Investigation

The distinct CMO review initiated a great level of marketing invention throughout the epidemic, using CMOs report nearly 5.6 out of 7 (where 1 means "not at all" and 7 means "very much"). Regardless, the assessment outcomes also record a decrease in the proper investigation on social media platforms, as 31% of dealers said they led the research to see the effect of their marketing activities throughout the epidemic, and 29% of marketers described investing resources in production (https://cmosurvey.org/results/). This statistic points out that marketers regularly apply new, unplanned strategies but do not fully understand their effects. Therefore, this trend needed to be corrected in the previous year, and social media platforms offer great chances to explore creative advertisements, and brand messages post and get direct or specific feedback from target customers (Lata & Kumar, 2021b). Marketers should use such tools to learn.

6.6 Play Using Advanced Channels and Features on Current Platforms

Social media planners must know what is original on current platforms, such as Instagram Reels, launched in the summer of last year, which offers an innovative channel that delivers the short video style and has taken the internet by storm. TikTok and Facebook gift cards for businesses, which were also issued before 2022 (https://cmosurvey.org/results/), are similar examples. This type of innovative tool offers the opportunity to establish an exclusive connection with customers (Lata & Kumar, 2022). The social media promoting approach includes the method of finding different innovative features as well as channels and, after that, rapidly producing content for them.

6.7 Invest in the Best Social Media

Social media management is being asked to cope with an expensive as well as an extremely actual part of the marketing budget. Also, taking a part in the social media marketing campaigns often needs wearing several fedoras, such as customer service representative, graphic designer, copywriter, etc. Marketing leaders must consider prudently who must fill this crucial place. Even though the greatest social media supervisor can have a progressive effect, an unprofessional or unfair one can damage a firm's brand. The nationwide regular income of social media supervisors is $50,500, as stated by Glassdoor, with marketing managers averaging $65,500, copywriters averaging $58,500 and advertising managers averaging $71,000. Obtaining the highest ability or talent in this area, the reward should correspond to the increasing value of the role (https://cmosurvey.org/results/).

6.8   Make Sure Social Media Management Is Agile

In 2020, social media sites or landscapes were rising promptly. Based on the fact, CMOs have placed the capacity to pivot on Social Media as peak ability they are looking in marketing professionals. As a result, while it derives towards social media management, CMOs should make sure that processes, talent as well as organizations' supporters can react and take advantage of these quick modifications. Administrations are prepared to rethink their social media plans in a quickly varying environment to maximize opportunity and minimize risk in connecting with customers (https://cmosurvey.org/results/; Lata & Kumar, 2021a).

6.9   Harness the Power of Inventors and Influencers

Influencer marketing finance plans are expected to grow to 7.5% from 6.5% in 2020 and is expected to grow to 12.7% in 2022 (https://cmosurvey. org/results/). As online spread remains to grow, it becomes serious for products' logos to recognize the correct influencers who invite target clients as well as recognize growing sections. It also becomes essential for social media network administrators to finance influencer preparation as well as correlation making. Influencers create trustworthy as well as accurate interactions with supporters who can turn out as remunerating clients.

6.10   Prudently Deliberate the Appropriate Platforms for a Specific Brand

It is substantial to deliberate how the chosen platform affects customers' awareness of the related brand. Customers specified that the association of trust is essential for the brand (inventing low price, innovation and even product quality. Therefore, constantly deliberate how the strategies of social media platforms (regarding privacy and hate speech in particular) can undermine customer trust.

6.11   Reducing Friction Between E-commerce and Social Media Platforms

To create online shopping stress-free, social media administrators should make sure they have a uniform procedure for redirecting customers from

132 *Manju Lata and Saurabh Mittal*

social media to e-commerce sites (Kumar & Kumar, 2017). Fraudulent consumer knowledge in this zone can lead to lost sales, and a good consumer can increase the same. Therefore, digital tools are developing (Kumar & Mittal, 2012; Lata & Kumar, 2022), and social media players need to regularly collaborate using advanced teams to make sure there is a smooth drive for consumers from social networks and mobile apps to a company's e-commerce site.

6.12 Keep Resourceful and Inventive Content Relevant to the Times

It is essential for the brands to sustain the inventive content, which is significant toward the truth about Covid-19 wherever possible. For example, a social media post showing a brand at a great indoor public gathering might not be noticed by customers who observe it as old-fashioned or, poorer, unresponsive. On the other end of the spectrum, several customers are tired of content that centers on the virus. For social media content to resonate with followers, it should be balanced. For example, the Stella Artois Staycation Swap, which is a competition in which travelers who have planned trips that have been cancelled due to Covid-19 match each other to exchange tours on TripAdvisor for an all-expenses-paid stay at their own location.

Therefore, during the Covid-19 epidemic, customers are spending maximum time online, and social media is gradually becoming an essential phase of the linking among brands and their consumers, as well as for communication with each other, existing and possibly innovative. Now is the time to spend creating a unified and active social media management resolution that adapts to the innovative environment. Because the Covid-19 pandemic is seriously damaging the healthcare system, society and the economy as a whole, pandemic prevention and response strategies and measures are directly required. Of these, trust management mechanisms with the promoter, response and mobilization of social media play a crucial role.

7. Conclusion

As the Covid-19 pandemic continues to worsen, more effective approaches and strategies are required to combat it. Although the social media and other online platforms have played an important role, these should be further used to improve trust during the pandemic, build social solidarity, reduce false or misinformation, reduce health problems in facilities and educate the public about prevention measures. Although during the pandemic there is a continuous development of information technology as well as social media, including use of visual dashboards and open data, there is a scope to utilize social media for promoting public health campaigns. Social media users need to be educated and made aware about the risk of unverified information, especially those related to remedies and treatments. It may be concluded that social

Social Media and Trust Management During the Pandemic   133

media has been a great support in keeping the users entertained, informed and giving them opportunities to utilize their precious time.

References

Anwar, A., Malik, M., Raees, V., & Anwar, A. (2020). Role of mass media and public health communications in the COVID-19 pandemic. *Cureus*, *12*(9), 1–12.

Assensoh-Kodua, A. (2016). Social purchasing and the influence of social networking: A conceptual view. *Banks & Bank Systems*, *11*(3), 44–57.

Auxier, B. (2020). 64% of Americans say social media have a mostly negative effect on the way things are going in the U.S. today. *Pew Research Center*. www.pewresearch.org/fact-tank/2020/10/15/64-of-americans-say-social-media-have-amostly-negative-effect-on-the-way-things-are-going-in-the-u-s-today/

Caulfield, T. (2020). Pseudoscience and COVID-19- we've had enough already. *Nature*. Retrieved April 27, 2020, from www.nature.com/articles/d41586-020-01266-z

Chen, R., & Sharma, S. K. (2013). Self-disclosure at social networking sites: An exploration through relational capitals. *Information Systems Frontiers*, *15*(2), 269–278.

Cheung, C., Lee, Z. W., & Chan, T. K. (2015). Self-disclosure in social networking sites: The role of perceived cost, perceived benefits and social influence. *Internet Research*, *25*(2), 279–299.

Choden, T. (2022). Effect of fake news on government action in combating COVID-19. *Bhutan Journal of Management*, *2*(1), 29.

Chronicle of Higher Education. (2007). *Michael Gorman vs. Web 2.0. 53(44)*, B4–B4. www.chronicle.com/article/michael-gorman-vs-web-2-0/

De, A., Bandyopadhyay, D., Gain, B., & Ekbal, A. (2021). A transformer-based approach to multilingual fake news detection in low-resource languages. *Transactions on Asian and Low-Resource Language Information Processing*, *21*(1), 1–20.

Dixon, S. (2022). *Social media use during COVID-19 worldwide statistics & facts*. www.statista.com/topics/7863/social-media-use-during-coronavirus-covid-19-worldwide/#dossierKeyfigures

Egan, L. (2020). Trump calls coronavirus Democrats' "new hoax". *NBC News*. www.nbcnews.com/politics/donald-trump/trump-callscoronavirus-democrats-new-hoax-n1145721

Garrett, L. (2020). COVID-19: The medium is the message. *The Lancet*, *395*(10228), 942–943.

Guess, A., Nyhan, B., & Reifler, J. (2018). Selective exposure to misinformation: Evidence from the consumption of fake news during the 2016 US presidential campaign. *European Research Council*, *9*(3), 4.

Hsieh-Ano, I. (2021). Can we trust social media? *Internet Reference Services Quarterly*, *25*(1–2), 9–23.

Kamel Boulos, M. N., & Geraghty, E. M. (2020). Geographical tracking and mapping of coronavirus disease COVID-19/severe acute respiratory syndrome coronavirus 2 (SARS-CoV-2) epidemic and associated events around the world: How 21st century GIS technologies are supporting the global fight against outbreaks and epidemics. *International Journal of Health Geographics*, *19*(1), 1–12.

Kumar, P., & Mittal, S. (2012). The perpetration and prevention of cyber crime: An analysis of cyber terrorism in India. *International Journal of Technoethics (IJT)*, *3*(1), 43–52.

Kumar, S., & Kumar, V. (2017). Technology integration for the success of B2C M-commerce in India: Opportunities and challenges. *IUP Journal of Information Technology*, *13*(1).

Kumar, V., & Mittal, S. (2020). Mobile marketing campaigns: Practices, challenges and opportunities. *International Journal of Business Innovation and Research*, *21*(4), 523–539.

Kushner, J. (2020). *The role of social media during a pandemic*. Retrieved November 25, 2022, from https://khoros.com/blog/social-medias-role-during-covid-19

Lata, M., & Gupta, A. (2020). Role of social media in environmental democracy. In *Examining the roles of IT and social media in democratic development and social change* (pp. 275–293). IGI Global Publications.

Lata, M., & Gupta, A. (2021). Education during the pandemic: Technology-based solutions. In *Stakeholder strategies for reducing the impact of global health crises* (pp. 209–224). IGI Global Publications.

Lata, M., & Kumar, V. (2021a). Smart energy management in green cities. *In Handbook of green engineering technologies for sustainable smart cities* (pp. 105–120). CRC Press.

Lata, M., & Kumar, V. (2021b). Internet of energy IoE applications for smart cities. In *Internet of energy for smart cities* (pp. 127–144). CRC Press.

Lata, M., & Kumar, V. (2022). IoT networks security in smart home. In *Cybersecurity for smart home* (pp. 155–176). ISTE-WILEY Publications.

Limaye, R. J., Sauer, M., Ali, J., Bernstein, J., Wahl, B., Barnhill, A., & Labrique, A. (2020). Building trust while influencing online COVID-19 content in the social media world. *The Lancet Digital Health*, *2*(6), e277–e278.

McKnight, D. H., Choudhury, V., & Kacmar, C. (2002). Developing and validating trust measures for e-commerce: An integrative typology. *Information Systems Research*, *13*(3), 334–359. https://doi.org/10.1287/isre.13.3.334.81

Mittal, S., & Kumar, V. (2018). Adoption of mobile wallets in India: An analysis. *IUP Journal of Information Technology*, *14*(1), 42–57.

Mittal, S., & Kumar, V. (2020). A framework for ethical mobile marketing. *International Journal of Technoethics (IJT)*, *11*(1), 28–42.

Mittal, S., & Kumar, V. (2022). A strategic framework for non-intrusive mobile marketing campaigns. *International Journal of Electronic Marketing and Retailing*, *13*(2), 190–205.

Moorman, C., & McCarthy, T. (2021). CMOs: Adapt your social media strategy for a post-pandemic world. *Harvard Business Review*. Retrieved December 23, 2022, from https://hbr.org/2021/01/cmos-adapt-your-social-media-strategy-for-a-post-pandemic-world

Murphy, J. (2007). International perspectives and initiatives. *Health Information & Libraries Journal*, *24*(1), 62–68.

Naeem, S. B., Bhatti, R., & Khan, A. (2021). An exploration of how fake news is taking over social media and putting public health at risk. *Health Information & Libraries Journal*, *38*(2), 143–149.

Organization for Economic Co-operation and Development. (2020). *Transparency, communication and trust: The role of public communication in responding to the wave of disinformation about the new Coronavirus* (pp. 1–12). OECD Publishing.

Petrosyan, A. (2023), *Global number of internet users 2005–2022*. Statista. Retrieved February 5, 2023, from www.statista.com/statistics/273018/number-of-internet-users-worldwide/#:~:text=As%20of%202022%2C%20the%20estimated,66%20percent%20of%20global%20population

Shu, C., & Shieber, J. (2020). Facebook, Reddit, Google, LinkedIn, Microsoft, Twitter and YouTube issue joint statement on misinformation. *TechCrunch*. Retrieved May 30, 2023, from https://techcrunch.com/2020/03/16/facebook-reddit-google-linkedin-microsoft-twitter-and-youtube-issue-joint-statement-on-misinformation/

Sneep, R., Cantle, F., Brookes, A., Jina, R., Williams, S., Galloway, J., Norton, S., Udukala, M., Birring, S., & Zuckerman, M. (2020, September 4). *Early epidemiological and clinical analysis of the first 200 patients with COVID-19 admitted via the emergency department in Kings College Hospital*. A Retrospective Cohort Study. Available at SSRN. Retrieved May 30, 2023, from https://ssrn.com/abstract=3576791. http://dx.doi.org/10.2139/ssrn.3576791

Stewart, R. (2020, May 15). *Advertising and social media face fresh trust issues amid global crisis*. www.thedrum.com/news/2020/05/15/advertising-and-social-media-face-fresh-trust-issues-amid-global-crisis

Ströhle, A., & Hahn, A. (2009). Vitamin C and immune function. *Medizinische Monatsschrift fur Pharmazeuten*, 32(2), 49–54.

Svare, H., Gausdal, A. H., & Möllering, G. (2020). The function of ability, benevolence, and integrity-based trust in innovation networks. *Industry and Innovation*, 27(6), 585–604.

Trew, B. (2020). Coronavirus: Hundreds dead in Iran from drinking methanol amid fake reports it cures disease. *Independent*. Retrieved April 29, 2020, from www.independent.co.uk/ne ws/world/middle-east/iran-coronavirus-methanol-drink-curedeaths-fake-a9429956.html

Van Dijck, J., & Alinejad, D. (2020). Social media and trust in scientific expertise: Debating the COVID-19 pandemic in the Netherlands. *Social Media+ Society*, 6(4), 1–11, 2056305120981057.

Venkataraman, A., Siu, E., & Sadasivam, K. (2016). Paediatric electronic infusion calculator: An intervention to eliminate infusion errors in paediatric critical care. *Journal of the Intensive Care Society*, 17(4), 290–294.

Vigdor, N. (2020). Man fatally poisons himself while self-medicating for coronavirus, Doctor Says. *The New York Times*. Retrieved March 24, 2020, from www.nytimes.com/2020/03/24/us/chloroquine-poisoning-coronavirus.html

Wang, Y., Min, Q., & Han, S. (2016). Understanding the effects of trust and risk on individual behavior toward social media platforms: A meta-analysis of the empirical evidence. *Computers in Human Behavior*, 56, 34–44. https://doi.org/10.1016/j.chb.2015.11.011

Warner-Søderholm, G., Bertsch, A., & Søderholm, A. (2018). Data on social media use related to age, gender and trust constructs of integrity, competence, concern, benevolence and identification. *Data in Brief*, 18, 696–699.

Wong, A., Ho, S., Olusanya, O., Antonini, M. V., & Lyness, D. (2021). The use of social media and online communications in times of pandemic COVID-19. *Journal of the Intensive Care Society*, 22(3), 255–260.

Yan, Q., Tang, S., Gabriele, S., & Wu, J. (2016). Media coverage and hospital notifications: Correlation analysis and optimal media impact duration to manage a pandemic. *Journal of Theoretical Biology*, 390, 1–13.

Yao, X., Ye, F., Zhang, M., Cui, C., Huang, B., Niu, P., Liu, X., Zhao, L., Dong, E., Song, C., Zhan, S., Lu, R., Li, H., Tan, W., & Liu, D. (2020). In vitro antiviral activity and projection of optimized dosing design of hydroxychloroquine for the treatment of severe acute respiratory syndrome coronavirus 2 (SARS-CoV-2). *Clinical Infectious Diseases: an Official Publication of the Infectious Diseases Society of America*, 71(15), 732–739. https://doi.org/10.1093/cid/ciaa237

8 Telegram as a Pedagogical Tool During the COVID-19 Pandemic

Kershnee Sevnarayan

1. Introduction

Online education has become an integral aspect of how teaching and learning take place in higher education institutions after the coronavirus (COVID-19) pandemic (Lata & Gupta, 2021). The transition from the traditional face-to-face teaching and learning approach to online instruction has been accelerated by the pandemic crisis (Singh & Kumar, 2022). Due to the circumstances, all educators are working efficiently to reorganize their curricula, study plans, and instructional materials to maintain the continuity of their lessons (Zha & He, 2021). Numerous studies have shown that social interaction among students and between them and their lecturers is crucial for knowledge acquisition and the development of successful learning (Chukwuere, 2021; Don et al., 2022; Jia et al., 2022; Sevnarayan, 2022; Kumar & Nanda, 2020). A variety of systems, including Google Classroom, Microsoft Teams, Webex, and a platform through social media, including WhatsApp, Telegram, and YouTube, can be used for mobile learning (m-learning) (Chung et al., 2020). According to Edward (2007), m-learning may help online students in many ways as he points out that

- mobile learning assists students with their talents recognition;
- it can be effective for both independent and team-based learning acts;
- learners can identify their weaknesses or strengths through mobile learning;
- the gap between the application of information and communications technology and mobile phone literacy can be bridged by m-learning;
- learning experience can be achieved in an informal environment through m-learning, which may satisfy some students with new learning experiences;
- learners have more time to focus on learning experience through m-learning; and
- m-learning helps with the raise of self-confidence and self-esteem.

Lecturers may find m-learning beneficial due to the pandemic concern which resulted in limited face-to-face interaction with students (Bhardwaj & Kumar, 2022a). In most of the studies that were reviewed, Telegram is an m-learning or social networking site that is frequently disregarded.

DOI: 10.4324/9781003315278-8

Since its launch in 2013, Telegram has shown extraordinary user growth, becoming the most downloaded and popular social media application with 500 million monthly users (Mansoor, 2022). Like other social networking sites, Telegram is cost-free, offers limitless Cloud storage space, facilitates media sharing regardless of file size or type, and can be viewed from numerous devices (Aladsani, 2021). Additionally, Telegram provides unique features including high security, video calls, chat channels and groups, polls, and bots. Telegram is a distinctive social networking programme due to its use of encryption and security. The software has several security options that provide users more privacy. These include preventing the public from viewing user phone numbers, enabling two-step authentication, limiting who can view the 'last seen' status, profile pictures, and banning other users so they cannot access the messages of the blocker. The results of polls, which may or may not be anonymous, can be used to resolve disputes between users or to record their availability for events. Polls also have a Quiz Mode option, which only allows for one right response.

This chapter investigates lecturers' perceptions of creating a social presence on Telegram. Additionally, the researcher goes further by observing the instructional techniques that lecturers use to create a social presence. Since online education was disregarded until the pandemic broke out and demonstrated the importance of educational technology in sharing information, this chapter will assist researchers in identifying important components of the online teaching process. Despite the significance of online contact, little research has been done on using Telegram as one of the networking sites to improve social presence in online educational environments. This study is conducted in an open distance and e-learning institution (ODeL) in South Africa and uses an academic writing module, ENG321, to understand the phenomenon of social presence. Using a qualitative approach and a community of inquiry theoretical grounding, this study investigates the following research questions:

RQ1: How do lecturers perceive Telegram as a platform to create social presence?
RQ2: Which instructional techniques are used to create a social presence by lecturers on Telegram?

2. Literature Review

2.1 Telegram as a Tool for the Dissemination of Educational Information

Research shows that social media includes veritable tools for disseminating and receiving information during the COVID-19 pandemic (Abdulazeez & Sunday, 2022). Literature also revealed that social media was a fertile ground for disseminating fake news (Bhardwaj & Kumar, 2022b).

This fake news had negative effect on the people's perceptions of social media applications such as WhatsApp and Telegram. This could be a reason lecturers are reluctant to use social networking sites in their teaching (Bansal et al., 2021). This chapter argues that Telegram as a social networking site provides the feeling of safety and inclusion to online students during the COVID-19 pandemic in the context under study. The results of a study conducted in Nigeria by Janavi and Mardnai (2022) revealed that social networking sites are very influential in people's lives and that many people think that training and information are published in these networks. They also believe that these networks can be an appropriate and useful platform for information, education, and awareness. According to Swartz et al. (2022), the Telegram app for teaching and learning was effective in a South African university under study. It is significant because the software enables the creation of a socially fair online classroom environment while also providing students with an inclusive and enabling learning environment at a time when the world is experiencing great disruption and fear.

2.2 Telegram as an Online Social Tool for Lecturers

Lecturers can utilize Telegram as a helpful pedagogical tool. According to Mohamad et al. (2020), students engaged in greater social conversation when the lecturer gave them exercises in the form of games and quizzes, like Kahoot!, because it may pique their attention and demand a quick response. Gamification provides a new trajectory for students to be more engaged in their online learning (Mohamad et al., 2020; Don et al., 2022). At a university of technology in Malaysia, Don et al. (2022) investigated the impact of teacher presence on online learning and discovered that online learning activities aided students in creating the explanations and solutions. Due to pandemic scenarios and the e-learning educational system, the online classroom must be tailored efficiently within a community of inquiry theory. Similar research was conducted by Jia et al. (2022) who gathered information from 354 full-time undergraduate students at a public Chinese university and looked at the impact of social presence, teacher-student interaction, and student-student interaction on learning engagement. This study's conclusions showed that social presence and learning engagement in online contexts were strongly impacted by teacher-student and student-student interaction. Additionally, social presence affected learning engagement directly. Social presence also acted as a mediator in the connections between student-student and teacher-student contact and learning engagement. This study verified the important influences of social presence, teacher-student interaction, and student-student interaction on learners' engagement in online environments. It would be interesting to investigate how social presence mediation by the Telegram messenger facilitates lecturer-student engagement.

3. Theoretical Framework

Through the interaction of social, cognitive, and teaching presences, the community of inquiry (CoI) theory, put forth by Garrison et al. (2000), has been acknowledged as having the capacity to foster learning and cooperation. The concept was initially developed by Garrison et al. (2000) to look at interactions that can encourage students' engagement and cognitive learning in online learning environments. The cognitive presence, teaching presence, and social presence were the three key components in the development of the CoI framework, which aimed to be a tool to examine the effectiveness of the learning process in online environments (Kumar & Sharma, 2021). A fourth presence was later added on to the theory, emotional presence. To make it easier for the reader to grasp how the four presences are interconnected, the researcher illustrates the diagram in Figure 8.1.

While 'social presence' helps students connect socially and emotionally with others, 'cognitive presence' refers to the capacity of students to create knowledge based on social interaction. Emotional presence is the external expression of emotion and feeling by lecturers and among students in a CoI. Additionally, the term 'teaching presence' describes how lecturers create and organize the learning experience, which is frequently thought to promote learner, social, and cognitive presence (Garrison et al., 2000). As a result, the development of a CoI framework must include teaching presence as it is essential to the success of an online environment. The CoI is a valuable idea to comprehend how pupils engage with one another and are motivated using the Telegram app. This claim is supported by the arguments made by Law et al. (2019) and Zuo et al. (2022), who contend that social presence has a higher influence on online learning engagement and motivation. According to Zuo et al. (2022), the relationship between CoI presences, technological acceptability, and online learning motivation is supported by CoI as

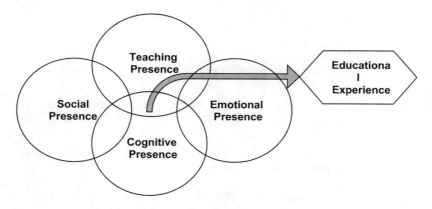

Figure 8.1 The four interrelated presences of a community of inquiry

140 *Kershnee Sevnarayan*

a theoretical model. It would be intriguing to conduct a CoI analysis on the study's findings.

There is a vast body of material available that focuses on suggestions for best practices in online learning as the field of online education has grown exponentially during the pandemic (Kovid & Kumar, 2022; Kumar & Gupta, 2021; Kumar & Malhotra, 2021). Researchers have suggested that there should be more opportunities for learner-to-learner interaction while using online learning. More research is now required to concentrate on the distinctive interaction between the lecturer and student through a range of tactics. Higher education institutions are searching for more ways to foster experiential learning using different technologies by enhancing the social presence of the various instructional methodologies (Kumar & Rewari, 2022).

4. Methodology

4.1 *Research Method and Design*

To better understand how lecturers utilize Telegram to promote social presence, this qualitative study uses Telegram as a pedagogical tool in an Academic Writing module (ENG321). A successful qualitative action research study offers a thorough grasp of the circumstance in which the researcher develops claims about the overall meaning derived and reports at the conclusion of a study. To better understand how lecturers perceive and act to establish a social presence in the ENG321 Telegram group, this study uses one-on-one interviews with lecturers as well as observations of the Telegram group.

A PAR design was selected for this study as it involves researchers and participants working together to understand a problematic situation and change it for the better. PAR admits that within educational settings, teachers are the individuals with authority and advantage; consequently, PAR studies motivate lecturers or researchers to participate eagerly alongside other participants such as students.

4.2 *Participants and Context*

In semester one of 2022, the ENG321 module consisted of 16,000 students and ten lecturers. To answer the first research question, purposive sampling was used where all ten lecturers were invited to participate in the one-on-one Microsoft Teams meeting with the lecturer. To answer the second research question, an observation of the Telegram group, which consisted of approximately 7900 ENG321 students, was conducted. Students agreed that, by being part of the group, they consented to their chats being used for data purposes.

One-on-one interviews with the lecturers were held over a one-hour Microsoft Teams meeting. All ten lecturers were invited to be part of the study;

Telegram as a Pedagogical Tool During the COVID-19 Pandemic   141

however, only four were available and took part in the study. Since qualitative studies focus on the experiences and thick descriptions of its participants, the four lecturers will suffice in this study. The four lecturer participants provided enough data for the researcher to come to a conclusion in the study. The lecturers are named lecturer 1, 2, 3, and 4. The name of the module is also given the name 'ENG321' for confidentiality purposes. PAR requires a great willingness on the part of both students and lecturers to disclose their personal views of their module interaction, their own opinions, and experiences. The two questions from the one-one-one interviews with lecturers that were asked and that will be analyzed and discussed in this chapter are the following:

1 Do you think that the Telegram group enhanced social presence in the module?
2 How has the Telegram group enhanced social presence in the module?

To corroborate what the lecturers have said in the one-one-one interviews discussed earlier, an observation schedule was used to understand how the ENG321 Telegram group facilitated social presence:

1 Discuss the instructional techniques that lecturers use to facilitate social presence.

4.3   Data Collection and Analysis

Data was collected during the first semester of 2022. Thematic analysis, which aligned with the research questions, was used to analyze the data. In line with the research questions, the following themes emerged:

- Lecturers' perceptions of social presence on Telegram.
- Instructional techniques used to create social presence.

5.   Findings and Discussion

In the data analysis, the researcher identified two themes related to lecturer's participation in Telegram to create a social presence. They are (1) lecturers' perceptions of social presence in Telegram and (2) instructional techniques used to create social presence.

5.1   Lecturers' Perceptions of Social Presence on Telegram

To understand lecturers' perceptions of social presence on the ENG321 lecturer-student Telegram group, two questions were asked in the one-on-one interviews with lecturers. Two of the respondents were a part of the Telegram group (including the researcher). The other two lecturers chose not to be part of the Telegram group from the beginning of the semester. The first question sought to understand lecturers' perceptions of social presence on Telegram: 'Do you think that the Telegram group enhanced social presence in the module?' Below are the verbatim responses of lecturers' perceptions of social presence on Telegram:

> The ENG321 group did increase social presence in the group. You (the researcher) did a fantastic job at creating that presence. I was available from time to time to answer basic queries, but I loved how you allowed students to express themselves and to be themselves in the group. Because of your presence, the students felt free to open and share information freely (Lecturer 1). Our students are even excited to see us in our livestreams and that has never happened before.
>
> To be honest, I have my reservations about Telegram. I have been against it from the start. The LMS (Learning Management System) is our main teaching communication and social media apps can cause distractions between students so that is why I have not joined the group and I cannot comment on the social presence of lecturers. It is great if there is one, but we should not be using social media apps as they cause distraction to the real learning process (Lecturer 2).
>
> I have not been on the Telegram group because I have had other module-related commitments but yes, the students did send us emails to express their satisfaction about the Telegram group. I noticed a lot less queries on the LMS because I am sure that they used the Telegram group to be social and discuss their queries. It is great that students can engage with the content and ask questions through other mediums (Lecturer 3).
>
> Yes, it did enhance social presence in the module. In distance education, we do not know our students, so I got to engage and interact with them on a personal level. For example, we all mourned with Zolani when her brother passed away with Covid. We saw students helping each other and I know we struggled to get student collaboration going before, but I really feel with Telegram, our students are getting to help each other. The Telegram group is helping them to think critically about the module. As lecturers we should be socially there for our students. (Lecturer 4).

From the responses above, three of the four lecturers agreed that the Telegram group did increase social presence in the module. They noted that the Telegram group allowed the students to be more social with lecturers. Lecturer 1 noted that students were never as social with them on ENG321 before the creation of the Telegram group. Lecturer 4 noted that the group allowed lecturers to communicate with students on a personal level, and the students enjoyed the level of social presence as they reciprocated it by being social with other students as well. In addition, the social presence of the lecturer on the group enhanced collaboration between students themselves and between the lecturer and students; this is something that the module

Telegram as a Pedagogical Tool During the COVID-19 Pandemic   143

has struggled to get right previously. The research findings above reveal that the Telegram group did foster a community of inquiry. The teaching and social presence of the lecturers on the group, in addition to their emotional presence, may have enhanced students' cognitive presence (Garrison et al., 2000). Students seemed to engage more with the ENG321 content material due to their interactions with their lecturer. This is confirmed by Law et al. (2019) who contends that social presence has a positive effect on online learning interaction and motivation. This indicates that social presence and the other presences in CoI do not operate in isolation; they are all interdependent. The findings above also reveal that the emotional and affective relationships lecturers form with their students positively affect the social presence they create within a module. In CoI, interaction with others (students and lecturers) may also promote critical thinking and understanding (cognitive presence). It is interesting that one of the participants (Lecturer 2) did not perceive Telegram to be a useful social application for educational purposes. Lecturers are opposed to the use of Telegram and other social media applications, as they are unaware of its benefits (Dollah et al., 2021). This notion, paired with the researcher's observation that lecturers in the South African ODeL university under study lacked m-learning knowledge and skills, set in motion the study's investigation into the participatory action research study regarding the use of Telegram to understanding social presence in online learning during the COVID-19 pandemic. The same lecturers shared their ideas about how the Telegram group enhanced social presence in the module. Below are some verbatim responses from each of the four lecturers:

> I really liked the way in which you pinned messages on the group so that students do not miss the valuable information in the module. Sometimes as lecturers we expect students to know certain things, but the reality is that our students are busy, they work a full-time job and pinning messages helps them to stay on track and not fall behind. I was not as active as you were (to the researcher) but when I was online, I did answer a few queries and did be in contact with a few students who were confused about the module content (Lecturer 1).
>
> I really think that we can be social on the LMS and not resort to complicate our jobs with the addition of social media apps like Telegram. (Lecturer 2).
>
> Like I mentioned, I was not part of the Telegram group as I did not have time, but I am aware that lecturers are very social on the group as students are made aware of important information about the module on Telegram, for example, links to Microsoft Teams meetings, important announcements that are replicated from the LMS announcements, and the posting of motivational videos. It is important that students receive information in different ways as the LMS may not be appealing to every student (Lecturer 3).

144   *Kershnee Sevnarayan*

> As the Telegram group owner, I made sure to pin important messages on the group that I did not wants students to miss, I asked students questions on a regular basis, I used polls to get an idea of what students' strengths and weaknesses are in the module, I elected another astute student as a group admin to facilitate interaction when I was not available. . . . I continually praised students in the group which I believe made them open up more. There wasn't a case of a single or few students dominating the discussions, all students felt like they belonged in the group. At one stage, a student said that the Telegram group felt like a real classroom, which made me happy (Lecturer 4).

According to the lecturers in the interviews, social presence was created through various lecturer activities on Telegram. To create a social presence, lecturers pinned important messages on the group, they answered students' questions, they asked questions, lecturers repeated essential information from the LMS on Telegram, and they used polls to understand students' strengths and weaknesses. The findings from the lecturers above reveal that the lecturers' teaching presence through their instructional techniques, mentioned above, may have established clear expectations in a social learning environment which encourages interaction. According to Lecturer 4, learning was regulated in the group by encouraging interaction between students. This leads to researcher to assume that lecturers encourage students to be responsible for their own learning; this is an important skill to learn in ODeL and online learning contexts. From a community of inquiry perspective (Garrison et al., 2000), the findings show how the lecturers have shown a teaching and social presence through the implementation of a variety of instructional techniques to maintain students' social engagement and interaction through different modes of communication, activities, progress monitoring, and peer feedback. These instructional techniques made by the lecturer facilitate communication between lecturers and students and students and students to form a CoI (Janavi & Mardnai, 2022). It is argued that a lack of these instructional techniques may have decreased the amount of interaction between stakeholders. These findings are further corroborated by Jia et al. (2022) who argue that social presence is directly affected by learning engagement. Social presence also acted as a mediator in the connections between student-student and teacher-student contact and learning engagement. The challenge remains that many lecturers are not open to participate in social media platforms such as Telegram, as it is not the official study platform, they do not have time for engaging with students on social media, and lecturers may not be digitally competent to participate with a younger, techno-savvy, diverse cohort of students.

5.2   *Instructional Techniques Used to Create Social Presence*

The second research question seeks to understand (through observations of the group chats) the instructional techniques that lecturers use to create a social space. In the interviews, the lecturers mentioned that pinning messages was one instructional technique that they used to alert students to important messages and announcements. The screenshot of the chat in Figure 8.2 below shows the lecturer alerting students to an important announcement which requires their attention.

As can be seen in Figure 8.2, the students have interacted with the lecturer's message by 'loving' it (24 heart emoticons) and liking it (19 thumbs-up emoticons). The researcher also observed that the lecturer used polling as another instructional technique, as shown in Figure 8.3.

As mentioned earlier in this chapter, the Telegram group consisted of 7900 students. In Figure 8.2, the reader can see that 924 students participated in this pole, and the lecturer was able to understand what their strengths and weaknesses are in academic writing. With this information, the lecturers were then able to tailor their pedagogies to assist students. The next technique that the lecturer used, which was not mentioned in the interview, was the use of casual language: 'Just joking, guys,' 'That was fun,' and memes, as shown in Figures 8.4 and 8.5.

The lecturer exhibited a sense of humour with her students, which made her popular with the students. This is seen by laughing emoticons and other emoticon reactions by the students. The students enjoyed the light-heartedness and the use of memes by the lecturer, which allowed them to communicate socially with the lecturer and other students. In addition to this, the lecturer answered questions in the group throughout the day (22:19 at night) as shown in Figure 8.6 below. This technique allowed the students to see that the lecturer was accessible and approachable to them.

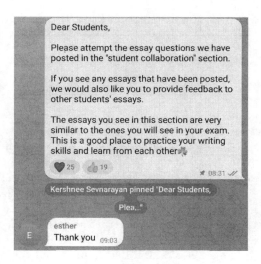

Figure 8.2 Lecturers' pinned messages on the Telegram group

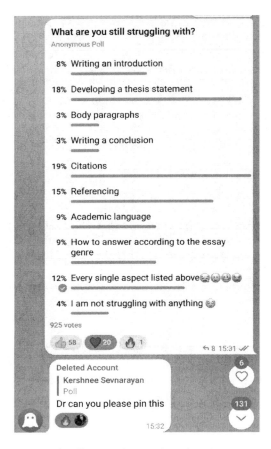

Figure 8.3 Lecturer's use of polls to understand students' content needs

Finally, the lecturer at all times directed students to the Moodle LMS, which is their official learning platform. In Figure 8.7, the lecture is observed to be redirecting students to the resources on Moodle so they can understand their module concepts.

As can be seen in the findings, the lecturer used a variety of instructional techniques which corroborated with what they had stated in the one-on-one interviews. The techniques that they used to facilitate social presence were pinning messages, using polls, usual casual language, and memes, being accessible by answering questions and directing students to the Moodle LMS for further module interaction. The findings confirm that Telegram can be configured and used as an educational social space that allows for the implementation of instructional techniques that seek to promote and collaborate construction of knowledge (Mohamad et al., 2020). This may lead the researcher to say that the careful configuration of a social presence on a Telegram group may

Telegram as a Pedagogical Tool During the COVID-19 Pandemic 147

Figure 8.4 The use of casual language by the lecturer on Telegram

enhance the cognitive presence of students (Garrison et al., 2000). It is also worth mentioning that the Telegram group was constantly busy throughout the day; it is assumed that is because there were over 7900 students on the group. I am not sure if the interaction would be the same if there were 300 students on the group, for example. The group was observed to be a safe place for students (Mishra et al., 2020); the group was devoid of any bias, nepotism, discrimination and resulted in a group that was inclusive. The students constantly expressed their love for the inclusivity and efficiency of the group and the leadership of the lecturer in the way the group was managed. Another finding worth underscoring is that whenever a message is sent over the Telegram group, such as, 'This is fun,' 'Hey, guys,' and 'Goodnight, students,' these words may be coded as social presence. The immediate response time between sending a message and responding may mimic a face-to-face interaction. Thus, the opportunity presented to lecturers during the pandemic

Figure 8.5 The use of memes by the lecturer

to promptly respond to students may have influenced the number of social presence occurrences, which were also driven by the feeling of belonging to a community that the lecturer created. The size of the Telegram group, the nature of the assigned instructional techniques, and the relationship between the lecturer and students are among the contextual variables that the researcher believes may have an impact on how social presence is established and maintained in online courses and social networking sites.

6. Limitations and Ethical Considerations

Although the CoI approach informs the deductions and inferences made in this chapter, there are limitations to this study. Firstly, because this study was conducted in a module with over 16000 students, a quantitative analysis might have enriched the data obtained; however, to overcome this limitation,

Telegram as a Pedagogical Tool During the COVID-19 Pandemic 149

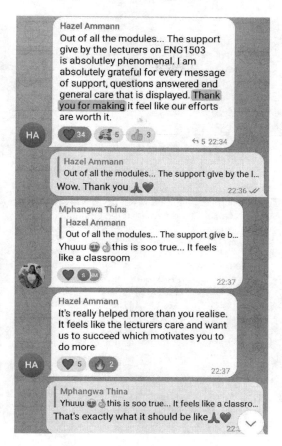

Figure 8.6 Lecturer being accessible on Telegram

thick descriptions from lecturers and students were provided. Secondly, observations of only one lecturer are provided on Telegram; this is because other lecturers opted not to be part of the group. This would have corroborated (or not) some of the thick descriptions made by students, adding to the validity of the deductions. Thirdly, the timing of this study is premature. A more critical evaluation is needed over a period; the Telegram group was only implemented in February 2022 in the context under study. Before conducting the research, ethical clearance was applied and granted by the university's ethics committee (NHREC Registration #: Rec-240816–052).

7. Conclusion and Implications for Further Research

This study serves as a springboard for conversations on social presence in the context of mobile learning, educational technology, and online distance

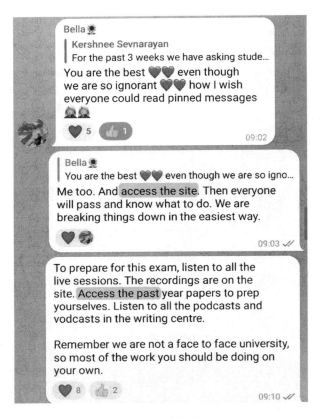

Figure 8.7 Lecturer directing students to their Moodle LMS

education. It also provides insight into how pedagogical educational experiences are created with the goal of encouraging collaborative learning. The research presented in this chapter shows that the social presence created by the lecturer significantly affects the educational consequences of teaching and learning. Social networking platforms like Telegram are successful because they incorporate social presence, teacher presence, cognitive presence, and emotional presence. To get more precise data based on the various presences in social networking sites, additional research using Telegram might be carried out with a bigger sample size of participants from diverse educational levels. In a similar vein, studies need to be conducted on how prepared the students are to reply and participate on Telegram. Additionally, to better understand how emoticons fit into CoI, researchers can try to decipher the meanings of the ones that students and lecturers employ. In the future, online learning techniques must be used in a more dynamic way to stimulate student participation in a range of more engaging teaching and learning activities. The use of interactive instructional learning techniques and teacher-student interaction during online learning sessions can therefore be investigated further. This is because, in the post-pandemic era, online teaching and learning will become more prevalent due to the complexity of technology and the development of the Internet of Things.

References

Abdulazeez, I., & Sunday, A. A. (2022). Social networking sites as tools for disseminating fake news during the 2020 COVID-19 pandemic. *Sau Journal of Management and Social Sciences*, 5(1), 147–156. www.journals.sau.edu.ng/index.php/sjmas/article/view/849.

Aladsani, H. (2021). University students' use and perceptions of telegram to promote effective educational interactions: A qualitative study. *International Journal of Emerging Technologies in Learning (iJET)*, 16, 182–197. https://doi.org/10.3991/ijet.v16i09.19281

Bansal, R., Mittal, R., & Kumar, V. (2021). Popularity and usage analytics of social media platforms in higher education. In *2021 international conference on computational performance evaluation (ComPE)* (pp. 631–635). IEEE. https://doi.org/10.1109/ComPE53109.2021.9752143

Bhardwaj, A., & Kumar, V. (2022a). Web and social media approach to marketing of engineering courses in India. *International Journal of Business Innovation and Research (IJBIR)*, 27(4), 541–555.

Bhardwaj, A., & Kumar, V. (2022b). A framework for enhancing privacy in online collaboration. *International Journal of Electronic Security and Digital Forensics (IJESDF)*, 14(4), 413–432.

Chukwuere, J. E. (2021). The impact of social media on students' social interaction. *Journal of Management Information and Decision Sciences*, 24(7), 1–15.

Chung, E., Noor, N. M., & Mathew, V. N. (2020). Are you ready? An assessment of online learning readiness among university students. *International Journal of Academic Research in Progressive Education and Development*, 9(1), 301–317.

Dollah, M. H., Binti, M., Nair, S. M., & Wider, W. (2021). The effects of utilizing telegram app to enhance students' ESL writing skills. *International Journal of Educational Studies*, 4(1), 10–16. https://doi.org/10.53935/2641-533x.v4i1.55

Don, M. A. M., Rosli, M. R., Senin, M. S. M., & Ahmad, M. F. (2022). Exploring social presence theory in the online classroom: The case for online presence. *International Journal of Academic Research in Business and Social Sciences*, 12(1), 26–40.

Edward, Y. (2007, June). Setting the new standard with mobile computing. *International Review of Research in Open and Distance Learning*, 8(2), 1–16.

Garrison, D. R., Anderson, T., & Archer, W. (2000). Critical inquiry in a text-based environment: Computer conferencing in higher education. *Internet and Higher Education*, 2(2–3), 87–105.

Janavi, E., & Mardnai, F. (2022). The effect of information and education through social networks on the level of public awareness during the COVID-19 pandemic (Case Study: Tehran). *Sciences and Techniques of Information Management*, 8(1), 45–72. https://doi.org/10.22091/stim.2021.6698.1551

Jia, M., Jiangmei, C., & Li, M. (2022). Teacher—student interaction, student—student interaction and social presence: Their impacts on learning engagement in online learning environments. *The Journal of Genetic Psychology*, 183(6), 514–526. https://doi.org/10.1080/00221325.2022.2094211

Kovid, R. K., & Kumar, V. (Eds.). (2022). *Cases on emerging markets responses to the COVID-19 pandemic*. IGI Global Publications.

Kumar, V., & Gupta, G. (Eds.). (2021). *Strategic management during a pandemic*. Routledge; Taylor & Francis Group.

Kumar, V., & Malhotra, G. (Eds.). (2021). *Stakeholder strategies for reducing the impact of global health crises*. IGI Global Publications.

Kumar, V., & Nanda, P. (2020). Social media as a tool in higher education: A pedagogical perspective. In *Handbook of research on diverse teaching strategies for the technology-rich classroom* (pp. 239–253). IGI Global Publications.

Kumar, V., & Rewari, M. (2022). A responsible approach to higher education curriculum design. *International Journal of Educational Reform (IJER)*, *31*(4), 422–441.

Kumar, V., & Sharma, D. (2021). E-learning theories, components and cloud computing based learning platforms. *International Journal of Web-Based Learning and Teaching Technologies*, *16*(3), 1–16.

Lata, M., & Gupta, A. (2021). Education during the pandemic: Technology-based solutions. In *Stakeholder strategies for reducing the impact of global health crises* (pp. 209–224). IGI Global Publications.

Law, K. M. Y., Geng, S., & Li, T. (2019). Student enrollment, motivation and learning performance in a blended learning environment: The mediating effects of social, teaching, and cognitive presence. *Computers & Education*, *136*, 1–12. https://doi.org/10.1016/j.compedu.2019.02.021

Mansoor, I. (2022, June 30). *Telegram revenue and usage statistics*. www.businessofapps.com/data/telegram-statistics/

Mohamad, M., Arif, F. K. M., Alias, B. S., & Yunus, M. M. (2020). Online game-based formative assessment: Distant learners post graduate students' challenges towards quizizz. *International Journal of Scientific and Technology Research*, *9*, 994–1000.

Sevnarayan, K. 2022. Reimaging eLearning technologies to support students: On reducing transactional distance at an open and distance eLearning institution. *E-Learning and Digital Media*, *19*(4), 421–439. https://doi.org/10.1177/20427530221096535

Singh, J., & Kumar, V. (2022). Combating the pandemic with ICT based learning tools and applications: A case of Indian higher education. *International Journal of Virtual and Personal Learning Environments (IJVPLE) Platforms (IJVPLE)*, *12*(1), 1–21.

Swartz, B. C., Valentine, L. Z., & Jaftha, D. V. (2022). Participatory parity through teaching with Telegram. *Perspectives in Education*, *40*(1), 96–111. https://doi.org/10.18820/2519593X/pie.v40.i1.6

Zha, S., & He, W. (2021). Pandemic pedagogy in online hands-on learning for IT/IS courses. *Communications of the Association for Information Systems*, *48*, 80–87. https://doi.org/10.17705/ 1CAIS.04811

Zuo, M., Hu, Y., Luo, H. et al. (2022). K-12 students' online learning motivation in China: An integrated model based on community of inquiry and technology acceptance theory. *Education and Information Technology*, *27*, 4599–4620. https://doi.org/10.1007/s10639-021-10791-x

9 Social Media–Based Learning Platforms and the Pandemic

A Comparative Analysis

Pooja Nanda and Anu Gupta

1. Introduction

Learning is a repetitive process which involves creating, understanding, interpreting, practising, and refining a consistent set of information content. The presence of digital technologies has a greater influence on the learning process and enhances learning outcomes (Kumar & Sharma, 2016). The emergence of COVID-19 has put education in danger, even though it is unquestionably important for the prosperity of a country and the development of an individual. It has significantly impacted the lives of millions of children. Since the lockdown was put into place, several urgent goals needed to be accomplished. The economic crisis hindered education as well by lowering its output. Studies have shown that the disease has prevented around 32 crore young people from receiving an education (https://timesofindia. indiatimes.com/readersblog/zita-janice/covid-19-and-its-impact-on-education-system-35076/). Many institutions were also forced to close. According to Unicef (2021), lockdowns resulting from COVID-19 caused schools with more than 168 million children to be totally closed for over a full year. Using digital technology, a traditional learning environment was to be created. Teachers began establishing modules, frameworks, and explanations on whiteboards, much like how a classroom is set up, to grab students' attention. The emergence of the coronavirus pandemic in 2020 altered many aspects of daily life, including how people use the internet. The average daily time spent on social media by Americans in 2020 was 65 minutes, a significant increase from the 54 and 56 minutes spent the year before (Statista, 2022a). In light of this, there has been an explosion of social media platforms (Kumar & Nanda, 2022). People tended to use social media (SM) more frequently during the epidemic for the purpose of social isolation. In the first three months of the COVID-19 outbreak, social media sites experienced a 61% increase in web traffic compared to the norm (Khan et al., 2021). Due to the rapid advancement of technologies like social media platforms, the world offered tremendous opportunities for exchange of ideas, experiences, and intelligence. A social media network emphasizes on social practices such as collaboration, interaction, community, and creativity (Kumar et al.,

DOI: 10.4324/9781003315278-9

2022). According to El-Badawy and Hashem (2015), social media platforms give individuals opportunities for interaction and doing two-way communication. Some of the top social media platforms include Facebook, LinkedIn, Twitter, Google+, blogging, wikis, YouTube, and many other platforms. The exponential rise of mobile phone use, which had a significant effect on many aspects of people's lives, can be attributed to the growth of social media (Mittal & Kumar, 2022). Social networking has evolved from a direct electronic information exchange to a virtual meeting spot, a shopping portal, and a crucial twenty-first-century education tool in less than a decade (Gupta et al., 2021). The spread and scope of social networking sites (SNS) is changing the way modern societies handle their social networks. Market leader Facebook, which presently has more than 2.91 million monthly active users, was the first social network to cross one billion registered accounts, according to Statista (2022b). As per Global Media Insights (2022), YouTube comes at position two with 2.56 million users, and WhatsApp takes position three with 2.0 million users in 2022. The statistics clearly show that social media sites such as Facebook, YouTube, and WhatsApp have a huge user base. This is attributed to the proliferation of internet and social media (Kumar & Ayodeji, 2021). The internet is used by 4.66 billion people around the world in 2021, with 316 million new users joining in 2020 (Smart Insights, 2021). As per the same report, 5.22 billion people own smartphones. Social media has become an important part of the lives of many young people (Nanda & Kumar, 2021). Most people over the age of 13 have a social media account, such as Facebook, Snapchat, Instagram, and others. Students today are intimately involved with social media at every stage. This can be used as a great opportunity to use these social media tools as a platform for learning as students are very comfortable using these online tools for learning. Despite the obstacles, mobile devices and social media offer excellent educational e-learning platforms for collaboration among academics, access to course materials, and student mentorship (Gikas & Grant, 2013). Students who adopt and use mobile devices and social media gain access to a variety of modern learning resources, such as access to course materials and communication with peers and experts. The most affordable and practical means for students to get pertinent information are via social media and mobile devices (Singh & Kumar, 2022; Mittal & Kumar, 2020). According to estimates from the International Telecommunication Union (ITU), the number of internet users surged from 4.1 billion in 2019 to 4.9 billion in 2021 during the COVID-19 outbreak. However, due to social media platforms, many people now have access to remote education, remote employment, and remote medical care (www.un.org/sustainabledevelopment/blog/2021/12/as-internet-user-numbers-swell-due-to-pandemic-un-forum-discusses-measures-to-improve-safety-of-cyberspace/). Web 2.0 technologies are particularly common among the younger generation. Even among college students, social media has grown in popularity. Several million students around the countries are trying to use these tools on a regular basis for personal interactions (Guy, 2012).

2. Social Media and Education

Selwyn (2012) believes that technology innovations have produced a new learning culture based on collaborative discovery and interaction. Modern technology makes every effort to meet people's needs, especially those of the younger generation (Nanda & Kumar, 2022). Old education delivery methods are being surpassed by new technologies. The learner in the twenty-first century relies on modern technology to help them learn. Lata and Gupta (2021) are of the opinion that, due to the occurrence of the COVID-19 pandemic, there is a need to reidentify the new and emerging learning pedagogies. This has led to a worldwide accelerated growth and ubiquity of digital education platforms. Traditional educational approaches can now be supplemented by social media. Educators can use social media to effectively engage these students (Kumar & Bhardwaj, 2020). To aid the delivery of instruction, social media resources may be incorporated into the existing educational framework as a teaching and learning resource. These techniques are gradually integrating with learning management systems as well. Social media can also be used as a supplement to existing curriculum delivery, as well as to expand the learning environment to the real world and enhance students' learning experiences with real-world knowledge. Online communities and groups are mostly used by students to read, exchange notes, make shared decisions, and share learning materials (Kumar & Sharma, 2017). To connect with students and provide them with timely information, educational institutions often use social media sites such as Twitter, Facebook, and YouTube. Most of the students' free time is spent on social media platforms, according to studies (https://elearningindustry.com/5-ultimate-tricks-using-social-media-learning-tools). Students can share, edit, and create course content in text, video, and audio formats using social media and mobile devices. Students can engage with mentors and classmates by using mobile devices and social media to access tools, documents, and course information. It was discovered by Batsila and Tsihouridis (2016) that students were able to improve their reading and writing skills by using a social media platform for digital storytelling in an English class. Also, Vázquez-Cano (2014) explored the way middle school students successfully used Twitter for learning the Spanish language, and their social science and natural science classes for enhancing their imagination and self-directed learning skills. It is important for students to remain linked to their peers during social learning. Building relationships with friends of friends can help students establish a strong network. They will have the opportunity to meet and build new relationships with many new people. As a result, social media platforms play a vital role in linking students with the people who inspire them.

Students have turned to social media to engage, share thoughts, debate, express themselves in the most personalized way possible, raise awareness, post questions with the assurance of receiving the most important responses, and so on. For students, some of the most significant advantages of social media networks include the following:

Learn and Build Networks

A major advantage of social media platforms for students is learning and building networks. Learning has gone beyond the classroom walls and almost every major e-learning website encourages social media learning (Gon & Rawekar, 2017). Students can learn through e-learning websites and use social media to address their matters. For instance: NPTEL, Udemy, YouTube, and so on. Students can use live videos, which are available on many social networking sites, to engage in class. Course material and notes can also be shared by students with the help of social networking sites like Facebook, Instagram, and even WhatsApp. Student networking is facilitated through social media platforms, and they get knowledge about local events and activities. They can also learn about quizzes, sporting events, and cultural competitions, among other things. Students can get involved in a variety of extracurricular activities by participating in these events.

Creativity Expression

Students can express themselves in a variety of ways on social media. Many students are hesitant to speak up in class because they are afraid of being judged. Social media enables students to freely express themselves. Students can use social media to express themselves in a variety of ways, through publishing of images, blogs, individual articles, videos, and audio recordings, among other things (Kirby, 2016). This encourages students to think out of the box and to discover their unique abilities. Students may no longer wait for an opportunity to participate in an event and demonstrate their abilities because of social media. YouTube channels with video posts are common among teenagers. According to how many people watch their content, they are paid. A large number of them have their own blogs where they can write and earn money. For example, Around the World is a blog written by Sush, a girl from Delhi who is studying computer science at Cornell University (www.topuniversities.com/blog/10-best-student-blogs-millennial-life).

Global Connections

Students may communicate with anyone in the world on social media since it is such a vast platform (Froment et al., 2017). It is essential for students to stay connected to their peers during this social learning process. By making friends with friends of friends, students can build strong networks. They can get to know a lot of new people and start forming connections with them. Students get a plethora of knowledge when given the chance to converse with people from various walks of life on such a big platform. Additionally, they gain knowledge about the various civilizations that exist in the world. This includes their language, manner of life, eating patterns, culture, conventions, and a whole lot more. They can also find out about the various courses offered by institutions all across the world and can access the recorded sessions. On a worldwide platform, students may express their ideas and opinions. Each person has a unique identity on social media. The events organized on social media can boost the students' talents and give them opportunities further in life (www.emertxe.com/emertxe/top-5-benefits-of-social-media-for-students/).

Recruitment Openings

Getting a job is one of the most pressing challenges confronting today's pupils. Even if a student completes their degree, finding work is quite tough. With the usage of social media platforms, they are able to take the advantage of job openings posted on these platforms. Many businesses post job vacancies on their social media pages. Students who follow these businesses on social media can directly apply to them. For example, the popular social media network LinkedIn has 810 million members with over 57 million registered companies in 2022 (https://kinsta.com/blog/linkedin-statistics). According to Hootsuite, six individuals are hired on LinkedIn every minute, with 49 million users using the platform each week to look for work. (https://blog.hootsuite.com/linkedin-statistics-business/). LinkedIn makes it simple and requires the least amount of effort to create a professional profile. A lot of organizations post their jobs through social media. It also offers services like training and offers a talent intelligence platform that empowers one to make smart workforce and hiring decisions. It also helps in getting real-time updates on the leads and accounts and seeing recent company growth trends (www.linkedin.com/premium/products). Students can tap this while looking for their final placements and internships. Students may use LinkedIn to apply for internships and employment in a variety of ways (Kumar & Nanda, 2019). Additionally, by following the target organizations, students can stay current on their activities and be inspired to use these tools wisely (Kumar & Nanda, 2019). LinkedIn also provides services like advertisements and provides insights about some organization. Students can use social media to research the company and all of the fields they are interested in. They may read other people's evaluations and comments to gain a general impression of the firm. They can view the ratings given to a certain company. One can ask their connections to write a recommendation of work that can be displayed on their profile (www.linkedin.com/help/linkedin). Students could make themselves visible by speaking up and forming positive relationships with everyone. They can also use social media to show off their abilities. They are free to publish any of their completed projects or models. Students can also seek advice and assistance from the seniors and teachers. They can get references from their instructors or friends. Students can share their knowledge, expertise, and experiences.

Open Learning

Another significant benefit of social media in education is the ability to study through distance learning mode. The dynamic nature of social media can be advantageous for distance education as well. As per Kaya et al. (2012), helping students to feel less alone is also an important benefit of social media usage in distance learning. Instructors today can attract students to remote learning programmes by using numerous internet technologies and social media. This will become an inescapable feature of our modern education system in the near future (Kumar & Sharma, 2021). In order to provide students with access to education in many different regions of the world, live lectures are now conducted via Skype or webinars.

3. Social Media and Student Engagement

Technology helps individuals to engage in cyberspace as well as get information (Kusumawati et al., 2014). Information and communication technology (ICT) in higher education eliminates the major limits of time and place, allowing access at any time and from any location (Nayar & Kumar, 2018). For higher education institutions, a framework for social media engagement was developed by Kumar and Nanda (2019). The framework considers the most important processes for students' engagement and their social media learning. This engagement helps students feel more connected and involved. According to the social learning theory, which Kumar and Sharma (2016) correctly identified, students learn most effectively when they can learn from one another. Social media play a critical role in carrying out informative and engaging learning activities. Students can use social media sites like Facebook, Twitter, Instagram, Pinterest, YouTube, and others as part of this procedure. Discussion boards and content exchange are two of the process of on-campus engagement's most important activities. Learning management systems (LMSs) may play an important role in content distribution and feedback collection. To develop discussion forums and online groups, students may utilize WhatsApp, Facebook, and Twitter. Mentoring and career assistance are the two most crucial activities when it comes to alumni networking, and LinkedIn, Facebook, Twitter, and blogs may all help. LinkedIn connections allow students and learners to keep track of an alumni's professional milestones, whereas Facebook, Twitter, and blogs allow for ongoing conversation. Likewise, job hunting and profiling can also be done by students.

Each social media platform has a range of educational applications, including news publication, live lecture hosting, and much more (Bansal et al., 2021). Social media use also makes more e-learning alternatives possible. Teaching pupils how to work from a distance is a critical ability to master as remote employment and online classes become more prevalent, and social media may help in this extremely effectively. The following are some of the most well-known social media platforms and how they are used in the educational field:

Facebook

It is one of the most widely used social media platforms in the world. It allows users to stay in touch with their relatives and friends, exchange photos and videos, talk, and join groups with others who have common interests, regardless of gender, creed, or nationality. This now aids in the flow of potentially incomprehensible ideas and viewpoints. Students, in particular, get more ideas and inputs quickly and readily, resulting in a higher grade than they would have received if they had used physical books from the library. Some of the activities which can be performed by learners through Facebook include the following:

- Requesting information
- Participating in online lectures
- Virtual visits to museums, etc.
- Personal experiences
- Keeping track of politicians and experts
- Public surveys

Twitter

This is a free microblogging website that allows users to submit brief messages known as tweets. Students can benefit from this since they are able to follow the tweets and absorb and apply the concepts to their maximum potential. Twitter gives its members more creative writing exercise than any other social media platform. It may enable and encourage students to interact with political officials, subject matter experts, and people of their community in ways that would be impossible without social media usage. Some of the major uses of Twitter in learning include the following:

- Communicate homework and assignments via tweets
- Be updated with educational resources
- Can be used as a class message board
- Post submission notices for assignment due dates
- Follow hashtags which are relevant
- Do contests planning
- Offer easy to handle research tool for students
- Discuss subjects of interest with others

Instagram

It is a popular photo- and video-sharing social media platform. Instagram is a Facebook-owned social networking website that was established in 2010. The major feature allows users to post photographs and videos of a maximum 60-second duration that may be modified with various filters and

160   Pooja Nanda and Anu Gupta

tagged and commented on by using the hashtag sign (http://socialwebqanda. com/2013/12/8-smart-uses-of-instagram-for-smart-students/). The important activities which can be performed by students on Instagram include the following:

- Create picture essays
- Enhance language abilities and skills
- iPhoneography feature to learn how to take pictures
- Develop emotional intelligence
- Upgrade interpersonal skills
- Effective project-based learning
- Gain maximum visibility in short time

LinkedIn

It is a professional social networking service that connects people. It offers a forum for connecting with people and sharing professional information in a safe and secure manner, as well as expanding one's network and approaching and reaching out to corporations based on specific needs. Students, in particular, may benefit from making oneself approachable, and LinkedIn may help them obtain the job of their dreams with the appropriate type of network (www.colourmylearning.com/2013/02/how-linkedin-works-for-education/). The other activities for which LinkedIn can be beneficial for students are the following:

- Demonstrate abilities, expertise, and other ongoing initiatives
- Explore different career opportunities displayed there
- Research about firms in their area of interest, future employers, as well as their background and history
- Graduates can maintain their profile page on LinkedIn
- Setting up job alerts for new options
- Make connections with individuals in their field of study, network, and learn more about potential employers
- Possibility of working for multinational organizations who hire through LinkedIn
- Subscribe to networks for updates

Pinterest

This is another social networking platform that concentrates on photographs with a brief explanation. Students can be benefitted from it by selecting an image and landing on a page with a thorough description. For instance, if someone wants to learn more about Hampi's architecture, they can just click on the image, which will take them to a website that contains all of the necessary information. Some of the other advantages of Pinterest in learning and education include the following:

Social Media–Based Learning Platforms and the Pandemic   161

- Set up a Pinterest board for the class
- Create a digital bibliography for research projects, publications, or group projects
- Work in group projects
- Student portfolios in digital format
- Get feedback from peers
- Share a photo journal of adventures with the class

YouTube

Being a free web-based service, it offers millions of short videos about various education ideas. Educators can quickly find and study videos pertaining to a certain subject or knowledge, then send the link to students. Students may benefit from YouTube in a variety of ways, including complementing their study materials and improving their knowledge of educational subjects. Students utilize YouTube for educational, cultural, and behavioural purposes. As a result, the usage of YouTube is becoming more popular. Education, in conjunction with students, must also make efforts to generate new video material. Video is a prominent tool in social media trends that is effective. The other benefits of YouTube for learners have also been identified:

- Share useful videos to inspire and help other students in their subjects
- Multiple videos of the same course are accessible on YouTube
- Highly valuable in medical courses (Barry et al., 2016)
- Entertainment videos can be watched to relieve stress

4. Social Media–Based Commercially Available Tools for Education

Technological advancements and students' greater usage of the internet for e-learning in educational institutions have resulted in radical changes in communication patterns (Ansari & Khan, 2020). Technology has become more important in the instruction of children and adolescents in the new era of learning. In the classroom, a number of social media technologies (from traditional to high-tech) may be deployed to promote student learning. Whiteboards, index cards, posters, audience response systems, Google collaborative tools, 3D printing, and wikis are just a few examples. A number of digital education technologies have been created with the intention of boosting academic process management, empowering students, encouraging teamwork, and facilitating communication between instructors and students.

The progression of latest technologies tries to accommodate the requirements of people, particularly the young generation. These technologies make the world more approachable for exchange of ideas and provide more opportunities for acquiring intelligence. Some of these advanced technologies like social media tools have found their way in the commercial world. These are

162 *Pooja Nanda and Anu Gupta*

further being leveraged in the education field for supplementing the offline learning. Some of the important commercial tools being used excessively in learning are Facebook, wiki, YouTube, LinkedIn, blogs, and Twitter. Each of these tools has its own characteristics and are good for the purpose it has been created for.

Technology has become an important aspect in the instruction of children and adolescents in the new era of learning. In the classroom, there are plenty of tech-based tools to utilize. Following are some of the tools that help instructors and students to communicate more effectively, with an emphasis on those meant to encourage, enhance, and manage learning:

VoiceThread (https://voicethread.com/)

VoiceThread is an interactive platform for collaboration and sharing that allows students to create online presentations, upload and exchange pictures, videos, and documents, and then have an online discussion through audio, video, or text comments about each other's posts (Hoplamazian & Monthie, 2017). An individual can share a VoiceThread with friends, students and colleagues, and they can also record feedback on the slides as an alternative. VoiceThread, though specifically built for asynchronous conversations, can be used to accomplish a variety of student learning goals. The platform has unique opportunities for promoting education, including the opportunity to upload visual, textual, and audio material, as well as receiving such material from peers and instructors. The ability to download PowerPoint presentations is also another advantage of VoiceThread. There are both free and paid accounts available on VoiceThread. The free account has limited functionality up to 30 days; however, instructors can use advanced options with a paid service. Due to COVID-19, the Language Teaching Methodologies unit is now being delivered online. We studied its benefits and potential pitfalls before choosing such a novel application of VoiceThread in the now entirely online teacher training course. The practical course components were moved to the VT platform in accordance with the collaborative learning principles (Dooly, 2018), which makes everyone's work visible and is anticipated to encourage the learning community and the adoption of peer feedback. With this, VoiceThread educators can increase involvement of students in more focused, substantive discussions. A license option is also offered by VoiceThread, which can be integrated in many learning managements sites (LMSs) for increasing further capabilities and providing automatic class group formation and management. This tool has 750 user accounts after Covid (https://jan.ucc.nau.edu/d-elc/tutorials/voicethread/voicethread.html). The primary factors of this online microteaching methodology include the continuous achievement of the Unit Learning Outcomes (ULOs), improved feedback literacy (Carless & Boud, 2018), and ICT skills for students, as well as the growth of autonomy as learners and teachers. Furthermore, VT promoted interaction and assisted in the creation of a community.

TeacherTube (www.teachertube.com/)

It is committed to all forms of schooling, from basics to work that is more challenging. Interestingly, some of the more helpful tools inside it are the tabs for docs and audio. Members are invited to share educationally relevant videos, as well as to make supportive comments and utilize the grading system to show their support for particular educationally beneficial videos. TeacherTube has been offering college students, high school students, middle school students, and primary school students an online network for exchanging instructional and educational films throughout the pandemic. Additional advantages include using the rating system, creating and joining video communities of like-minded people, and adding assessment and lesson plan files to your video as support. One can set up videos to be either public or private, with invite-only access. Teachers can grade the value of videos using the user rating system, but users can also report videos for being offensive. Users may also help protect the site's reputation by reporting inappropriate videos. The service is free for everyone. They can also scroll through hundreds of videos that members of the group have uploaded. They can join and build video groups to meet people who share their interests (www.edutopia.org/blog/teacher-tube-educational-video-resource). More than a million page visits are being generated by the site each month (Patil, 2021). Major libraries are using the service to spread knowledge. The website has hosted several imaginative educational competitions in collaboration with businesses like Texas Instruments and Interworked Institutions. The ability to upload, tag, and distribute videos globally, along with the ability to upload lesson plans, evaluations, and other file types to videos, are some of the elements that contribute to TeacherTube's popularity. To meet individuals who share your interests, establish, join, and connect with video groups. Utilize application programming interfaces (APIs) to embed TeacherTube videos into your website.

SlideShare (www.slideshare.net)

During the pandemic, SlideShare became one of the top 100 most visited sites in the world (www.slideshare.net/about). SlideShare is a slide-hosting-based Web 2.0 service. It is a LinkedIn-owned site that lets you upload and distribute presentations online. SlideShare for presentations to be shared is the world's largest community. With 80 million monthly users till 2021 and 130 million page views, it is running free of cost (https://expandedramblings.com/index.php/slideshare-statistics/). SlideShare has recently been voted in the Top 10 World Tools for Education. SlideShare has plenty of content that is professional. Presentations from classroom lessons can be uploaded to SlideShare for students who might have missed the session or need access to the slide content after the class is over. In addition to seeing slides submitted by teachers, students can upload their lectures and browse presentations on a variety of subjects. It is a great way to drive initial traffic to the content from other social channels. The number of users of SlideShare is 80 million per month in 2022 (https://expandedramblings.com/index.php/slideshare-statistics/).

WizIQ (www.wiziq.com/)

WizIQ includes a learning management system which provides live and self-paced learning in a virtual classroom. It helps the production of research, video streaming with a comfortable mobile environment. Universities during the COVID-19 situation could provide technical help to the instructor and students through their IT department and other outsources for upgrading or installing software for online teaching, as well as arrange some technical training through online mode. Academic staff members in universities frequently used WizIQ for online instruction. It possesses the ability to provide live and on-demand webinars and is furnished with enough resources, including presentations, desktop sharing tools, audio, and video. Teachers can use the creation wizard to build hundreds of courses online, as well as the built-in evaluation tool. Instructional images, slideshows, and animations can also be created in the virtual classroom. For collaborative teamwork, WizIQ offers immersive apps for learners and their peers. WizIQ supports word processing, presentation of PowerPoints, and online posting and editing of spreadsheets. The students practice in collaborative teams in order to operate. It includes live text and audio chat, enabling students to post their questions and answers on the spot. This includes personal chat features, powerful whiteboard apps, and media players with interactive video streaming. This tool is absolutely free. This allows the content library to be uploaded and facilitates participation and evaluation. This encourages documentation to support students to revise and view the missed sessions. The platform has 400,000 educators and trainers (www.wiziq.com/es/). Powerful tools for course administration and pedagogical tasks, including synchronous and asynchronous communication tools, material generation and distribution, assessment, and control of students' activities, are available on e-learning systems like WizIQ.

Edmodo (https://new.edmodo.com/)

One type of educational technology that took advantage of the internet exclusively during the COVID-19 quarantine is virtual class, often known as online class. Edmodo is a teaching and learning forum for texts, calendars, and general correspondence for teachers and students. As students appreciate the presentation of it, communicating with students becomes easier and more efficient as well as more effective. Sharing useful apps with students makes it simple. It helps the entire group to learn with all-in-one LMS, networking, collaboration, and Zoom video conferencing resources from anywhere. It is a forum that is loved by learners as it enhances their confidence and experience

Social Media–Based Learning Platforms and the Pandemic   165

of what it means to be a digital citizen. Also, parents can get updates from the class, keep in touch with teachers, and help home learning. An internet network connection-connected personal computer (PC) or laptop is used to implement the online learning system. Groups on social media sites like WhatsApp (WA), Telegram, Edmodo, Instagram, Zoom, and other platforms can be used by educators to learn together at the same time. The tool is entirely free but also offers several paid apps which can be downloaded as per the users' needs. To help learners keep on track, they can also see classroom events and grades immediately. It has helped over 100 million users till 2019 (https://go.edmodo.com/about/) learn well together in hundreds of thousands of schools all over the world.

TEDEd (https://ed.ted.com/)

TEDEd aims to blast and celebrate the ideas of educators and students from around the globe. From building a growing collection of unique animated movies to giving teachers around the world a place to create their own interactive lessons, we support interested students everywhere. The COVID-19 pandemic's unparalleled impact on educational systems around the world led to the creation of TED's award-winning youth and education programme. Their goal was to assist students, teachers, and families in swapping out negative emotions like anxiety, loneliness, chaos, and exhaustion for positive emotions like curiosity, connectivity, predictability, and renewal by offering a wide range of educational resources and stimulating learning opportunities. It is a platform that allows one to organize an assignment around a video and determine the interaction of students with the content. The format of the lesson consists of the title of the lesson, a written introduction, a set of multiple choice or open-ended questions, a place for additional resources to facilitate further discovery, and an interactive class discussion. It offers several TED Talks with condensed, frequently animated segments covering subjects including science, technology, social studies, literature, language, art, health, psychology, business, and economics. In return for an annual subscription, TED offers an ad-free video experience that allows users to stream TED speeches without advertisements. Only TED presentations provide an ad-free video experience, podcasts, and other forms of TED material. They may have commercials supplied by the platform where they are distributed, as well as references to sponsors, if relevant. The subscription provides users of the TED iOS app an ad-free experience by paying a yearly membership directly to the Apple Store, which may be cancelled up to 24 hours before the following yearly term. The site also makes communication simple with groups and clubs. Students are able to complete the lesson and can review a description of the results and comment on their individual responses. TEDEd has a global network of over 650,000 teachers (https://ttaconline.org/Resource/JWHaEa5BS75xzwDLo-MpCQ/ Resource-ted-ed-discover-create-support).

Vimeo (https://vimeo.com/)

The coronavirus pandemic continuously presented challenges for everyone, both offline and online. Vimeo is a website where videos can be uploaded, posted, and viewed by customers. The primary goal of Vimeo is to distribute high-definition video on a variety of devices. Software as a service is how Vimeo conducts business. Teachers can use it to upload and store videos and then use it as a tool to teach students more about video creation. A basic, free Vimeo subscription is available; however, it is limited to 500 MB of storage each week. Alternately, one can create a YouTube video for free and host it for a required time. Instead of monthly or annual payment schemes, YouTube concentrates on generating money through advertising. Vimeo Video School offers classes and tutorials on a variety of topics. It had 1.53 million subscribers at the end of 2020 (www.statista.com/statistics/705598/vimeo-subscribers-worldwide/). It is highly engaging, capable of exciting and affecting people; it creates greater interaction, leads to the dialogue and assimilation of content; video classes lead to creating a closer partnership between teacher and student through the use of picture and sound. The fact that Vimeo's video quality is clear, precise, and simpler to read is one of the things that makes it good. With Vimeo, one can publish updated copies of the video while maintaining the original URL, as well as upload improved recordings of live streams that can be altered before posting. The monthly bandwidth cap for Vimeo is 2 TB. As a result, Vimeo is able to handle a massive volume of large-sized videos.

WordPress (https://wordpress.com/)

WordPress developed into the ideal instrument for all online education requirements as the coronavirus caused the harshest and quickest spreading epidemic the world has ever seen. Schools, teachers, and students all across the world are attempting to use this platform's potential for their educational requirements. The user can instantly create a blog using this internet service. WordPress has developed into a terrific tool for educators to create a web of communication and instruction for their pupils because it offers a variety of template options. Teachers may also use it to encourage learners to write more by helping them create their own blogs. Students may easily construct an ePortfolio of concepts over the term they have studied. They can demonstrate their learning online by incorporating connections, multimedia, and original content without having to deal with physical documents and books. The ability to store their work electronically enables them to access the data anywhere a computer and internet connection is available. This is a free tool. A specific template for ePortfolios has recently been introduced to WordPress, which improves WordPress's function as a place to store and organize work. This helps students and professionals to expose their work to a global audience of peers, consumers, and employers in a realistic and simple way. Most of the popular universities, distance education institutions, charter schools, etc., make use of the WordPress multisite feature. The site offers Edublogs. They are mostly used by students to share the content they created with teachers rather than information exchange by institutions. Students write articles and create other forms of content and share them here. Teachers exclusively use this platform to share class schedules, homework, lesson plans, etc. Over 400 million people visit WordPress websites every month (www.cminds.com/ultimate-guide-wordpress-statistics%E2%80%A8%E2%80%A8/#:~:text=Looking%20 at%20websites%20built%20with,visit%20WordPress%20websites%20 every%20month).

Skype (skype.com)

COVID-19 placed a strong emphasis on the requirement to accept various and adaptable teaching and learning techniques. In order to lessen the disruption to educational activities, e-learning arose as a supplemental solution. One such platform was Skype, which provided innovative and adaptable teaching and learning methods while adhering to the precautions against the spread of the pandemic. The platform not only ensures that students engage with teachers but allows students to widen their world view. By connecting other teachers and then connecting students to each other, it helps set up virtual links. Skype also has a full forum for educators who can use it to teach various lessons that are already available on it. It can be used to connect with friends, learn about new cultures, learn a new language, and/or exchange teaching materials with other teachers in the classroom and also contact another classroom anywhere in the world. Skype also offers the ability for students and teachers to participate in virtual tours of historical sites, connect with writers and scholars, and engage in discussions with classrooms around the world. As per Statista, 1.67 billion users are estimated for Skype in 2020 (www.statista.com/statistics/820384/estimated-number-skype-users-worldwide/). Teachers and even students frequently use Skype for educational purposes, and it provides services like Skype in the classroom. With the use of Skype-based online classes, students may maintain continual communication with their professors. Some of the factors that make it unique include virtual field trips, Skype lessons by experts, Mystery Skype, which is a guessing game which can be used by kids to improve geography, and Guest Speakers option, which is used to connect with experts on various subjects around the world.

GoClass (www.goclass.com)

The pandemic caused a broad suspension of face-to-face activities at educational institutions in order to stop the virus's transmission and lessen its consequences. Some different tools and techniques were highlighted to maintain the continuity of learning. One such emerging platform is GoClass. This is a collaborative virtual space based on internet that combines documents and presentations. Through the Show-Explain-Ask method, this tool offers a space to build, revise, and maintain the lesson plan. This allows the lesson plan and assignment upload to be connected to pictures, videos, instructions, and evaluation. It provides an informative dashboard and capacity assessment to view student development. Using GoClass, teachers may develop lessons and send them to students' mobile devices. The free account enables features including lesson and course building, content sharing, and learner evaluation. GoClass is an e-class platform that enables teachers to hold in-person lessons and concurrently share content with their students. GoClass aids in boosting student engagement, classroom management, and productivity. The enhanced teacher dashboard gathers rich performance data from students and presents this data in easy-to-use visual snapshots that inform instruction and assist with task management. The GoClass's mobile function of this enables content to be given to the student. The improved GoClass+ teacher dashboard gathers rich student progress information and presents this information in graphic snapshots that are simple to utilize, that advise instruction and assist in task management. GoClass, which first launched in January 2012, now has over 50,000 users in more than 70 countries (https:// learningmate.com/news/goclass-announces-its-next-generation-learning-platform-for-classroom-mobile-devices-at-iste-2013/). A few key features are that it is a fantastic web tool or app that enables teachers to develop content on the web and then share it with students on an iPad while conducting real-time evaluations. Using a simple access code, it also enables teachers to use several lessons with different grade levels. By allowing parents to view their child's growth, it's also a terrific place to promote parental involvement.

5. Conclusion

The present work clearly highlights the social media tools that played a vital role in improving the learning and education at the time of the pandemic. Due to the lack of physical interaction required between/among teachers and students, all of the applications have assisted in reducing the rate of COVID-19 virus propagation by preserving social distance. Teachers have a greater possibility of engaging and interacting with the younger generation of pupils since they feel more at ease with the new educational techniques. Institutions that use these technologies correctly and integrate them into the educational process can benefit from students' digital capabilities for learning while minimizing the institution's budgetary burden at the same time. Most of these tools include cost-effective, free versions that can be used. To reach the full potential of technology for education, the education systems must embrace social media learning, and all these should be included as part of the educational pedagogy. Teachers should not limit themselves to a specific tool and can select the appropriate tool based on the needs of the class.

References

Ansari, J. A. N., & Khan, N. A. (2020). Exploring the role of social media in collaborative learning the new domain of learning. *Smart Learning Environments*, 7(1), 1–16.

Bansal, R., Mital, N., & Kumar, V. (2021). Popularity and usage analytics of social media platforms in higher education. *2021 international conference on computational performance evaluation (ComPE)* (pp. 631–635). IEEE. https://doi.org/10.1109/ComPE53109.2021.9752143

Barry, D. S., Marzouk, F., Chulak-Oglu, K., Bennett, D., Tierney, P., & O'Keeffe, G. W. (2016). Anatomy education for the YouTube generation. *Anatomical Sciences Education*, 9(1), 90–96.

Batsila, M., & Tsihouridis, C. (2016). "Once upon a Time there was . . ." A digital world for Junior High School learners. *International Journal of Emerging Technologies in Learning*, 11(3), 42–50.

Carless, D., & Boud, D. (2018). The development of student feedback literacy: Enabling uptake of feedback. *Assessment & Evaluation in Higher Education*, 43(8), 1315–1325. https://doi.org/10.1080/02602938 .2018.1463354

Dooly, M. (2018). Collaborative learning. In J. I. Liontas (Ed.), *The TESOL encyclopedia of English language teaching* (pp. 1–7). Wiley. https://doi.org/10.1002/9781118784235.eelt0394

El-Badawy, T. A., & Hashem, Y. (2015). The impact of social media on the academic development of school students. *International Journal of Business Administration*, 6(1), 46–52.

Froment, F., García González, A. J., & Bohórquez, M. R. (2017). The use of social networks as a communication tool between teachers and students: A literature review. *Turkish Online Journal of Educational Technology-TOJET*, 16(4), 126–144.

Gikas, J., & Grant, M. M. (2013). Mobile computing devices in higher education: Student perspectives on learning with cellphones, smartphones & social media. *Internet and Higher Education Mobile*, 19(2013), 18–26.

Global Media Insights. (2022). Retrieved December 29, 2022, from www.globalmediainsight.com/blog/youtube-users-statistics

Gon, S., & Rawekar, A. (2017). Effectivity of e-learning through WhatsApp as a teaching learning tool. *MVP Journal of Medical Science*, 4(1), 19–25.

Gupta, G., Kumar, V., Paruthi, M., & Giri, P. (2021). Determinants of the quality and acceptability of Moocs: International Vs Indian perspective. *Webology*, 18(6), 1265–1283.

Guy, R. (2012). The use of social media for academic practice: A review of literature. *Kentucky Journal of Higher Education Policy and Practice*, 1(2), 7.

Hoplamazian, G. J., & Monthie, S. (2017). A review of voicethread as a tool for advertising education. *Journal of Advertising Education*, 21(1), 46–52.

Kaya, S., Özgür, A. Z., & Koçak, N. G. (2012). Integrating social media into distance learning. In *EDULEARN12 proceedings* (pp. 2566–2575). IATED.

Khan, M. N., Ashraf, M. A., Seinen, D., Khan, K. U., & Laar, R. A. (2021). Social media for knowledge acquisition and dissemination: The impact of the COVID-19 pandemic on collaborative learning driven social media adoption. *Frontiers in Psychology*, 12, 648253.

Kirby, T. R. (2016). *Networking and connecting creative minds: Understanding social media's role in today's visual arts instruction* [Master's theses], p. 754. Available at https://scholarworks.wmich.edu/cgi/viewcontent.cgi?article=1767&context=maste rs_theses. Last accessed: June 17, 2023

Kumar, V., & Ayodeji, O. G. (2021). Determinants of the success of online retail in India. *International Journal of Business Information Systems (IJBIS)*, 37(2), 246–262.

Kumar, V., & Bhardwaj, A. (2020). Role of cloud computing in school education. In *Handbook of research on diverse teaching strategies for the technology-rich classroom* (pp. 98–108). IGI Global Publications.

Kumar, V., & Nanda, P. (2019). Social media in higher education: A framework for continuous engagement. *International Journal of Information and Communication Technology Education (IJICTE)*, 15(1), 97–108.

Kumar, V., & Nanda, P. (2022). Social media as a learning tool: A perspective on formal and informal learning. *International Journal of Educational Reform (IJER)*, 1–26.

Kumar, V., Nanda, P., & Tawangar, S. (2022). Social media in business decisions of MSMES: Practices and challenges. *International Journal of Decision Support System Technology (IJDSST)*, 14(1), 1–12.

Kumar, V., & Sharma, D. (2016). Creating collaborative and convenient learning environment using cloud- based moodle LMS. *International Journal of Web-Based Learning and Teaching Technologies*, 11(1), 35–49. https://doi.org/10.4018/ IJWLTT.2016010103

Kumar, V., & Sharma, D. (2017). Cloud computing as a catalyst in STEM education. *International Journal of Information and Communication Technology Education (IJICTE)*, 13(2), 38–51.

Kumar, V., & Sharma, D. (2021). E-learning theories, components, and cloud computing-based learning platforms. *International Journal of Web-Based Learning and Teaching Technologies (IJWLTT)*, 16(3), 1–16.

Kusumawati, R. D., Oswari, T., Utomo, R. B., & Kumar, V. (2014). The influence of 7P's of marketing mix on buying intention of music product in Indonesia. *Procedia Engineering*, 97, 1765–1771.

Lata, M., & Gupta, A. (2021). Education during the pandemic: Technology-based solutions. In *Stakeholder strategies for reducing the impact of global health crises* (pp. 209–224). IGI Global Publications.

Mittal, S., & Kumar, V. (2020). A framework for ethical mobile marketing. *International Journal of Technoethics (IJT)*, 11(1), 28–42.

Mittal, S., & Kumar, V. (2022). Strategic framework for non-intrusive mobile-marketing campaigns. *International Journal of Electronic Marketing and Retailing (IJEMR)*, 13(2), 190–205.

Nanda, P., & Kumar, V. (2021). Social media analytics: Tools, techniques and present day practices. *International Journal of Services Operations and Informatics (IJSOI)*, 11(4), 422–436.

Nanda, P., & Kumar, V. (2022). Information processing and data analytics for decision making: A journey from traditional to modern approaches. *Information Resources Management Journal (IRMJ)*, 35(2), 1–14.

Nayar, K. B., & Kumar, V. (2018). Cost benefit analysis of cloud computing in education. *International Journal of Business Information Systems*, 27(2), 205–221.

Patil, S. (2021). New dawn of teaching—learning—a teacher tube. *Aayushi International Interdisciplinary Research Journal*, 8(2), 68–70.

Selwyn, N. (2012). Making sense of young people, education and digital technology: The role of sociological theory. *Oxford Review of Education, 38*(1), 81–96.

Singh, J., & Kumar, V. (2022). Combating the pandemic with ICT based learning tools and applications: A case of Indian higher education. *International Journal of Virtual and Personal Learning Environments (IJVPLE) Platforms, 12*(1), 1–21.

Smart Insights. (2021). Retrieved May 5, 2021, from www.smartinsights.com/social-media-marketing/social-media-strategy/new-global-social-media-research/

Statista. (2022a). Retrieved December 29, 2022, from www.statista.com/topics/7863/social-media-use-during-coronavirus-covid-19-worldwide/#topicHeader__wrapper

Statista. (2022b). Retrieved April 16, 2022, from www.statista.com/statistics/272014/global-social-networks-ranked-by-number-of-users/

Unicef. (2021). Retrieved December 29, 2022, from www.unicef.org/india/press-releases/covid-19-schools-more-168-million-children-globally-have-been-completely-closed

Vázquez-Cano, E. (2014). Mobile distance learning with smartphones and apps in higher education. *Educational Sciences: Theory and Practice, 14*(4), 1505–1520.

10 The Scope and Challenges of Learning Through Social Media Sites During the Pandemic

What Really Matters

Irtifa Mukhter, Richa Choudhary, Aasim Ur Rehman Ganie, and Syed Seerath Mukhter

1. Introduction

In recent years, students and academics have adopted social media tackles such as Facebook, Twitter, YouTube, blogging platforms, etc., as alternate learning and teaching methods (Kumar & Nanda, 2019). For example, as reported, faculty members used Facebook and YouTube for online and offline teaching purposes and to upload educational videos. Studies have shown that students enjoy using online social media sites for learning objectives to enrich their knowledge domain due to their helpful element in their learning activities and its ability to enhance learning experiences (Veletsianos & Navarrete, 2012). In addition, social media tools are also preferred and viewed favourably in e-learning courses, particularly for accessible communication between students and academics as a vehicle for quick and easy communication amongst students and scholars (Brady et al., 2010). However, not all students can benefit from social media due to their diverse backgrounds or learning styles (Balakrishnan & Gan, 2016). Most of the lessons on the ground of social media and instruction have discovered the ways of possibilities of using some of the popular social media tools popular among the youth in teaching and learning, considering the vast popularity of such tools among the younger generation (Everson et al., 2013; Greenhow & Robelia, 2009; Roblyer et al., 2010; Kumar & Nanda, 2020). On the other hand, a review of the literature revealed attempts to develop other social media-enabled tools that can be used clearly to teach and learn the field of education (Kapoor et al., 2018). For example, Edmodo combines certain features of Facebook and Twitter, allowing teachers and students to communicate and collaborate. Other educational tools include Pizza, a Q&A web service that caters to students and educators, and Diego, a social bookmarking website that allows users to bookmark and tag web pages. Socrative, Quizizz, and Kahoot! enable educators to assess students via conducting fun and engaging self-paced assessments during lecture classes in the form of quizzes. Screencast-O-Matic allows educators to create short educational videos for their students, which can be saved or uploaded on YouTube. However, these tools are not

DOI: 10.4324/9781003315278-10

considered social media applications but instead categorized as educational technologies. The individual social media platforms that have been very common among teachers and learners over the past few years are individually discussed briefly. These platforms have become very popular and have attracted many subscribers to study using these handles.

Facebook

Facebook, a famous social networking site, has gained huge popularity among people because of its various features. Users on this site can interact, talk, and exchange ideas. With 2.7 billion users in January 2021 (Statista, 2021b), it has numerous uses in formal educational settings. As a result of Facebook's growing adoption, its application to education is crucial. Enrolling students requires no additional labour, and the platform is always available. Facebook is used by a lot of teachers and shares educational content and material for the users. This platform has been famous and successful among aspirants preparing for competitive or job-related exams. There is various success where educators have used Facebook groups to improve student learning. (Kumar & Nanda, 2022).

YouTube

Another common platform is the online video streaming handle called YouTube, developed and managed by Google. This platform is the world's third most popular online destination (Holland, 2016). As of January 2021, this platform had crossed more than 2.29 billion users worldwide (Statista, 2021b). The reason for the popularity of YouTube is that the videos make the classroom more engaging and interactive. Academicians have been making numerous efforts worldwide to make smart lectures that are video-based, especially in the form of MOOCs (Kumar & Sharma, 2017). Educationists can use YouTube to publish their videos for free and can interact with the learners through the option of comments. This interaction through comments serves as inputs or feedback and helps them improve the video content, quality, and ease. Students from all around the world can access the material using computers and mobile devices. YouTube has become a valuable medium for classroom-based learning since it is simple to use, accessible globally, affordable, and has feedback systems. (Kumar & Nanda, 2022)

LinkedIn

Many people use LinkedIn nowadays, mostly those looking for jobs and for business networking. This platform enables one to build a professional profile quickly and in a standardized way (Kumar & Nanda, 2019). LinkedIn has established itself as an effective SM tool for business networking and jobs. Students interact with senior academicians as well as business executives for insightful conversations and guidance. Many students do connect with particular individuals on LinkedIn for higher education and job prospects. Students read the posts made by their mentors or another individual, which might serve as a useful starting point for discussions in class. The use of LinkedIn in the classroom has effectively brought the most recent advances in the industry. (Kumar & Nanda, 2022)

Instagram

Students use Instagram to share images or videos connected to their education and topic of discussion. Their followers on Instagram profiles can comment on them, which may result in the pupils' learning in groups (Kumar & Nanda, 2019). Teachers typically need to prepare many charts, pictures, and quota holders for classroom demonstrations. Instagram is being used to create particular galleries that correspond to a course and share them with the students forever. This can be a valuable tool for teaching pupils definitions and formulas while making them always available. (Kumar & Nanda, 2022)

Twitter

A common way to write about specific subjects and make it public is through blogging. However, creating a blog requires significant time and work to adhere to a particular writing style and create the desired content. Twitter, a microblogging platform, has aided educators in producing clear and succinct content within the confines of 280 characters. This makes it easier for professors to interact with pupils in real time and provide important information in a concise form. Sharing relevant links and content on Twitter, information about schedules, curricular changes, future events, etc., may be quickly shared. Writing messages is a standard method for learning since it is simple and does not require a rigid framework (Kumar & Nanda, 2022).

WhatsApp

Over the last few years, WhatsApp has become more popular among students and academicians. Through the specially designed chat groups, it offers a forum for both students and teachers. Through the chat groups, they may discuss a subject on a single platform (Baguma et al., 2019). It also assists instructors in resolving issues even when they are not physically present in the classroom (Akulwar, 2019). WhatsApp has become a helpful forum for the teacher to address the concerns of a single student, who may also be able to help other students in the neighbourhood. With this live platform, students can get their problems resolved at any time (Zan, 2019). In addition

The Scope and Challenges of Learning Through Social Media 175

to students and teachers, parents have also been added to the chat groups, where teachers share material, such as a curriculum, tuition, past years' papers, etc. (Kumar & Nanda, 2022).

2. Models of Social Media Learning

The central idea of social construction is that knowledge building is a social process through communication and collaboration with others (Mittal & Kumar, 2019). The architectural theory states that human knowledge is constructed and that the learner creates new knowledge based on previous learning. In a constructive approach to education, the learner is no longer a simple passive recipient of knowledge. They are motivated to play an essential role in building their knowledge (Kumar & Sharma, 2021). The learning process can also be through complex conversations such as games, discussions, case-based work, and collaboration with peers and friends (Kumar & Rewari, 2022). Social learning can be described as a prosperous form of knowledge (Mondahl et al., 2009). Recent studies have shown that the digital generation of students learns differently from the previous generation and relies on the web to access information and communicate with others (Benson & Avery, 2009). Some information and communication models and their applicability in learning and education are discussed here.

2.1 Virtual Networks and Web 2.0 Applications

The term "Web 2.0" has received massive popularity since the Web 2.0 conference held in 2005 and hosted by O'Reilly Media and MediaLive (O'Reilly, 2005). The emergence of Web 2.0 applications and subsequent availability of broadband networks have tremendously increased the capacities of the internet. Web 2.0 is described as "Web as Platform," where entrepreneurs, software developers, and end consumers have transformed the internet and made it available through microcomputers, smartphones, and MP3 players. Their applications are very promising to use in educational settings. In a more traditional learning environment, limited simulation scenarios and collaborative services are offered initially. In addition to that, action-based information sharing and learning are limited in the traditional learning environment. With an evident focus on case-based teaching in the Web 2.0 dynamic e-learning platform, the results show that understanding is practical if students solve communication problems in a collaborative environment (Sharma & Kumar, 2017). Nowadays, enthusiastic academicians and commentators are focusing much on casting the internet in a new light with the help of Web 2.0 application and technologies. These platforms place the learners or students at the centre of online activities and help in forming new creations, collaborations, and consumptions (Kumar & Nanda, 2020). In particular, the emergence of Web 2.0 technologies has received growing popularity where students and learners are interconnected and can collaborate in varied forms

176 *Irtifa Mukhter et al.*

of joint interactions (Bhardwaj & Kumar, 2022). Despite the considerable contribution, some minorities of educationalists have related the emergence of "Web 2.0 transformation of learning" with "potentially groundbreaking implications for the field of education" (Selwyn, 2007).

2.2 *Case-based Learning Environments*

The case-based models primarily include the actions of written synchronized and non-serious communication components. Theoretically, this model enables the students and learners to reflect on and monitor their progress while learning with successes and failures. Designing suitable learning actions is critical to further develop the learning platform with a more social, user-friendly interface that allows students to collaborate, share information and experiences, and communicate through synchronous and asynchronous communication services. In the new version of the available platform, students can critique and comment on other students' work, quote and submit content related to their portfolio assignments, assign tasks to each other, and submit. They can use mobile solutions, video conferencing, and podcasts. Teachers expect that students gain communication, critical, and collaborative skills useful for academic and professional contexts using the platform (Redecker et al., 2010).

2.3 *Multimedia Learning Model*

The multimedia learning model was first introduced by Richard Mayer in 1997. The broad cognitivism idea asserts that the three components of the multimedia learning theory aid in improving student learning. The first is the multimedia principle, which states that there are two channels—audio and visual—for processing information. According to this idea, students learn more effectively from words and images than just words alone. The second feature is that each channel can only process a certain amount of data. In other words, because humans have a limited capacity for processing information, they attempt to make sense of it by constructing mental models based on information sources. This paradigm can be applied in various ways in the classroom, such as assisting pupils in global exploration. Using a computerized global map that incorporates both auditory and visual information, teachers can utilize this technique to teach geographic locations, like the highest mountain or the longest river in geography class. Students can digest information from multiple sources, which might lead to greater comprehension. Because it is challenging for them to digest the information without visualization, most students struggle to comprehend information from texts. Teachers need to be aware that having two sources of information allows students to digest more information simultaneously, improving learning. They will be able to commit the information to long-term memory thanks to this procedure (McTigue, 2009).

The Scope and Challenges of Learning Through Social Media

2.4 Social Media Instructional Design Model

The social media instructional design model aims to reduce the requirement to be knowledgeable about the various instructional design models available and/or an expert in learning technology. Instead, this dynamic instructional tool is intended to assist in boosting instructional designers' and educators' abilities to effectively create teaching that makes appropriate use of social media's affordances. Additionally, it could contribute to the widespread adoption of social media as a trustworthy and useful resource in the classroom by giving instructional designers and teachers a much-needed model for using social media as learning tools (Conley & Sabo, 2015).

2.5 Blended Learning Theory

As the Web 2.0 applications attracts huge popularity, it demands for the teachers and instructors to be more deliberate while using multimedia platforms in the classrooms. One of the approaches that inclines with the multimedia classroom learning is blended learning theory. This model has been used to scrutinize the usage and scope of YouTube in a classroom setting by Fleck et al. (2014). The blended approach learning has been defined by Garrison and Kanuka (2004) as "Thoughtful integration of classroom face to face learning experiences with online learning experiences." Over the years, the use of YouTube in the classroom has ought to fall under this definition. It is important to note that the major aim behind the development of blended-based learning models is face-to-face interactions with online learning experiences. Under the blended model, it is maintained that the two should complement one another in a well-balanced, uniform, harmonious mixture (Hussey et al., 2013; Osguthorpe & Graham, 2003). Instructors need to be mindful that merely adding videos to a course in a haphazard way will not have the positive effects on learning that a truly blended learning theory class will have. Fleck et al. (2014), after scrutinizing the feasibility of the blended model of classroom learning, found that students were more familiar with online learning tools and more interested in audiovisual learning than traditional classroom lectures. Some of researchers have held that introducing multiple social media sites can change the blended form of learning in higher education and can have a significant positive effect on the teaching and learning processes (Artal-Sevil et al., 2015).

2.6 Distance Learning

Distance learning has become increasingly popular, particularly during the COVID-19 pandemic, and has become a must (Kovid & Kumar, 2022). Distance education learning can happen in multiple forms and with the assistance of various systems and applications (Singh & Kumar, 2022). Distance learning is often called e-learning, blended, or mobile learning (Ajayi et al., 2019). The use of social media over the years has increasingly been used for entertainment, interactions with people, as well as for professional purposes. Still, these applications have added a new dimension to learning through virtual platforms. Many educational institutions have started offering courses, knowledge sharing, and MOOCs through the social media platforms (Whiting & Williams, 2013; Edegoh et al., 2013; Papoola, 2014). The history of distance or open learning goes back to the sixties, when the Open University of the UK started courses to make them accessible to common people. Distance learning provides flexibility and makes learning easy while removing all the traditional barriers such as eligibility criteria, attendance, the timeline for the course, etc. (Kumar & Nanda, 2020). The two common forms of distance learning which has encouraged and attracted the learner over the past few years are MOOCs and SPOCs. Various institutes nationally and internationally have started massive online courses, which has played a vital role in the upliftment of open learning and the educational sector on the whole. The role of social media in open learning is well-acknowledged and made it possible for learners to join courses irrespective of geographical and other logistical barriers.

2.7 Social Media as a Space of Learning

Before the development of social media, the dominant learning ideas were attitudes, knowledge, and construction. According to Siemens (2005), the limit of these theories is that they all have an individual concept of learning. It means that, despite their differences, all approaches consider knowledge to exist in individuals. According to Siemens, even the social seven constructivist is individualistic. As Stephenson (1998) described it: "I keep my knowledge to my friends." It reflects that people act fast and make decisions not based on what they know but on what they can understand when they feel the need. In the spirit of the principle of learning communication, it considers the sample experiences of learners from the net generation that use social media tools—made to adapt. Connectivity means that social media facilitating communication between people and information resources should enhance learning because knowledge is the product of those connections rather than the learner's head.

Social media allows learners to connect with tutors and other information resources. The results are probably best understood in the light of the connectivism theory of learning. The learning process is enhanced by anything that improves the connection between students and online resources. The increase in engagements related to the use of social media reflects the contribution made through connectivity. However, the results can also be explained from a socially constructive point of view as social rather than academic relations proved necessary. Findings are essential for educational practitioners because they illustrate how social media can influence education. The selective effect of using social media suggests ways to be best used as the medium to increase communication between students, students, and their teachers and between students and educational resources. In particular, it appears that technology

The Scope and Challenges of Learning Through Social Media 179

is an effective way to engage students, and teachers need not fear that this will result in reduced attendance at lectures or seminars. Unlike personal tweets, it will be of great interest to study what aspects of the learning process can be improved through social media (Liu, 2010).

3. Opportunities of Social Media Learning

The use of social media in education has made learning smooth and allowed the instructors to share the course content very easily. It has led to a space where learners can accomplish their learning goals irrespective of their geographical or geopolitical situation. Nowadays, more and more students are interested in using social media and mobile devices in their career enhancement and skills building (Evans, 2014). Social media has done an excellent job during the COVID-19 pandemic. It increased academic collaboration, enhanced the accessibility to course contents, and made it possible for learners and instructors to talk and meet each other despite the lockdown measures. Introducing social media in education provides enough opportunities for learners or students to interact with peers, tutors, and experts while saving precious time. Besides these factors, the use of social media has economical value as it is a very cheap and convenient tool to access relevant information and educational material (Ansari & Khan, 2020). The use of social media has not only increased accessibility and reduced costs but has also significantly contributed to the learner's academic performance and satisfaction (Zhu, 2012). Since the last few years, social media has gained much popularity and momentum at an unimaginable speed. It indicates that, as social beings, we need constant connection with each other and the outside world. Social media has made the world much more open than it used to be before. It has brought numerous opportunities for exchanging information and ideas due to the development of advanced technologies. Social media found its way quickly into the commercial world; at the same time, educators are seeking possibilities of leveraging social media tools in the educational arena. It also provided means for educators and learners to become independent in their study and research.

3.1 Scope of Social Media Learning

The Council on Communications and Media Strasburger et al. (2013) study shows that the increasing use of social media applications outside of formal educational settings has helped modernize educational and training institutions and help them learn for the twenty-first century. It provides new opportunities to prepare and allow people to access information. Evidence suggests that social media is already influencing people's ways of finding, creating, sharing, and learning knowledge through the abundance of media opportunities and collaborating. These exercises are fundamental to education and training to develop the skills needed for future jobs. Social media enable new tools for educational institutions to transform themselves into

180 *Irtifa Mukhter et al.*

places that participate in a knowledge-based society. It supports the capabilities required for strengthening education and training, lifelong learning, and acquiring new skills. Social Performance Organizations such as the Brussels Think Tank and the Lisbon Council are now debating how to quickly address this challenge on a broader front, based on the social consensus around expertise, which is key to Europe's future (Council, 2009). The education and training system must embrace social media and current learning opportunities and methods that keep evolving as new technologies evolve and prepare learners for the rest of the twenty-first century (Gruzd et al., 2016).

3.2 *Uses of Social Media Learning*

In most schools, on-campus technology integration is a top-down process. Teachers and students use the technology that IT people have chosen. Rarely will IT people investigate between teachers and students. The possibilities are what students and teachers use; not what schools have implemented. There is no limit to the creative minds that use technology. Social media sites such as YouTube have many features that can help educators deliver content. For example, it can enhance the presentation, translate video captions into different languages to increase access to other language learners, and allow anyone to embed the required videos anywhere to improve the teaching effect. Social media, such as YouTube, Facebook, Instagram etc., has become a fast-learning tool due to their ease of use and availability of videos and content for viewers wherever there is an internet connection. It does not require a browser plug-in or a third-party application to handle content like iTunes podcasts. A spring 2009 study at UH involved a large chemistry class using both iTunes podcasts and YouTube videos, and results show that more than 70% of students use YouTube videos and less than 30% use podcasts (Arrington, 2009). The reason is simple; access to YouTube is effortless. When educational videos and information operate as an academic learning resource, one precaution that students should be aware of is the content's credibility if public content is for educational purposes. Both teachers and students should ensure the credibility and reliability of the source, so that the data is accurate and correct. Students can improve their analytical skills through this process. Using social media tools in teaching can sometimes be very difficult for teachers. Students can be great mentoring tools because they are experts and understand mechanisms well. Integrating technology into future education should focus on what students use rather than what the school wants them to use, to guarantee maximum performance (Ankit et al., 2012).

4. The Merits of Social Media Learning

Different reports explain the impact of increasing access to information and social media. One of the studies conducted by (Abbas et al., 2019) among university students aged 16–35 years examined students' behaviour using social satisfaction theory while practicing social media. The study identified 18 negative and constructive factors in social media from previous literature. The results show that using social media has improved students' academic performance and has opened the ways for e-learnings and research. However, this study also showed that social media in developing countries harms student behaviour compared to the positive aspects. This study presents a link between contrast and creativity and provides opportunities for future research by facilitating a better understanding of social media features and web-based social networks (Guy & Marquis, 2016).

Information Sharing and Awareness

The other positive features include sharing opinions with others, raising awareness, sharing knowledge, building relationships, identity, reputation, and connections, improving social influence, and developing other communication skills. Social media is growing worldwide, and many student communities and others join these social media sites to interact with friends, family, and strangers. Social media influences human behaviour, and technological advances have helped improve learning and retrieval through social networks, information exchange, etc. (Balakrishnan & Gan, 2016). Social media applications are helpful in educational institutions, medical sciences, and businesses. Over the past decade, social media has significantly changed how people, social communities, and other organizations create, share, and use information. The information and knowledge during the COVID-19 pandemic as shared through social media platforms spread a considerable awareness and helped contain the virus (Kumar & Malhotra, 2021). Social media during the pandemic played a huge role, and all agencies used it as the first medium to reach out to people (D'Souza et al., 2020).

Contribution During Emergencies

The explosion of the COVID-19 pandemic worldwide, and the exposure of entire populations to the disease with no specific pharmacological treatment and rapid levels of infection, have highlighted the importance of digital media as the preferred health communication channel (Kumar & Gupta, 2021). Thus, aside from traditional media, other social agents have emerged as drivers of the social communication thread in crises. They contribute significantly by providing a true, informative story. Social networks support these new agents, and they are massively and effectively contributing to the management of communication in a global pandemic accompanied by social instability (Pérez-Escoda et al., 2020).

Social media has a big advantage due to rapid proliferation of educational materials in the era of COVID-19. When it comes to publishing, studies show that the dissemination of scientific literature on social media platforms (Facebook, Twitter, etc.) increases the number of downloads, queries, and citations

182   *Irtifa Mukhter et al.*

with which the COVID-19 pandemic has characteristics that are undoubtedly permitted. The rapid spread of knowledge worldwide and a significant reduction in editorial times have gone from months of processing to months or even weeks after its reception (Abbas et al., 2021).

Web Rendezvous

The online meetings on Zoom, Google Meet, etc., discussions, and streaming of videos have now become the new normal, and learners like to share information through social media. By doing this, they get engaged with each other instantly. Social media has made it possible to share communications easier and faster with learners and instructors. It has made younger learners or school students experts in interacting with others on the internet.

Social Media Marketing

Social media has made the marketing of products very easy (Mittal & Kumar, 2022). The concept of "new media" has led business enterprises, professionals, and entrepreneurs to build a social media strategy to publicize their products and service. In this era, social media marketing has attracted people to build up skills, and social media marketing is a career option. It not only prepares the workers to become successful but also helps them to learn skills that business and corporates use to strengthen their customer circles.

5.   Demerits of Social Media Learning

Apart from the several merits of social media learning, social media in educational settings also has certain disadvantages. Excessive use of social media makes students emotionally and physically unbalanced and results in sluggishness or irritability. Given the advantages and disadvantages of social media, parents of students should regulate their children's use of social media, as the adverse effects of social media can affect a student's academic performance (Abbas et al., 2019).

Effects on Human Health

Prolonged sitting is one of the most dangerous factors affecting human health; adolescents are significantly more prone to various diseases as they sit for long hours using social networking sites. The adverse effects of prolonged sitting are widespread and are growing every year. Many health concerns are related to people's actions, sitting down, and focusing on social networking sites or other intelligent devices.

Effects on Mental Health

The rise of social media has shaped the world in many ways, affecting people from all walks of life. As explored in this study, negative social media factors,

The Scope and Challenges of Learning Through Social Media   183

such as depression, stress, anxiety, and other health issues, affect student communities. Students from selected universities prefer social media to create awareness, reduce stress, gain helpful information, and make new friends. In contrast, some students spend too much time on social media and waste much time. Several reports have found that increased use of social media and mobile devices have led to depression, attention and concentration issues, stress, and anxiety among young people (Barry et al., 2017).

These factors help encourage parents to keep an eye on their children, as excessive use of social media is detrimental to teens. This balanced approach is practical, as using social media during the learning process benefits students. However, the adverse effects of social media can harm health through disproportionate use. Such adverse effects can lead to health problems with too much social media. In general, students prefer to interact with classmates and friends in person (Subrahmanyam et al., 2000).

Malpractices

One of the dangerous consequences of relying on online technology is that some fraudulent institutions have provided fake degrees through online learning, and students fall into their trap. Furthermore, some students use online words when completing homework and writing exams and papers, suggesting that social media and social networks have blurred the distinction between formal and informal writing. Students may encounter fraud or deception while using social media, as social sites are used from time to time to take advantage of other users. Social media has severely and negatively affected students by setting unrealistic expectations and creating stressful situations (Katete & Kalonga, 2019).

Fake Information

Among the disadvantages, there is the possibility that the information transmitted is not correct, has not been subjected to peer review, does not apply to our environment, or is even incorrect. Another major barrier to social media and information dissemination is "bubble filters," a concept coined by Eli Pariser in (2011). It describes a "personalized access team" for the user, with a collection of algorithms through data from a single user, predicting their preferences and getting results considered like this user's favourite.

Cyberbullying

While social media provide a huge opportunity to the students and instructors, they can also be weapons of cyber abuse and malicious activities even in campuses. There is an increasing trend of cybercrimes worldwide, and young people are becoming victims of cyber abuse and crimes through the social networking sites (Almuneef et al., 2016).

184 *Irtifa Mukhter et al.*

The Problem of Miscommunication

Learning on social media does not guarantee the learners the same opportunity to communicate and explain topics as face-to-face interaction (Hameed et al., 2008). Face-to-face interactions allow people to understand the physical cues such as expressions, tone, tempo, and volume of speech, behaviour, and body language than an online learning system.

6. Conclusion

Overall, as we have described here, we get a multimedia approach that looks at the combined effects of social networks and topic discussions, a promising way to discover new ways of learning. Combined with understanding local contexts and behavioural patterns across multiple contexts, we expect significant research contributions to emerge to help us know twenty-first-century learning practices. Finally, the popularity of social media can encourage learning and its widespread popularity and learning by creating virtual online study groups, supporting the sharing of ideas, and promoting active interactions between students and lecturers. It can be accessible and encouraging. However, the adoption of social media should be integrated as part of higher education teaching and learning curriculum; only after in-depth analysis were both clear guidelines for using such tools provided for lecturers and students. Learning activities should also use various social media tools and a comprehensive approach to helping students with multiple learning styles. Learners are already immersed in the presence and use of social media and come to learn through social media as an additional means of finding and acquiring information, helping and engaging the community, and building knowledge. Future technology integration in education should focus on what students use rather than what the school wants them to use, guaranteeing maximum performance. When students become stakeholders in their education, there will be a revolution in education through effective collaboration between teachers and students. Suggestions to provide a balanced approach to social media can help avoid the negative health consequences of the overuse of social media. Government officials can also benefit from these suggestions. They can take appropriate steps to protect students' health and other members of society by increasing their use of social media. In short, student communities shared their observations about online posts or content that prompted them to develop behaviours to prevent adverse emotional reactions.

References

Abbas, J., Aman, J., Nurunnabi, M., & Bano, S. (2019). The impact of social media on learning behavior for sustainable education: Evidence of students from selected universities in Pakistan. *Sustainability, 11*(6), 1683.

Abbas, J., Wang, D., Su, Z., & Ziapour, A. (2021). The role of social media in the advent of COVID-19 pandemic: Crisis management, mental health challenges and implications. *Risk Management and Healthcare Policy, 14*, 1917–1932.

The Scope and Challenges of Learning Through Social Media   185

Ajayi, A., Ayo, C. K., Olamide, O., & Amoo, E. O. (2019). Mobile learning and accounting students' readiness in tertiary and professional institutions in Nigeria. *Cogent Arts & Humanities, 6*(1), 1–25.

Akulwar, I. S. (2019). What's up! WhatsApp: An additional teaching-learning tool in physiotherapy education. *Communication Society and Media, 2*(4), 136–145.

Almuneef, M., Anton-Erxleben, K., & Burton, P. (2016). *Ending the torment: Tackling bullying from the schoolyard to cyberspace United Nations office of the special representative of the secretary-general on violence against children* (p. 116). United Nations Publications.

Ankit, A., Abou Naaj, M., & Nachouki, M. (2012). Using interactive video conferencing for blended teaching at Ajman University of science and technology. In *IADIS international conference* (pp. 20–28). Retrieved May 31, 2023, from https://www.iadisportal.org/digital-library/using-interactive-video-conferencing-for-blended-teaching-at-ajman-university-of-science-and-technology

Ansari, J. A. N., & Khan, N. A. (2020). Exploring the role of social media in collaborative learning the new domain of learning. *Smart Learning Environments, 7*(1), 1–16.

Arrington, M. (2009). *YouTube EDU launch, So go to learning something.* Retrieved April 23, 2010, from http://techcrunch.com/2009/03/26/you tube-edu-launches/#ixzz0m5GoZUtZ

Artal-Sevil, J. S., Romero-Pascual, E., & Artacho-Terrer, J. M. (2015). Blended-learning: New trends and experiences in higher education. In *8th international conference of education.* Seville.

Baguma, R., Bagarukayo, E., Namubiru, P., Brown, C., & Mayisela, T. (2019). Using WhatsApp in teaching to develop higher order thinking skills: A literature review using the activity theory Lens. *International Journal of Education and Development Using Information and Communication Technology, 15*(2), 98–116.

Balakrishnan, V., & Gan, C. L. (2016). Students' learning styles and their effects on the use of social media technology for learning. *Telematics and Informatics, 33*(3), 808–821.

Barry, C. T., Sidoti, C. L., Briggs, S. M., Reiter, S. R., & Lindsey, R. A. (2017). Adolescent social media use and mental health from adolescent and parent perspectives. *Journal of Adolescence, 61*, 1–11.

Benson, V., & Avery, B. (2009). Embedding web 2.0 strategies in learning and teaching. In Miltiadis D. Lytras, Ernesto Damiani, & Patricia Ordonez de Pablos. *Web 2.0* (pp. 1–12). Springer. https://doi.org/10.1007/978-0-387-85895-1

Bhardwaj, A., & Kumar, V. (2022). A framework for enhancing privacy in online collaboration. *International Journal of Electronic Security and Digital Forensics (IJESDF), 14*(4), 413–432.

Brady, K. P., Holcomb, L. B., & Smith, B. V. (2010). The use of alternative social networking sites in higher educational settings: A case study of the e-learning benefits of Ning in education. *Journal of Interactive Online Learning, 9*(2).

Conley, Q., & Sabo, K. E. (2015). The social media instructional design model: A new tool for designing instruction using social media. *International Journal of Social Media and Interactive Learning Environments, 3*(4), 290–304.

Council, L. (2009). Innovating indicators: Choosing the right targets for EU 2020. *Lisbon Council e-Brief, 4*, 2009.

Council on Communications and Media. (2013). Children, adolescents, and the media. *Pediatrics, 132*(5), 958–961. https://doi.org/10.1542/peds.2013-2656

D'Souza, R. S., D'Souza, S., Strand, N., Anderson, A., Vogt, M. N., & Olatoye, O. (2020). YouTube as a source of medical information on the novel coronavirus 2019 disease (COVID-19) pandemic. *Global Public Health, 15*(7), 935–942.

186 Irtifa Mukhter et al.

Edegoh, L. O. N., Asemah, E. S., & Ekanem, I. B. (2013). Facebook and relationship management among students of Anambra State University, Nigeria. *International Review of Social Sciences and Humanities*, 6(1), 205–216.

Evans, C. (2014). Twitter for teaching: Can social media be used to enhance the process of learning? *British Journal of Educational Technology*, 45(5), 902–915.

Everson, M., Gundlach, E., & Miller, J. (2013). Social media and the introductory statistics course. *Computers in Human Behavior*, 29(5), A69–A81.

Fleck, B. K., Beckman, L. M., Sterns, J. L., & Hussey, H. D. (2014). YouTube in the classroom: Helpful tips and student perceptions. *Journal of Effective Teaching*, 14(3), 21–37.

Garrison, R. D., & Kanuka, H. (2004). Blended learning: Uncovering its transformative potential in higher education. *The Internet and Higher Education*, 7, 95–105. https://doi.org/10.1016/j.iheduc.2004.02.001

Greenhow, C., & Robelia, B. (2009). Old communication, new literacies: Social network sites as social learning resources. *Journal of Computer-Mediated Communication*, 14(4), 1130–1161.

Gruzd, A., Paulin, D., & Haythornthwaite, C. (2016). Analyzing social media and learning through content and social network analysis: A faceted methodological approach. *Journal of Learning Analytics*, 3(3), 46–71.

Guy, R., & Marquis, G. (2016). The flipped classroom: A comparison of student performance using instructional videos and podcasts versus the lecture-based model of instruction. *Issues in Informing Science and Information Technology*, 13, 1–13. www.informingscience.org/Publications/3461

Hameed, S., Badii, A., & Cullen, A. (2008, May 25–26). Effective e-learning integration with traditional learning in a blended learning environment. *European and Mediterranean conference on information systems 2008 (EMCIS2008)*. A1 Bustan Rotana Hotel, Dubai.

Holland, M. (2016). How YouTube developed into a successful platform for user-generated content. *Elon Journal of Undergraduate Research in Communications*, 7(1), 1–1.

Hussey, H. D., Fleck, B. K. B., & Richmond, A. S. (2013). Promoting active learning through a flipped course design. In J. Keengwe, G. Onchwari, & J. Oigara (Eds.), *Promoting active learning through the flipped classroom model*. IGI Global Publications.

Kapoor, K. K., Tamilmani, K., Rana, N. P., Patil, P., Dwivedi, Y. K., & Nerur, S. (2018). Advances in social media research: Past, present and future. *Information Systems Frontiers*, 20(3), 531–558.

Katete, R. S., & Kalonga, G. (2019). Student model and elimination of examination malpractices-the Zambian case. *The Journal of Educational Development*, 7(3), 186–196.

Kovid, R. K., & Kumar, V. (Eds.). (2022). *Cases on emerging markets responses to the COVID-19 pandemic*. IGI Global Publications. ISBN13: 978-16-6843-504-5. https://doi.org/10.4018/978-1-6684-3504-5

Kumar, V., & Gupta, G. (Eds.). (2021). *Strategic management during a pandemic*. Routledge; Taylor & Francis Group. ISBN 9780367646479.

Kumar, V., & Malhotra, G. (Eds.). (2021). *Stakeholder strategies for reducing the impact of global health crises*. IGI Global Publications. ISBN13: 978-17-9987-495-9. https://doi.org/10.4018/978-1-7998-7495-9

Kumar, V., & Nanda, P. (2019). Social media in higher education: A framework for continuous engagement. *International Journal of Information and Communication Technology Education (IJICTE)*, 15(1), 97–108, 109–120.

Kumar, V., & Nanda, P. (2020). Social media as a tool in higher education: A pedagogical perspective. In *Handbook of research on diverse teaching strategies for the technology-rich classroom* (pp. 239–253). IGI Global Publications.

Kumar, V., & Nanda, P. (2022). Social media as a learning tool: A perspective on formal and informal learning. *International Journal of Educational Reform*, 10567879221094303.

Kumar, V., & Rewari, M. (2022). A responsible approach to higher education curriculum design. *International Journal of Educational Reform (IJER)*, *31*(4), 422–441.

Kumar, V., & Sharma, D. (2017). Cloud computing as a catalyst in STEM education. *International Journal of Information and Communication Technology Education (IJICTE)*, *13*(2), 38–51.

Kumar, V., & Sharma, D. (2021). E-learning theories, components and cloud computing based learning platforms. *International Journal of Web-Based Learning and Teaching Technologies*, *16*(3), 1–16.

Liu, Y. (2010). Social media tools as a learning resource. *Journal of Educational Technology Development and Exchange (JETDE)*, *3*(1), 8.

Mayer, R. E. (1997). Multimedia learning: Are we asking the right questions? *Educational Psychologist*, *32*(1), 1–19.

McTigue, E. M. (2009). Does multimedia learning theory extend to middle-school students? *Contemporary Educational Psychology*, *34*(2), 143–153.

Mittal, S., & Kumar, V. (2019) Study of knowledge management models and their relevance in organisations. *International Journal of Knowledge Management Studies*, *10*(3), 322–335.

Mittal, S., & Kumar, V. (2022). Strategic framework for non-intrusive mobile-marketing campaigns. *International Journal of Electronic Marketing and Retailing (IJEMR)*, *13*(2), 190–205.

Mondahl, M., Razmerita, L., Rasmussen, J., & Remenyi, D. (2009). Social software, thinking styles, personalization and case-based foreign language learning: The quest for new pedagogical models in higher education. In *8th European conference on e-learning* (pp. 383–391). Academic Publishing Limited.

O'Reilly, T. (2005). *What is Web 2.0?* 2. Retrieved September 12, 2022, from http://oreilly.com/web2/archive/what-is-web-20.html

Osguthorpe, R. T., & Graham, C. R. (2003). Blended learning environments: Definitions and directions. *The Quarterly Review of Distance Education*, *4*(3), 227–233.

Papoola, M. (2014). New media usage for communication and self concept among journalism and mass communication students in Oyo State, Nigeria. *New Media and Mass Communication*, *26*, 22–34.

Pariser, E. (2011). *The filter bubble: What the Internet is hiding from you*. Penguin.

Pérez-Escoda, A., Jiménez-Narros, C., Perlado-Lamo-de-Espinosa, M., & Pedrero-Esteban, L. M. (2020). Social networks' engagement during the COVID-19 pandemic in Spain: Health media vs. healthcare professionals. *International Journal of Environmental Research and Public Health*, *17*(14), 5261.

Redecker, C., Ala-Mutka, K., & Punie, Y. (2010). Learning 2.0: The impact of social media on learning in Europe. Policy brief. *JRC Scientific and Technical Report*. EUR JRC56958 EN. Retrieved September 11, 2022, from http://bit.ly/cljlpq

Roblyer, M. D., McDaniel, M., Webb, M., Herman, J., & Witty, J. V. (2010). Findings on Facebook in higher education: A comparison of college faculty and student uses and perceptions of social networking sites. *The Internet and Higher Education*, *13*(3), 134–140.

Selwyn, N. (2007, October). Web 2.0 applications as alternative environments for informal learning-a critical review. In *Paper for CERI-KERIS international expert meeting on ICT and educational performance* (Vol. 16, p. 17). Retrieved May 31, 2023, from https://www.oecd.org/education/ceri/39458556.pdf

Sharma, D., & Kumar, V. (2017). A framework for collaborative and convenient learning on cloud computing platforms. *International Journal of Web-Based Learning and Teaching Technologies (IJWLTT)*, 12(2), 1–20.

Siemens, G. (2005). Learning development cycle: Bridging learning design and modern knowledge needs. *Elearnspace Everything Elearning*, 48(9), 800–809.

Singh, J., & Kumar, V. (2022). Combating the pandemic with ICT based learning tools and applications: A case of Indian higher education. *International Journal of Virtual and Personal Learning Environments (IJVPLE) Platforms (IJVPLE)*, 12(1), 1–21.

Statista. (2021b). Retrieved April 17, 2021, from www.statista.com/statistics/ 272014/ global-social-networks-ranked-by-number-of-users/

Stephenson, J. (1998). The concept of capability and its importance in higher education. *Capability and Quality in Higher Education*, 1–13.

Subrahmanyam, K., Kraut, R. E., Greenfield, P. M., & Gross, E. F. (2000). The impact of home computer use on children's activities and development. *The Future of Children*, 123–144.

Veletsianos, G., & Navarrete, C. (2012). Online social networks as formal learning environments: Learner experiences and activities. *The International Review of Research in Open and Distributed Learning*, 13(1), 144–166.

Whiting, A., & Williams, D. (2013). Why people use social media: A uses and gratifications approach. *Qualitative Market Research: An International Journal*, 16(4), 362–369.

Zan, N. (2019). Communication channel between teachers and students in chemistry education: WhatsApp. *US-China Education Review A*, 9(1), 18–30.

Zhu, C. (2012). Student satisfaction, performance, and knowledge construction in online collaborative learning. *Journal of Educational Technology & Society*, 15(1), 127–136.

Index

accusation 17
administration 44, 103, 131, 164
afraid 124, 156
algorithm 9, 10, 21, 101, 102, 183
amateur 1, 5
amplification 5, 8
angiography 24
anonymous 24, 29, 137
anxiety 16, 18, 69, 88, 125, 165, 183
artificial intelligence 9
assessment 18, 113, 129, 130, 163, 164,
    168, 172
assistance 42, 122, 157, 158, 177
astronomy 29
attitudes 4, 26, 27, 73, 78, 115, 130, 178
authentication 120, 137

baseless 99
beliefs 9, 38, 106, 108
budgetary 168
bureaucrats 115

campaign 5, 15, 86, 87, 88, 93, 94, 105,
    130, 132
capitalism 24, 36, 37, 38, 39
catastrophe 36, 100, 103
catastrophes 100, 103
censorship 4, 5, 9
challenges 9, 19, 39, 56, 87, 103, 113,
    125, 130, 157, 166, 172
citation 60, 63, 181
cognitive 9, 17, 41, 67, 76, 139, 143,
    147, 150
collection 41, 63, 90, 102, 112, 113,
    158, 165, 183
commercialization 40
communal 93
compatriots 30
complexity 19, 22, 105, 151

component 36, 38, 100, 103, 137, 139,
    176
comprehension 9, 56, 176
computational 21, 103
confronting 157
confusion 16, 29, 85, 86, 100
consensus 2, 18, 39, 100, 104, 125, 180
consortium 22
constant 102, 103
constructive 175, 178, 181
consumption 5, 10, 36, 102
contradictions 44
controversial 2, 23, 25
conventional 22, 38, 41, 120
coordination 15, 17, 107
correlation 68, 77, 111
counteract 106
credible 99, 106, 107
criticism 25, 26, 38, 106
crowdsourcing 103, 104, 112, 113
curfew 87, 89, 91, 94
curriculum 69, 155, 175, 184
customization 77

damage 99, 103, 114, 127, 131
deliberate 131, 177
dendritic 19, 22, 24, 25, 26, 29, 30
depopulation 6
deregulation 39, 40
disorder 88
dissemination 8, 9, 78, 99, 100, 102,
    103, 104, 181
domestic 25, 27, 45, 125, 126
droplets 85
dynamic 39, 108, 150, 158

efficacy 29, 31, 76, 101
egalitarian 41
electoral 36

190 Index

embracing 56, 123
emotions 77, 85, 104, 165
emphasis 35, 42, 45, 94
emphasis 35, 42, 45, 94, 162, 167
empowers 157
enabler 62, 75, 95
endurance 77
enthusiastically 92, 94
entrepreneurial 40
epidemiological 101
epistemic 17, 18
equalization 38
escalate 86, 106
evaluate 18, 42, 44, 47, 66, 110
expertise 28, 104, 106, 108, 157

fearmongering 127
feedback 13, 144, 158, 161, 162
fundamental 35, 38, 39, 50, 56, 57,
    107, 108

genetics 22
globalization 35, 36, 39
governance 16, 18, 30
growth 35, 37, 39, 42, 121, 122, 137,
    154, 155, 157, 162

hardship 16, 114
harmful 4, 40, 100
healthcare 102, 106, 120, 122, 132
heparin 24
homeschool 124
hygienically 4
hyper-globalization 36

ideological 38, 41, 43, 55
inadvertently 10
independently 111, 112
indispensible 88
inequalities 35, 37, 38, 39, 40, 41, 42,
    43, 45, 47, 49, 50
infectious 3
influence 76
infodemic 87, 88, 91, 93, 94, 95, 100,
    105, 106, 120
informatics 62
initiatives 100, 105
innovation 24, 25, 28, 56, 131, 155
innovations 25, 56, 155
integrated 102, 124, 162, 184
interpersonal 57, 67, 76, 107, 109, 110,
    112, 113, 160
interventions 18

intuition 29
invasion 114

journalism 11
judgments 107, 108

legitimacy 8, 19, 99, 120
legitimization 38, 43
lockdown 54, 85, 87, 89, 91, 92, 93,
    94, 95, 123, 124, 125, 126,
    153, 179

magnitude 16, 54, 94
mandate 54, 92
manufactured 28, 88
marginalized 36
mentoring 158, 180
misconceptions 100
misfortune 17
misrepresentation 6
mitigation 100
m-learning 136
moderator 66
MOOC 173, 178
morale 88, 95, 105
motivated 9, 123, 139, 175
multidimensional 16, 18, 127

nationalistic 30
negligible 5, 76
neocolonialism 39
neoliberalism 37, 38, 40, 46, 49, 50
nonprofessional 2
non-therapeutic 21

objectionable 4
observation 110, 126, 140, 141, 144
orchestrate 17, 18
orthodox 92
outbreak 103, 115, 153, 154
outburst 88
outrageously 104

panic 86, 88, 92, 114, 123, 126
perpetuate 41
pervasive 38
phenomenon 39, 78, 85, 137
plethora 156
policymakers 37, 39, 94, 120
prescriptions 3
prevalence 100, 102
problematic 17, 39, 44, 45, 86
prodigious 86

Index 191

productivity 55, 168
proliferate 100
prosperity 153
psychological 75, 78, 122, 124

quarantine 49, 93, 99, 103, 123, 126
quasi 110, 111
questionable 100

rationally 9
rebellious 28
redistributing 47
redistributive 42
reidentify 155
reliability 44, 106, 108, 127, 180
religious 115
rescuing 8, 93
reskilling 37
resolution 122, 124, 127, 128, 132
responsible 4, 9, 39, 109, 120, 127,
    128, 144
rigorous 86, 87

sanitizers 6, 88
scientifically 99
security 5, 127, 137
self-interest 108
seminar 122, 179
sensitive 4, 124
sentiment 15, 17, 20, 27, 30, 31, 42,
    45, 110

severity 42, 46, 94, 100
skyrocket 100
spreading 3, 6, 85, 86, 87, 88, 93, 94,
    114, 115, 124, 125, 166
standard 24, 25, 30, 44, 100, 106, 111,
    173, 174
stigma 85, 115
stressful 17, 183
susceptibility 67, 76
suspicion 22, 26, 28, 29, 30
sustain 120, 132
symptoms 86
systematically 19, 128

technology-enabled 54
theories 12, 18, 19, 29, 35, 100
thrive 18
transcript 58
transmission 3, 100, 104, 167
transparent 25

unabated 100
unanticipated 16, 110
uncontrolled 87, 128
unemployment 36, 38, 45, 46, 47, 48, 50
unreasonable 30, 31

VoiceThread 162
vulnerabilities 37

willingness 29, 71, 72, 76, 141

Printed in the United States
by Baker & Taylor Publisher Services